Hiking Grand County, Colorado

A Backcountry Guide to Winter Park, James Peak Area, Fraser Valley, Indian Peaks, Never Summer Range, Troublesome Valley, Williams Fork Mountains, Vasquez Mountains, and Beyond

Deborah Carr and Lou Ladrigan

Third Edition

Backcountry Bound, Tabernash, Colorado

Hiking Grand County, Colorado

A Backcountry Guide to Winter Park, James Peak Area, Fraser Valley, Indian Peaks, Never Summer Range, Troublesome Valley, Williams Fork Mountains, Vasquez Mountains, and Beyond

by Deborah Carr and Lou Ladrigan

Published by:
Backcountry Bound
Post Office Box 537
Tabernash, CO 80478-0537 U.S.A.
Orders @ backcountrybound@mindspring.com
http://backcountrybound.home.mindspring.com

Library of Congress Card Number: 2002101264

ISBN-13: 978-0-9717327-1-1

Copyright © 2002 and 2006 by Deborah Carr and Lou Ladrigan
First Printing 2002, Second Printing 2006 - revised, Third Printing 2012 - revised

Printed in Hong Kong

Cover design by Deborah Carr
All Photographs by Deborah Carr and Lou Ladrigan
USGS Topographic Maps by National Geographic TOPO! Mapping Software for Colorado 2000, 2003, and 2008 with routes and waypoints plotted by Deborah Carr and Lou Ladrigan using a Garmin GPS.

Table of Contents

PREFACE

This book has been written because very little detailed information has been documented regarding Grand County's extensive hiking trail system. Some of the maps available date back to the 1970's and many of the roads and trails have been rerouted over the years. USDA Forest Service trail maintenance monies and manpower have been reduced, resulting in wonderful trails being forgotten and unused. This book is intended to provide accurate information for both popular and little known hikes providing the reader with a rewarding and successful journey through Grand County's backcountry.

Most of the trails are well marked and can be followed easily. However, many of the hikes presented in this book are described in great detail because trail markers disappear, forks are unclear, and little used trails can be hard to follow. There are many variations and combinations of hikes that can be done with the information provided in this book. It is with great anticipation that this book be used as a foundation for additional exploration. This book includes all USDA Forest Service recognized system hiking trails plus many social trails (non-designated user created trail), and some forgotten trails.

The trails described are classified predominantly as "primitive" modes of travel, which include foot and horse traffic. Please consult the USDA Forest Service for accessibility for horse travel. Some trails permit bike travel, but bikes are rarely seen on them. Several trail descriptions recommend the use of bikes for part of the trip because of the distance to the destination and the accessibility for the bikes. Summer motorized vehicle traffic is not permitted on any of the trails in this book, with the exception of a few shared trailheads.

Every hike in this book was traveled on foot and recorded with a Garmin 12 CX GPS or a Garmin GPSMap 76S. It was then mapped onto National Geographic TOPO! Mapping Software for Colorado. Local hike masters, USDA Forest Service authorities, and outfitters reviewed facts for accuracy and clarity. Using the latest technology, the knowledge of local experts, and personal experience, this book was carefully written to be the best overall hiking handbook in Grand County. This book cannot replace a good map, compass, or common sense.

The first edition research for this book required hiking 866 miles with a total elevation gain of 213,240' completed in 484 hours. This is exactly the life span of a good pair of hiking boots. Additional miles, elevation gain, and hours were spent to confirm second and third edition updates.

Disclaimer: All of the information in this book is thought to be correct. Neither the publisher nor the authors are responsible for the actions of the reader.

ACKNOWLEDGEMENTS

Special thanks go to the following organizations and people, without whom this book would not have been possible:

USDA Forest Service, Sulphur Ranger District for their enthusiasm about this venture, their endless hours of answering questions, and their review of this book,

USDA Forest Service, Parks Ranger District for providing all the information on the Troublesome Valley,

The late Dennis Larson for his software support, his hiking knowledge, and his review of this book,

Snow Mountain Ranch – YMCA of the Rockies, especially Mark Birdseye and Rod Lee for sharing their hiking knowledge and their review of this book,

Jim Noel for his printing advice and for sharing his technical knowledge of the printing business,

Grand County Historical Association and all the local historians and long time residents who's wonderful stories brought the past of Grand County back to life, including John Gubbins, Jean Miller, George and Barbara Mitchell, Bob Temple, Joe Kelley, and Fran Holzwarth Needham,

Jim Nelson's Fly Tackle Shop, the late Jim Nelson for his help with all the fishing questions,

Samuelson Outfitters, Dick and Cathy Samuelson for providing directions to lost trails in the Troublesome and their review of this book.

Second edition update thanks go to:

Donn Manly, Sharon Fender, Bob Freeman, Dan Minnick, and Richard Carande for letting us know about trail changes, feature changes, and typos.

Third edition update thanks go to:

USDA Forest Service, Sulphur Ranger District for their continued support and help,

Keith Greenwell for his suggestion to include our GPS coordinate Datum as NAD83.

Valley between Mirror Lake and Triangle Lake

1. HIKING AWARENESS

Hiking Musts

1. **Always prepare for bad weather.** Mountain weather changes from warm and sunny to frigid and raining or snowing without warning. Dress in layers and carry rain gear and warm clothing. Exposure to the elements can result in hypothermia. Lightning strikes are very common and very deadly. When bad weather approaches head down below timberline, especially if you hear thunder. Get below timberline before you see lightning. You do not want to be the highest point or near the highest point above timberline. Most lightning occurs outside of rain, sometimes as far as 10 miles away. Therefore, just because the storm has passed overhead, lightning is still a major concern if thunderclouds are still in the area. Mountain thunderstorms generally occur in the early afternoon. Schedule hikes so that you are below timberline before then.

2. **Always pack plenty of water.** Although water is the heaviest item in your pack, it is the most precious. Pack more than you think you will use. If bad weather hits, you lose your way, or even get hurt, you will need water. Do not depend on using water in streams. What may be a roaring river in the spring and early summer may be no more than a trickle or a dry river bed in late summer or early fall. If creek water is used, always use a certified water purification system that will filter at a minimum, bacteria and protozoan cysts such as Giardia.

3. **Always protect against sunburn.** The sun's rays are much more intense at higher elevations. Wear a brimmed hat and sunglasses with UVA and UVB protection. Wear plenty of sunscreen. The reflection off the snow increases the sun's intensity. Sunburns at high altitude can ruin a vacation.

4. **Always bring a First Aid Kit** with a minimum of supplies including Band-Aids, moleskin for blisters, antiseptic, aspirin, mirror, matches, and a jack knife.

5. **Always bring a map and compass** and know how to use them. If you lose your way, you will need to know where you are in order to find your way back.

6. **Always consider altitude.** All of the hikes in this book begin above 7000'. Altitude sickness affects people differently and has nothing to do with physical conditioning. If dizziness, loss of breath, disorientation, or nausea occur, return to a lower elevation. Sometimes a few days to acclimate reduces altitude sickness symptoms, sometimes it does not. Drink plenty of fluids. This will help alleviate the headache that sometimes accompanies high altitude sickness. If symptoms persist, seek medical attention.

7. **Always hike with someone** and leave word with a third party regarding your destination and anticipated return time.

8. **Always prepare physically for hiking <u>before</u> the hike**. Physical conditioning is essential for an enjoyable trip. Being in good physical condition results in increased endurance, reduced effort of elevation gains, and decreased fatigue. Not being physically prepared for high altitude hiking can result in muscle cramps, loss of breath, dizziness, dehydration, and an overall miserable time.

Hiking Shoulds

1. Pack enough food for your anticipated hike. Remember that you will be burning a lot of calories during the hike so pack high-energy foods.

2. Wear good hiking shoes. A good pair of boots will make your trip much more enjoyable.

Hiking Extras

Additional items that make hiking more enjoyable include the following: camera, GPS and extra batteries, water purification system, binoculars, books on flowers and wildlife, warm gloves, mosquito repellent, whistle, trowel, and a fishing rod. Cell phones are nice to have for emergencies, but signals are often blocked due to the mountains.

Hiking Etiquette

1. Hikers traveling uphill have the right of way. Please move to the side of the trail and allow them to pass. Also, please allow faster hikers to pass. Backpackers (not daypacks) always have the right-of-way.

2. Horses have the right of way over hikers and bikers, while hikers have the right of way over bikers. When passing a horse/rider always verbally communicate with the horse rider to provide a safe encounter.

3. Be considerate of other hikers. If someone is distressed, please offer assistance. Professional medical attention is not quickly available on a trail.

4. Always pack out all of your trash. That includes all uneaten foods, peels, and bio-degradables. Provide the next hiker with the same pristine experience you experienced. If trash is already on the trail, pick it up and keep the forests clean. Be

a responsible hiker and follow the rules of "Pack In-Pack Out" and "Leave No Trace".

5. Do Not Vandalize or Remove Trail Markers.

6. Several trails run through Private Property. In these cases, please be respectful and do not litter, camp, hunt, or fish.

7. Do not short cut switchbacks. This causes erosion.

8. When walking on the tundra where there is no visible trail, avoid walking single file to reduce erosion. Spreading out reduces the impact to the fragile ground.

9. Do not throw cigarette butts or matches on the forest floor. Pack these out with your trash. Forest fires are a major concern in the mountains.

10. Bury human waste by digging a hole with a small trowel and covering the waste and any tissue with plenty of dirt away from the trail or water.

Wildlife

1. Do not approach wildlife. The animals are wild and should be treated as such. Please keep a safe distance. Animals that look harmless can become fierce if they feel threatened or feel that their young are in danger. Also, wildlife can carry diseases/viruses that can be transmitted to humans, including Tuberculosis, Brucellosis, and Rabies.

2. Never feed wildlife. Human food is foreign to their bodies and can make them sick or even kill them. Human food can stop an animal's digestive system, change their migration, and increase the spread of disease. The salt content alone in human snack food can kill small animals like squirrels and chipmunks. In addition, it is against Colorado State Law to feed large animals including deer, elk, antelope, mountain goats, bighorn sheep, mountain lions, and bears.

Dogs

Dogs are permitted on most of the trails in this book. Some of the trails require dogs to be leashed and are identified as such. However, at all times dogs must be under control. Dog owners who allow their dogs to chase wildlife and intimidate other hikers are increasing the probability of having dogs banned permanently from the National Forest. Most National Parks prohibit dogs, including Rocky Mountain National Park.

Logging and Trail Reroutes

Recently, the lodgepole pine forests in Grand County have been mostly left dead as a result of the Mountain Pine Beetle Epidemic. The trees are falling and the USDA Forest Service is logging many of our recreational areas for safety. Trails may be closed during this process or even rerouted when these operations are completed. It is our hope to keep this book up-to-date, but in some cases the changes may take place before we can publish the updates. In all cases, for the most updated trail information, please contact the USDA Forest Service, Sulphur Ranger District at (970) 887–4100.

Hiking Season

Generally the hiking season in Grand County begins around Memorial Day and extends into October, depending on winter snow fall. Hunting season begins in late August. Please consult the local Colorado Division of Wildlife office (970) 725-6200 or local hunting stores for hunting season dates.

Road Gates

Each fall many of the road gates are closed due to the restricted access during the winter months. If a gate is not open for a particular trail or you would like to inquire before taking a hike, call the USDA Forest Service Sulphur Ranger District at (970) 887–4100, Walden Office (970) 723-8204, or Rocky Mountain National Park (970) 627-3471 for road status.

Trail Gates

Some of the trails cross private property and other trails cross land that is leased to ranchers. Gates may be present to contain cattle or otherwise. For this reason, leave a gate the way you found it, either open or closed.

Search and Rescue Card

For a minimal fee per year, a Colorado Outdoor Recreation Search and Rescue Card (CORSAR) is offered by the Colorado Department of Local Affairs. This fee covers all costs incurred by local government if a search and rescue operation becomes necessary while hiking, backpacking, canoeing, kayaking, cross-country skiing, climbing, etc.. This coverage includes helicopter service, which can run into the thousands of dollars. To obtain your CORSAR card, contact any Colorado Parks and Wildlife office or local hunting, boating, or fishing store. Hunting, fishing, and boating licenses include this Search and Rescue feature. The local Colorado Parks and Wildlife office number in Hot Sulphur Springs is (970) 725-6200.

2. WILDERNESS AREAS
and Protection Areas

A Wilderness Area is land set aside by Congress to provide a "wilderness" experience in an area of generally undisturbed land. The 1964 Wilderness act prohibits any motorized and mechanized access, the building of new roads, structures, and facilities in wilderness areas.

The Vasquez Wilderness, Byers Peak Wilderness, Never Summer Wilderness, and Indian Peaks Wilderness all lie in Grand County. The Ptarmigan Peak Wilderness lies on the Summit County/Grand County boundary.

In general, the following restrictions apply:

1. No camping within 100' of any lake, stream, or trail.
2. No fires within 100' of any lake, stream, or trail.
3. No livestock within 100' of any lake, stream or trail (except for watering or through travel).
4. No riding or pack animals to be grazed 100' of any lake, stream, or trail.
5. No groups larger than a combination of 12 to 15 people and livestock depending on the Wilderness Area. The Never Summer Wilderness group size is 10.
6. No wagons, carts, or vehicles, including bicycles.
7. Dogs must be under control at all times – sometimes leashed.
8. All hay and straw used on National Forest Land must be certified "Weed Free". Hay and straw are allowed in the Vasquez and Byers Peak Wilderness Areas, but are prohibited in the Never Summer and Indian Peaks Wilderness Areas.
9. No storing of equipment, personal property, or supplies for more than 14 days within a 30 day period.

In addition, the following restrictions apply:

1. Indian Peaks Wilderness – Dogs must be leashed. Contact the Sulphur Ranger District for more information regarding camping permit regulations.
2. Never Summer Wilderness – No open fires within ½ mile of Parika Lake.
3. Ptarmigan Peak Wilderness – Dogs must be leashed.

A Protection Area and a "Special Interest Area" in Grand County are managed similarly to a Wilderness Area. The same regulations apply except the Protection Areas permit bicycle use in summer and snowmobile use in winter on designated routes; whereas the Special Interest Area permits bicycle use in summer on designated routes, but no snowmobile use in winter.

Bowen Gulch Protection Area and the James Peak Protection Area and Special Interest Area all lie in Grand County.

Mother Moose and calf walking across Columbine Lake Trail

3. HOW TO USE THE BOOK

The trails have been categorized by trail location, not by Wilderness designation or National Forest.

HIKE NAME – identifies the name of the trail, the trail destination, or a point of interest.

Level of Difficulty is based generally on elevation gain for the entire trip, both going and returning. The ratings are as follows:

Easy is 0' - 499',
Moderate is 500' – 1999',
Difficult is 2000' – 2999',
More Difficult is 3000' – 3999'
Most Difficult is 4000' +.

Additional factors are taken into consideration, such as the condition of trail and length. However, the general guideline for Level of Difficulty is elevation gain. Any of the hikes can be made easier by shortening them, thus lessening the elevation gain. Evaluate the profile drawings to pick a distance that suits your individual preference.

Overnight trip "Level of Difficulty" is based on the highest level of difficulty of any day on the entire trip. For example, if a hike is recommended as a 3 day trip and the first day is of Moderate Difficulty, the second day is More Difficult, and the third day is Easy, then the final "Level of Difficulty" rating for this hike would be More Difficult. In addition, the level of difficulty increases when a backpack is carried for overnight stays.

One-way Mileage is taken directly off the TOPO! mapping software. It takes into account the elevation gains and losses.

One-way Hiking Time is an approximate time for an intermediate hiker. Some people hike straight to the top of a mountain, turn around, and hike back down. Others hike at a slower rate, take pictures, look at flowers, rest, and take it all in. Physical condition and age are big factors when considering time. These hiking times took into consideration stops for photos and brief breaks, but please adjust them for your own personal level.

Round-trip Mileage is noted when the hike is a loop.

Round-trip Hiking Time is noted when this hike is a loop.

Altitude, GPS Reading at Trailhead, Destination, or Point of Interest is the elevation, longitude, and latitude at the starting point, ending point, or point of interest on

13

the trip. The longitude and latitude accuracy is within 20'. Many factors influence elevation accuracy, so for the purpose of this book, all elevation data is taken from the TOPO! mapping software.

Trail Fee – Most of the trails in Grand County do not require a trail fee. Some areas that do require day use fees are the Arapaho National Recreation Area, Rocky Mountain National Park, and Snow Mountain Ranch.

🐕 - Dogs Permitted – Leashed where noted.

🐟 - Fishing Permitted with Colorado license (See current "Information and Wildlife Property Directory" for rules and regulations – available from the Colorado Division of Wildlife). Please be respectful of fishing regulations and adjacent private properties.

▲ - Overnight Camping Permitted. Most of the trails allow overnight camping without a permit. However, some trails require a permit and others do not allow camping at all. National Forest permits are available from the USDA Forest Service at either the Sulphur Ranger District on US Hwy 40 just south of Granby (970) 887–4100, or the Walden Office (970) 723-8204. Camping permits in Rocky Mountain National Park are available by calling (970) 627-3471.

WD – Wilderness Area or Protection Area Designation such as *BG* = Bowen Gulch Protection Area, *BP* = Byers Peak Wilderness Area, *IP* = Indian Peaks Wilderness Area, *JP* = includes both the James Peak Wilderness Area and the James Peak Protection Area and Special Interest Area, *NS* = Never Summer Wilderness Area, *PP* = Ptarmigan Peak Wilderness Area, *VQ* = Vasquez Wilderness Area. See Chapter 2 – Wilderness Areas for information on regulations.

Rocky Mountain National Park (*RMNP*) is managed as a Wilderness Area and is included here because special restrictions apply. Contact the National Park Service at (970) 627-3471 for details on these restrictions.

Trailhead Location – The directions given are the most direct from the closest major road. Sometimes there is more than one way to reach a trailhead and two access descriptions are given, but generally only the most direct route is provided. All mileages are approximate. Some trailheads may be identified with a trailhead sign, adequate parking, and restroom facilities. Other trailheads are unidentified, have limited parking on the side of the road, and have no restroom facilities. Be prepared for either condition.

Trail Description – Trail highlights and directions are detailed for an enjoyable trip.

Historical Note - Interesting information is included for the purpose of adding color to Grand County's trails. The information has been gathered by interviewing long time residents, historians, reviewing old maps, and interpolating folklore. Many historians have differing opinions on historical events and many of the records have been lost forever. For this reason the historical information included throughout this book should be regarded as one version of history and should not be regarded as absolute fact.

Map – The map provides information regarding the starting point, points of interest, unclear parts of the trail, and destination point. These items are numbered and correspond to the trail description and the profile. TN (true north) and MN (magnetic or compass north) are also identified. Scale is provided for additional information.

Elevation Profile – The profile is a graph of the grade (or elevation gain) vs. distance for each trail. The following information is displayed:

- The vertical axis is the trail elevation in feet above sea level.
- The horizontal axis is the trail length in miles.
- The number in the far left lower corner is the scale of the profile. For example: 1.0x means that the elevation and mileage are proportional (or 1:1). However, 2.4x means that the elevation is 2.4 times larger than the mileage (2.4:1). In other words, the elevation looks 2.4 times steeper than it is. This scale factor varies for each profile. It is important to remember when comparing levels of difficulty between trails.
- To the right of the scale factor is the total mileage and final elevation.
- In the lower right corner is the elevation gain. The first number is the elevation ascended, the second number is the elevation descended, and the final number is the net gain. Total gain is the first number plus the second number, which applies to the complete hike, both going and returning. For a One-way hike requiring two vehicles or a Round-trip hike, only the first number applies to the total gain.
- Horizontally along the top of the profile are the numbered points of interest, which correspond to the trail description and the map.

Boiler used at Lumber Mill at Monarch Lake

4. GLOSSARY AND LEGEND

Alpine - Life Zone between 11,500' – 14,400'. Trees do not grow in this life zone and it is often referred to as the tundra. It is made up of mostly mosses and lichens with occasional grasses and sedges.

Bouldering – non-technical climbing over large rocks, also referred to as scrambling.

Buck and Rail – fence made of logs to block a road or signify a trailhead.

Cairn - a pile of stones or rocks constructed as a landmark.

Cirque - concave excavation on a mountainside carved by glacial erosion.

Clear-cut - an area where trees have been removed generally for the purpose of logging.

Continental Divide - the Continental Divide is the mountain range, which divides the watershed between the eastern United States and the western United States. The Continental Divide is referred to in this book loosely. Many of the mountains in Winter Park, James Peak area, Vasquez Mountains, Indian Peaks, Never Summer Range, and the Troublesome Valley lie along the Continental Divide. When describing views along the Continental Divide, the geographic regions mentioned above are generally referenced for visual clarification.

CD Trail – **(CDNST or CDT)** Continental Divide National Scenic Trail is a 3100 mile trail that runs the length of the Continental Divide from Canada into Mexico through Montana, Idaho, Wyoming, Colorado, and New Mexico. It was designated a National Scenic Trail in 1978 by Congress and although not yet completed in its entirety, Colorado is 90% complete. The beginning of the CD Trail in Grand County is along the southeast border near Hagar Mountain. The trail follows the eastern border of the county, heads west through Rocky Mountain National Park, then follows the northern border before exiting the county at the northwestern corner near Rabbit Ears Pass. The trail generally follows close to or parallel to the Continental Divide ridgeline based on the terrain.

CR - County Road – most roads in Grand County are identified as CR, such as CR 8 or Grand County 8.

FSR - (FDR or FR) – Forest System Road (previously called Forest Development Route or Forest Route). Roads within Forest Service Boundaries are identified as FSR, such as FSR 140. Also previously known as USFR or United States Forest Road.

GPS - Global Positioning System – most commonly known as a hand held receiver, which identifies longitude and latitude coordinates calculated from satellite triangulation. Trailhead and final destination coordinates are listed on each hike. Additional GPS coordinates for points of interest are listed in the back of this book in the Appendix. Longitude and latitude are also noted on the edges of any USGS or Trails Illustrated topographical map. All coordinates use NAD83 datum.

Montane - Life Zone between 8000' – 10,000'. Usually timbered in lodgepole pine, aspen, blue spruce, and Englemann spruce.

RMNP – Rocky Mountain National Park.

Scramble – see Bouldering.

Scree – loose rock generally on a hillside.

Single-track – a narrow trail generally trodden by foot or horse traffic.

Subalpine - Life Zone between 10,000' – 11,500'. Usually timbered in Engelmann spruce and subalpine fir.

Switchback – where a trail ascends or descends a steep hillside and turns sharply in the opposite direction.

Tank Trap – large dirt berm built to deter bike, OHV, or vehicle traffic on a trail.

Tarns - small mountain lakes.

Timberline - the boundary between the subalpine and the alpine, usually about 11,500'. Stunted Engelmann spruce trees are found at timberline. The term Krummholtz (crooked wood) is commonly used to describe this region.

USFR – United States Forest Road – See **FSR**.

Water bar – generally made of logs which are placed in the ground to divert water off the trail. Sometimes berms are built to deter large water flows.

Waypoint – the longitude and latitude coordinates of the trailhead, destination, or a point of interest. The term is generally used by GPS enthusiasts.

🚲 ✝ 🚶 - combined bike and hike trip recommended.

🚐 🚐 - two cars recommended for one-way hiking.

🌙 - overnight trip recommended.

5. GPS USE

A GPS is a hiker's luxury and although it is not necessary to have one, it is an added safety feature and was found to be an invaluable tool for hiking and writing this book. GPS use has become a part of today's technology for many backcountry hikers.

The term GPS refers to "Global Positioning System", which locates longitude and latitude coordinates through the use of satellites. GPS units were originally designed for the US military, but have become increasingly popular among the general public for recreational navigation. Today's GPS receivers are capable of measuring longitude, latitude, altitude, and recording and storing information for specific locations. A GPS can track point to point routes and can provide direction for backtracking. Some GPS receivers have built-in maps that make navigation and orientation simple. They can even display distances traveled and distances remaining along with the rate of speed traveled. Today's GPS features are endless for the backcountry hiker.

When using this book with a GPS, note that trailhead and destination data are listed for each hike description. Additional waypoints for points of interest and junction points are listed in the Appendix. These points can be easily programmed into any standard GPS, allowing the user to create the described route and follow it with confidence. All our coordinates were recorded with our GPS datum set at NAD83.

The Garmin 12 CX GPS was used to compile the original data for this book because of its receiver type (parallel-channel), memory capacity, number of channels, routing map, download capabilities, size, ease of use, antenna configuration, and speed of information. Later updates were made using a Garmin GPSMap 76S because of its added features including a built-in base map and electronic compass.

When choosing a GPS, the options are based on personal preference. However, one important feature to consider in the high country is that mountains and trees can block satellite signals. Purchasing a GPS unit with a parallel-channel receiver is necessary for reliable responses of signals and information where these obstacles exist.

GPS receivers give hikers security in knowing where they are, where they are going, and how to get back. When route and location information is available, uncertainty is decreased and enjoyment is increased.

Note - When this book was originally GPS'd and published, GPS technology was not as accurate as it is today. Therefore, our waypoint data may vary slightly from current GPS read-outs. That being said, the directions in the book will cover any discrepancies which may occur.

Lone Eagle Peak and Mirror Lake

6. HIKES BY REGION

Troublesome Valley and Trailhead Map 225

Williams Fork Mountains and Trailhead Map 257

Additional Grand County Hikes 280

Gore Canyon and Routt Divide and Trailhead Maps 281

WINTER PARK

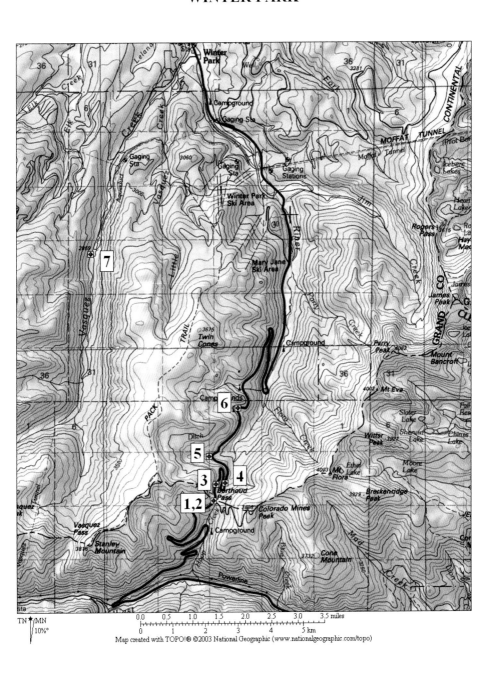

1. BERTHOUD PASS TO WINTER PARK SKI RESORT 🚗 🚗

Level of Difficulty - Moderate
One-way Mileage – 10.48 miles
One-way Hiking Time – 6 hours
Altitude, GPS Reading at Trailhead –11,300', 39°47'53"N, 105°46'39"W
Altitude, GPS Reading at Destination – 9104', 39°53'08"N, 105°45'48"W
Trail Fee Required – No

🐕 Leash, 🚫 N/A, ⚠ Yes, WD VQ

Trailhead Location – This hike is a one-way hike requiring two vehicles.
1st Car Parking - Park the first car at the Winter Park Ski Resort, south of the town of Winter Park, located off US Hwy 40 between mile markers 232 and 233. Parking is available near the Winter Park Ski Resort Base and village (8).
2nd Car Parking - Park the second car at the Berthoud Pass parking area located on US Hwy 40, south of the town of Winter Park, near mile marker 243. On the west side of the highway (at the crest of the pass) is the trailhead, next to mile marker 243 (1).

Trail Description – Climb steeply through the subalpine forest, breaking through to the tundra. Above timberline, the trail follows the Continental Divide ridgeline (2). During the winter, skiers race down the shear face on the left. Climb up several switchbacks (3) where the trail levels off slightly. On the left is a tarn with Englemann Peak behind it. On the right is a view of Twin Cones, which is the top of the Winter Park Ski Resort. Near the top of the hill is a cairn on the right, off the main trail (4). This cairn is visible when the pyramid shaped Vasquez Peak comes into view. Follow this cairn off the worn trail toward Twin Cones and head north onto the unsigned Nystrom Trail. There is no visible foot trail from this point and no sign, but there are several cairns to identify the way. Hike across the tundra and follow the cairns down to a small saddle with a shallow tarn (5). Pass around the left side of the tarn and hike up the hill following the cairns. At the top of this hill are terrific 360° views. Looking north and clockwise are Longs Peak, Indian Peaks, James Peak area, Colorado Mines Peak and the communications stations, the Continental Divide, Stanley Mountain, Vasquez Pass, Vasquez Peak, Mt. Nystrom and the Vasquez Mountains, White Cliffs, Sheep Mountain, and the Never Summer Range. Continue toward Twin Cones. Winter Park Ski Resort's Vasquez Cirque is on the left. Follow the ski area "Out of Bounds" markers and skirt the left side of Twin Cones. Pass the first cone and maintain the same elevation or begin downhill slightly. This leads to the "Primrose" Ski Trail. Parsenn Bowl is ahead and the Timberline chair lift is on the right, which ends at the top of the second cone. In the valley below, three chair lifts converge. This area is called Lunch Rock. Follow the trail left, down the ridgeline in the direction of Lunch Rock through a field of giant boulders. Return below timberline and head into the woods. A trail sign identifies the route to the Winter Park Complex. Follow this trail into the forest and pass several meadows filled with wildflowers. Follow the trail called "Upper Roof of the Rockies" (6). Hike through the woods and meadows and cross several ski runs and pass under several chair lifts.

Sections of this trail are shared with bikes so be alert to cyclists. At the intersection, turn right toward the Sunspot Lodge and at the next intersection turn left. Follow any other signs to the Sunspot. From the Sunspot (7), the Ute Trail to the Winter Park Ski Resort Base is between the Zephyr Chair Lift and the Sunspot. Follow the series of switchbacks, down across several ski trails and through the woods to the Winter Park Ski Resort Base (8).

Vasquez Peak and the Vasquez Mountain Range along the Continental Divide

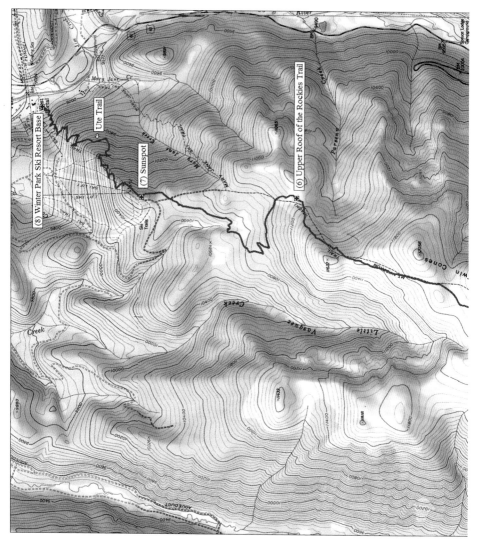

(8) Winter Park Ski Resort Base

Ute Trail

(7) Sunspot

(6) Upper Roof of the Rockies Trail

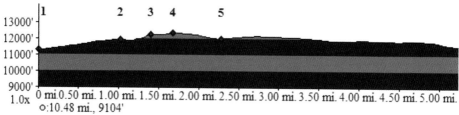

13000'
12000'
11000'
10000'
9000'
1.0x

0 mi 0.50 mi. 1.00 mi. 1.50 mi. 2.00 mi. 2.50 mi. 3.00 mi. 3.50 mi. 4.00 mi. 4.50 mi. 5.00 mi.
○:10.48 mi., 9104'

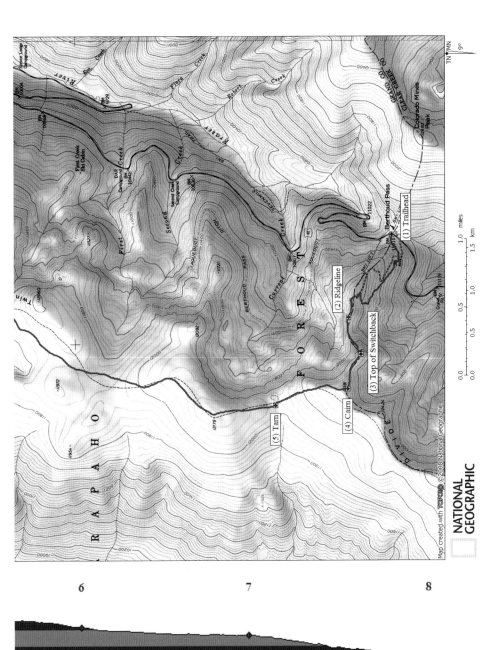

NATIONAL
GEOGRAPHIC

5.50 mi. 6.00 mi. 6.50 mi. 7.00 mi. 7.50 mi. 8.00 mi. 8.50 mi. 9.00 mi. 9.50 mi.10.00 mi.10.50 m
Gain: +1418' -3614' = -2196'

2. STANLEY MOUNTAIN, VASQUEZ PASS, AND VASQUEZ PEAK

Level of Difficulty – Most Difficult
One-way Mileage – 6.14 miles
One-way Hiking Time – 4 ½ hours
Altitude, GPS Reading at Trailhead – 11,300', 39°47'53"N, 105°46'39"W
Altitude, GPS Reading at Destination – 12,904', 39°47'47"N, 105°51'18"W
Trail Fee Required – No

🐾 Yes, ✦ N/A, ▲ Yes, **WD** VQ

Trailhead Location – On US Hwy 40, south of the town of Winter Park, at mile marker 243 is Berthoud Pass. Park at the parking area on the east side of the highway. On the west side of the highway (at the crest of the pass) is the trailhead, next to mile marker 243 (1).

Trail Description – This is a great challenge for the hiker who enjoys an interval training workout. Climb steeply through the subalpine forest, breaking through to the tundra. Above timberline, the trail follows the Continental Divide ridgeline (2). During the winter, skiers race down the shear face on the left. Climb up several switchbacks where the trail levels off slightly. On the left is a tarn with Englemann Peak behind it. On the right is a view of Twin Cones, which is the top of Winter Park Ski Resort. Approach the top of this hill, where there is a great view of the pyramid shaped Vasquez Peak. At the top of the hill looking west are views of the Vasquez Creek Valley with Mt. Nystrom to the right of Vasquez Peak. To the left is US Hwy 40 below. Follow the trail beside two unnamed peaks with views of several tarns to the left on the way to Stanley Mountain. The trail does not continue to the top of Stanley Mountain, but the short climb is worth the view. On top of Stanley Mountain (3), looking north and clockwise are Longs Peak, Indian Peaks, the James Peak area, Colorado Mines Peak with its communications stations, US Hwy 40, Engelmann Peak, Robeson Peak, Bard Peak, Jones Pass Road, Mount Parnassus, Henderson Mine, Woods Mountain, the Continental Divide, Vasquez Pass, Bill's Peak, Byers Peak, Unnamed Peak, the Never Summer Range, and the Fraser Valley.

From Stanley Mountain, do not continue on the worn trail. This trail leads to Jones Pass and is used when hiking the CD Trail while carrying heavy packs. Head northwest toward Vasquez Pass and follow the cairns and posts down the very steep slope. There is no visible trail and the best way down is to make several switchbacks, keeping the cairns in sight. Follow the cairns to a faint switchback trail near the bottom. At Vasquez Pass (4) the trail to Vasquez Peak is visible on the other side of the saddle. Follow the trail up a few switchbacks and climb along the ridgeline to the next unnamed peak (5). On the right side is a view of Winter Park Ski Resort's Vasquez Cirque. From the top of this unnamed peak, Vasquez Peak is due west. There are two cairns, one on the right and one on the left. From the cairn on the right is a beautiful view of the Vasquez Creek valley.

The cairn on the left (6) is the more direct route and heads west down a saddle. On the ridgeline above, there appears to be a giant cairn between the peak ahead and Vasquez Peak. This cairn (7) is "nature-made" and is conveniently located on the trail. Follow the bouldered hillside down through the grassy meadow to the saddle. Vasquez Peak is best reached by paralleling the Continental Divide ridgeline. Cross below the peak at the top of the saddle and follow the roller coaster hills. On the left is the Jones Pass Road crossing the Continental Divide. After the "nature made" cairn (7) is in view, there are a few more roller coaster dips. The hillside is almost entirely made up of boulders. The views are endless and breathtaking. From the top of Vasquez Peak (8), looking clockwise from Jones Pass are the Gore Range and the St. Louis Divide. Continuing west are Mt. Nystrom with Vasquez Lake below, Bill's and Byers Peaks, Ptarmigan Peak, Bottle Peak, Unnamed Peak, the Never Summer Range, Lake Granby, Longs Peak, the Fraser Valley below, Indian Peaks, Rollins Pass and the Moffat Road, the James Peak area, Colorado Mines Peak, and Englemann Peak.

Historical Note – Both Berthoud Pass and Vasquez Pass were discovered at the same time by Edward Berthoud's exploration party. Vasquez Pass was eventually abandoned and Berthoud Pass became the major wagon route into the Fraser Valley. There is some doubt as to whether Berthoud was the first to discover Berthoud Pass. A few years earlier several miners from Empire City were said to have discovered the pass, but Berthoud was responsible for promoting it as a major road into Middle Park.

Vasquez Peak

31

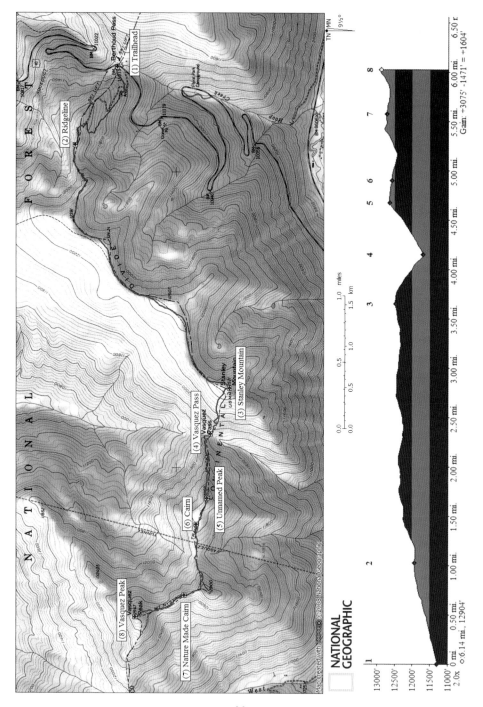

NATIONAL
GEOGRAPHIC

Map created with TOPO!® ©2005 National Geographic

(1) Trailhead
(2) Ridgeline
(3) Stanley Mountain
(4) Vasquez Pass
(5) Unnamed Peak
(6) Cairn
(7) Nature Made Cairn
(8) Vasquez Peak

Gain: +3075', -1471' = -1604'

32

3. BERTHOUD PASS AQUEDUCT TO SECOND CREEK 🚗 🚗

Level of Difficulty - Moderate
One-way Mileage – 4.39 miles
One-way Hiking Time – 2 hours
Altitude, GPS Reading at Trailhead – 11,212', 39°48'08"N, 105°46'38"W
Altitude, GPS Reading at Destination – 10,585', 39°49'22"N, 105°46'11"W
Trail Fee Required – No

🐾 Yes, 🚣 N/A, ▲ Yes, WD None

Trailhead Location – This is a one-way hike requiring two vehicles.
1st Car Parking – On US Hwy 40, south of the town of Winter Park, at mile marker 240 is a pullout on the west side of the highway. There is no trailhead sign, but there is an avalanche warning sign at the trailhead for winter backcountry skiers (11). This is also the parking area for the Second Creek Trailhead, Hike #6, page 40.
2nd Car Parking – On US Hwy 40, south of the town of Winter Park, just north of Berthoud Pass between mile markers 242 and 243 (closer to mile marker 243) is a pullout on the east side of the highway. Park at this pullout. The trailhead (1) is on the left (west side of the highway). There is no trailhead sign, but the trail begins on the service road beside a sign "National Forest means year round fun!" just south of the pullout.

Trail Description – Follow the service road and pass around the gate. This road is used to access a water collection site and measuring devices, which is just up the hill from the highway (2). Snow and water levels are measured here periodically to project the water supply that is transported to the Front Range. On the right, immediately after the collection site is an aqueduct and a view of Colorado Mines Peak. Follow the service road to a viewpoint (3), where US Hwy 40 is visible below, the Continental Divide is on the right and ahead (east and north), Current Creek Cirque is to the west, and a cut across the hillside above the highway, which is the Berthoud Pass Aqueduct.

Head west on the road and pass a shelf of boulders on the right below. Move into the subalpine forest and descend a short hill to a concrete water gate/diverter surrounded by a metal frame (4). The gate is used to regulate the flow of water to the Front Range. Ascend the hill where the road fades into a trail. The dirt has eroded away at several places on the trail and a metal water pipe is visible. At the top of this hill is another water diversion gate (5) which flows directly from the Berthoud Pass Aqueduct. Follow the trail along the right bank of the Berthoud Pass Aqueduct through the woods to Current Creek (6). At this location, Current Creek is regulated to flow into a series of aqueducts. To the west is the Current Creek cirque and drainage. To the east is a view of Colorado Mines Peak, Mt. Flora, Mt. Eva, and Parry Peak. Don't cross any waterways and continue to follow the ditch.

After Current Creek, the old aqueduct does not carry water as it did when it was built. Many sections of the aqueduct have caved in and filled in with dirt. However, long sections of the walls of the aqueduct are in great condition and it is amazing to think of the labor involved to create this aqueduct years ago. On the right is a pond (7) and beside and beyond the pond are the remains of a wooden aqueduct used to bridge the flow of water across this low spot in the topography. Pass the remains of the wooden aqueduct back onto the bank of the aqueduct. Continue beside the aqueduct where the trees have grown on the trail. The trees to the east of the aqueduct are sparse and there are occasional views of US Hwy 40 and the Continental Divide. Continue to follow the aqueduct and move away from the highway and back into the subalpine forest where the trees are more dense. Head west toward the Second Creek Cirque. There is an occasional view of the chair lift at the Winter Park Ski Resort to the north, just to the east of Twin Cones.

The trees along the ditch thin slightly and there is a view to the right (east) of Parry Peak and Mt. Eva. As the terrain and views open up, there is a great rock depression on the right caused by glacial movement and a small cirque on the left (8). Continue to follow the aqueduct to a small waterfall (9). At this waterfall, leave the aqueduct and bear right. Stay on the right outside edge of the willows and spruce trees through the meadow. Second Creek Cirque is to the left (west). At the edge of the woods near the promontory is the Broome Hut (10) slated to open December 2012. From the cabin, again are great views of James Peak and looking south are Mt. Eva with a small building on top, Mt. Flora, and the Colorado Mines Peak with all its communications stations.

Head east and pick up the worn trail. Descend through the meadows into the subalpine forest. Continue on this moderate descent into the montane forest of firs, lodgepole, and spruce trees. Wind near the creek to the Second Creek Trailhead (11).

Pond beside Aqueduct

34

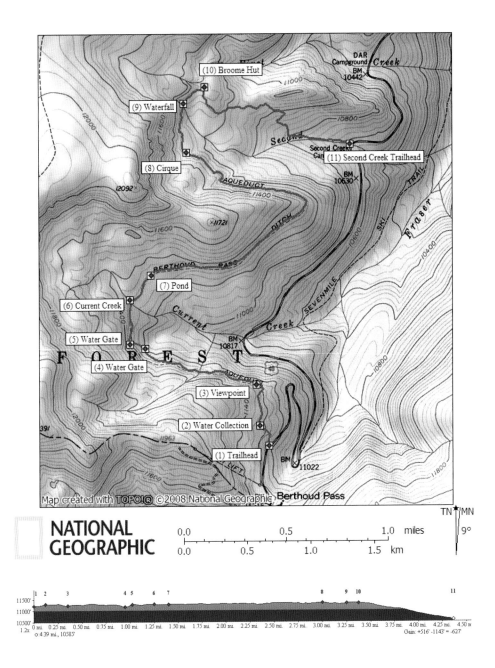

(10) Broome Hut

(9) Waterfall

(8) Cirque

(11) Second Creek Trailhead

(7) Pond

(6) Current Creek

(5) Water Gate

(4) Water Gate

(3) Viewpoint

(2) Water Collection

(1) Trailhead

DAR Campground
BM 10442

BM 10630

BM 10817

FOREST

Berthoud Pass

BM 11022

Map created with TOPO!® ©2008 National Geographic

NATIONAL GEOGRAPHIC

| 0.0 | | 0.5 | | 1.0 | miles |
| 0.0 | | 0.5 | | 1.0 | 1.5 | km |

TN /MN
9°

4. SEVEN MILE SKI TRAIL 🚗 🚗

Level of Difficulty - Moderate
One-way Mileage – 2.46 miles
One-way Hiking Time – 2 hours
Altitude, GPS Reading at Trailhead – 10,903', 39°48'09"N, 105°46'26"W
Altitude, GPS Reading at Destination – 9761', 39°49'39"N, 105°45'34"W
Trail Fee Required – No

🐾 <u>Yes</u>, 🐟 <u>N/A</u>, ▲ <u>Yes</u>, **WD** <u>None</u>

Trailhead Location – This is a one-way hike requiring two vehicles.
1st Car Parking – On US Hwy 40, south of the town of Winter Park at the first switchback from town, between mile markers 236 and 237 is a pullout. Park here (6).
2nd Car Parking – On US Hwy 40, south of the town of Winter Park on US Hwy 40, between mile markers 241 and 242 (closer to 242) is a pullout on the east side of the highway. Park at the far north end of this pullout (1).

Trail Description – This is a short hike with no elevation gain. It is rated as moderate because it follows an old road that is overgrown with trees and is challenging to follow in places. This was the original wagon road over Berthoud Pass and the Continental Divide into Middle Park. Edward Berthoud was responsibly for getting support to build this toll road.

To begin this hike, find the culvert at the north end of the pullout. Below the culvert is a level spot. The pullout is on top of part of the old road. Hike down the steep loose sandy hillside. Once on level ground, head north. The old Berthoud Pass Road is soon visible. It is about 12 feet wide and level with hard packed dirt. The old roadbed has been well preserved over time, but trees have grown up on the road. Although the road is easily identified, walking around the trees is a challenge. The road is a gentle downhill grade from start to finish.

Parallel US Hwy 40 to the first of several creeks (2). During the construction of US Hwy 40, this drainage was routed here and an avalanche of rocks obliterated the road. Cross the creek and continue at the same elevation through the woods. Follow the road through the woods to Current Creek (3). At Current Creek, the remains of a bridge are visible. Cross the creek to a clearing, where there is a view of the Berthoud Pass Aqueduct on the hillside ahead and US Hwy 40 on the right. From this clearing, the road disappears in the marsh. Continue through the marsh and make a slight turn to the right (north), where the road is visible again. Taller trees have grown on the road and walking around them is a challenge. Beyond a clearing is an old car with wooden spoke wheels (4) on the right side of the road.

Next, the road disappears under a rockslide, but the roadway is still obvious. Continue on the road where the trees are taller. Cross Second Creek (5) and follow the road through the jungle of trees to First Creek (6). After First Creek, the old road was again demolished when the new highway was created. Follow the creek to US Hwy 40.

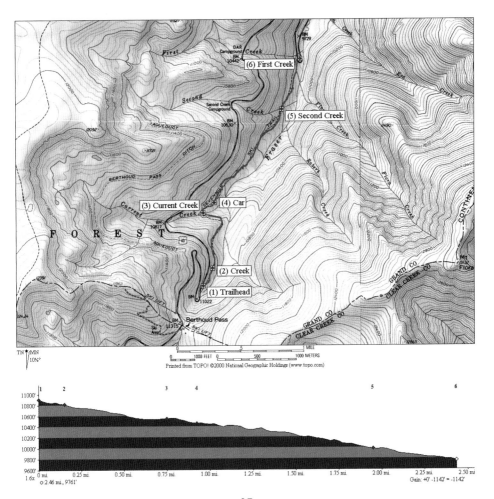

5. CURRENT CREEK LOOP

Level of Difficulty - Moderate
Round-trip Mileage – 2.89 miles
Round-trip Hiking Time – 2 hours
Altitude, GPS Reading at Trailhead – 10,805', 39°48'35"N, 105°46'47"W
Altitude, GPS Reading at 1st Pond – 11,513', 39°49'00"N, 105°47'24"W
Altitude, GPS Reading at 2nd Pond - 11,628' 39°48'43"N, 105°47'43"W
Trail Fee Required – No

🐈 Yes, 🐟 N/A, ▲ Yes, **WD** None

Trailhead Location – On US Hwy 40, south of the town of Winter Park, near mile marker 241 is a large pullout on the west side of the highway. There is no trailhead sign, but the trail is on the right of the creek (1).

Trail Description – Follow the trail on the right side of Current Creek upstream through the spruce-fir forest. Move away from the creek and come to a faint "T". Turn right at the "T", which leads to the aqueduct (2). At the aqueduct there is a gate that diverts water. Cross the aqueduct and continue to the right of this gate toward the cirque. The cascading creek on the left makes a beautiful picture with the cirque in the background and the flowers in the foreground. Move away from the creek and skirt the woods through the willows. At the boulder field (3), the trail disappears. Cross over the boulders and head up the hill to the north. It is a short walk through the trees where the first pond (4) hugs the cirque face. To reach the second pond, traverse the hillside left (southwest) of the first pond. Remain at the same elevation to reach a small tarn (5). Climb up the boulders behind the tarn and through the willows to the second pond (6). There are actually two ponds here, one above the other. This is a good place to view the cirque and valley below. From this pond, head down through the woods where Current Creek flows in the valley. Cross back over the aqueduct (2) and turn right. Follow the service road beside the aqueduct into the woods. The water eventually flows into a pipe and disappears into the mountain. Continue along the service road and just beyond the low spot in the road, the trail reappears on the left. Follow this trail down the hill and back to the creek to a small hut. This is known as the Peter Rabbit Hut (7). Follow the trail downstream where the inbound trail is visible. Cross the creek and follow the trail back to the trailhead (1).

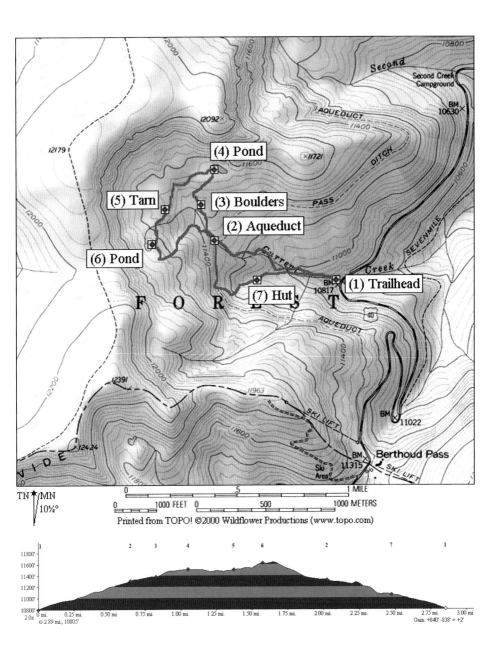

6. SECOND CREEK

Level of Difficulty - Easy
One-way Mileage - .99 miles
One-way Hiking Time - 45 minutes
Altitude, GPS Reading at Trailhead – 10,585', 39°49'22"N, 105°46'11"W
Altitude, GPS Reading at Destination – 11,322', 39°49'36"N, 105°46'59"W
Trail Fee Required – No

🐕 Yes, 🚳 No, ▲ Yes, **WD** None

Trailhead Location – On US Hwy 40, south of the town of Winter Park, at mile marker 240 is a pullout on the west side of the highway. There is no trailhead sign, but there is an avalanche warning sign at the trailhead for winter backcountry skiers (1).

Trail Description – Begin to the right of the avalanche sign and parallel Second Creek. There are several side trails that inter-twine with the main trail, but the main trail is distinguishable. This is a montane forest with spruce and fir, along with lodgepole pine trees. Move away from the creek. The trees thin and the cirque is visible ahead. At the crest of the long hill, the trail levels off slightly and an aqueduct is visible against the steep hillside. The trail turns to the right and the Broome Hut (slated to open December 2012) is straight ahead (2).

From the promontory beside the hut, the views of the James Peak area are spectacular. Looking as far north as possible along the Continental Divide is James Peak. From James Peak, looking south are Parry Peak, Mt. Eva with a small building on top, Mt. Flora, and the Colorado Mines Peak with all its communications stations.

Note – This area is a popular winter destination for tele-mark skiing, cross country skiing, and snowshoeing.

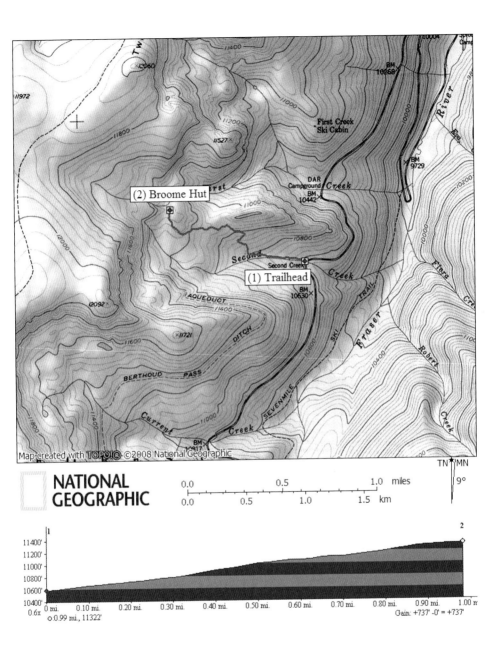

7. VASQUEZ CREEK TO VASQUEZ PASS 🚴 + 🚶

Level of Difficulty - Difficult
One-way Mileage – bike (2.85 miles) + hike (4.23 miles)
One-way Hiking/Biking Time – bike (1 hour) + hike (2 ½ hours)
Altitude, GPS Reading at Trailhead - 9430', 39°51'52"N, 105°49'22"W
Altitude, GPS Reading at Destination – 11,699', 39°47'15"N, 105°49'44"W
Trail Fee Required – No
🐾 Yes, 🎣 Yes, ▲ Yes, WD VQ

Trailhead Location – From US Hwy 40, in the town of Winter Park, head west on Vasquez Road. Follow this paved road for 1.1 miles and then continue on the rough dirt road for 1.7 miles, where it becomes FSR 148. Follow this for another 1.9 miles to the trailhead (1). Park on the side of the road. Do not park in front of the gate.

Trail Description –

Bike – Pass around the gate and follow the service road. Parallel Vasquez Creek and a marshy willow lined valley, which are on the left. It is a steady climb. About a mile from the trailhead is a clear view of the "V" shaped Vasquez Pass. Cross the creek and follow the trail through the dense forest. Cross a second creek and follow the trail to a fork (2). The left fork leads to the Vasquez Pass Trail and the right fork leads to the Vasquez Aqueduct. To continue to Vasquez Pass, park bikes here. Bikes are not permitted on the Vasquez Pass Trail because the trail crosses into the Vasquez Peak Wilderness.

For a short side trip, take the right fork for .5 miles to the aqueduct (2A). The Vasquez Aqueduct begins west of Jones Pass where water is collected from Bobtail Creek, McQueary Creek, and Steelman Creek. It flows through the Jones Pass Tunnel into Clear Creek, where it is diverted into the Vasquez Aqueduct and then flows through the Moffat Tunnel to Denver. Return to the fork (2).

Hike - Follow the Vasquez Pass Trail through the lush subalpine forest. Cross the creek in the bottom of the valley and begin a steady climb through the forest up a set of switchbacks. Cross a creek (3) into a meadow with a great view of Vasquez Pass. After the meadow, continue into the forest with peek-a-boo views of the Continental Divide. Hike up a second set of switchbacks nearing timberline. Stanley Mountain is visible on the left of the pass and ahead is an unnamed peak. Through the meadow the trail is faint. Follow the cairns and skirt the forest's edge to the top of Vasquez Pass (4). At the top of the pass looking south are Red Mountain and Pettingell Peak. The buzz from the Henderson Mine is audible below. The trail straight up on the left (east) leads to Stanley Mountain and the trail straight up to the right (west) leads to Vasquez Peak. To the north are the Vasquez Creek valley and the town of Fraser with the mountains of the Continental Divide in the background.

Side Trip to Berthoud Pass or Vasquez Peak - Refer to Stanley Mountain, Vasquez Pass, and Vasquez Peak Hike #2, page 30.

Note - Beneath Red Mountain is one of the largest deposits of molybdenum ore in the world. The Henderson Mine excavates the ore, transports it east through the Continental Divide on a 14 mile long conveyor to the Williams Fork Valley, and then processes it at the mill for commercial use.

Historical Note – This trail over Vasquez Pass originally started on the east side of the Continental Divide in the town of Empire and was one of the routes proposed by Edward Berthoud as a major road over the Continental Divide into the Fraser Valley.

Vasquez Creek was originally named Dennis Creek after a member of Edward Berthoud's exploration party.

Red Mountain from Vasquez Pass

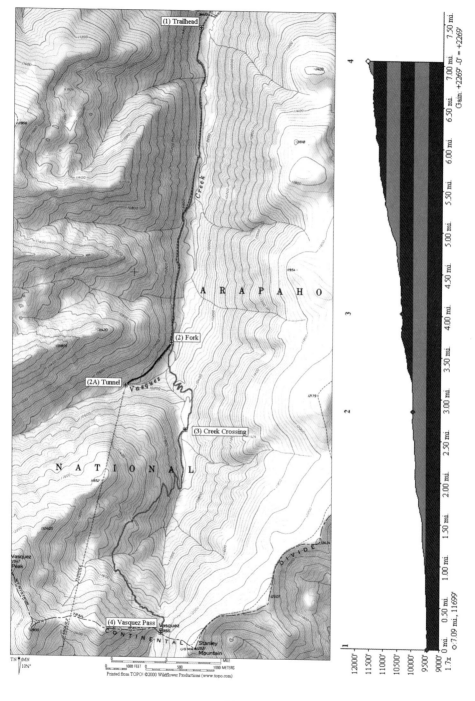

(1) Trailhead

A R A P A H O

(2) Fork

(2A) Tunnel

Vasquez

(3) Creek Crossing

N A T I O N A L

Vasquez
Peak

(4) Vasquez Pass

Vasquez
Pass

C O N T I N E N T A L

D I V I D E

Stanley
Mountain

TN /MN
10%°

1000 FEET   MILE
500   1000 METERS

Printed from TOPO! ©2000 Wildflower Productions (www.topo.com)

1.7x

0 mi.   0.50 mi.   1.00 mi.   1.50 mi.   2.00 mi.   2.50 mi.   3.00 mi.   3.50 mi.   4.00 mi.   4.50 mi.   5.00 mi.   5.50 mi.   6.00 mi.   6.50 mi.   7.00 mi.   7.50 mi.

◊ 7.09 mi, 11699'

Gain: +2269' -0' = +2269'

12000'
11500'
11000'
10500'
10000'
9500'

JAMES PEAK AREA

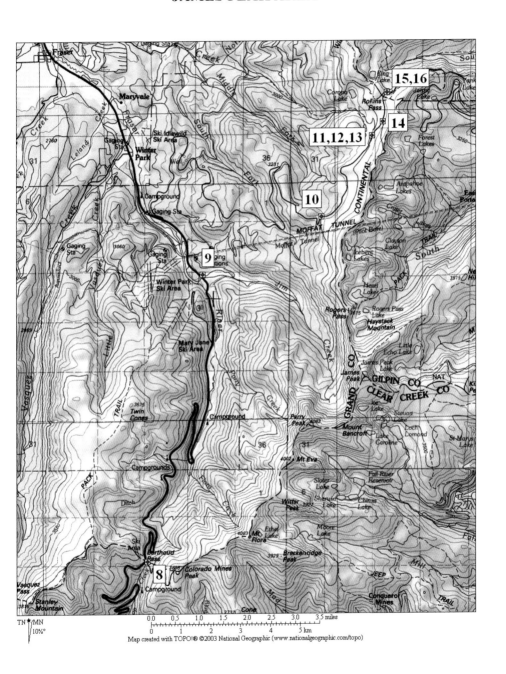

8. MT. FLORA, MT. EVA, PARRY PEAK, MT. BANCROFT, AND JAMES PEAK 🚗 🚗

Level of Difficulty – Most Difficult
One-way Mileage – 12.91 miles
One-way Hiking Time – 9 ½ hours
Altitude, GPS Reading at Trailhead – 11,290', 39°47'52"N, 105°46'36"W
Altitude, GPS Reading at Parry Peak – 13,324', 39°50'17"N, 105°42'47"W
Altitude, GPS Reading at Trestle – 11,124', 39°53'56"N, 105°42'28"W
Trail Fee Required – No

🐾 Yes, 🎣 N/A, ▲ Yes, WD JP

Trailhead Location – This is a one-way hike requiring two vehicles.
1st Car Parking – On US Hwy 40, north of the Winter Park Ski Resort main entrance between mile markers 231 and 232, turn east onto CR 80 (FSR 149), also known as the Moffat Road to Corona Pass. Follow FSR 149 for 10.7 miles to the top of the railroad trestle. Park on the side of the road near the Rogers Pass Trail sign (17). The Moffat Road is a good dirt road. This road is the old railroad bed where trains crossed the Continental Divide at Rollins Pass (near the town of Corona), traveling from Denver to Hot Sulphur Springs. For an interpretive self-guided tour of the Moffat Road stop by the Winter Park Visitor's Center.
2ⁿᵈ Car Parking - On US Hwy 40, south of the town of Winter Park, at mile marker 243 is Berthoud Pass. Park at the Berthoud Pass parking lot. The trailhead is at the gate to the south of the parking area (1).

Trail Description – Most of this hike is above timberline. Be aware of the ever-changing weather conditions. There is no quick route to escape below timberline during a thunderstorm. Pass around the gate along the CD Trail and follow the road through the trees to timberline and onto the tundra. It is a steady climb up several switchbacks. There are great views of Englemann Peak to the southwest, the Woods Creek valley, Hagar Mountain, Red Mountain, Stanley Mountain, the Current Creek cirque, and Twin Cones at Winter Park Ski Resort. On the left is a fork (2), where a single-track trail leaves the road.

For a short side trip to the top of the Colorado Mines Peak, continue on the road to the right. Colorado Mines Peak (2A) houses facilities for aviation and telecommunications systems. Return to the fork (2).

To continue to Mt. Flora, follow the single-track trail down across the tundra. To the left (west) and clockwise are the Vasquez Mountains, the Troublesome Valley, the Never Summer Mountains, Lake Granby, the mountains in Rocky Mountain National Park, Longs Peak, Indian Peaks, Parry Peak, Mt. Eva, and Mt. Flora. A lower trail joins the existing trail from the left (3). Continue straight (northeast) toward the saddle with Mt. Flora ahead and a small tarn below on the right.

46

Along the hillsides and valleys, the tundra is covered in short grasses, alpine flowers, mosses, and lichens. Most of the approaches and descents to the peaks are covered with rocks, boulders, short grasses, and tight sod. The peaks themselves are very rocky with little protection from the fierce cold and wind.

On the approach to Mt. Flora, there are several false pinnacles. From the top of Mt. Flora (4), both Ethel Lake and Byron Lake are visible to the east. Continuing clockwise are the Front Range Mountains with the Denver skyline in the distance, Breckenridge Peak, Mt. Evans, Grays and Torreys Peaks, Englemann Peak, Red Mountain, the Gore Range, the Vasquez Range, Byers Peak, Ptarmigan Peak, White Cliffs, Sheep Mountain, the Troublesome Valley, the town of Fraser and the Fraser Valley, Lake Granby, the Never Summer Range, the mountains in Rocky Mountain National Park, Longs Peak, Parry Peak, Mt. Eva, James Peak, Mt. Bancroft, and Witter Peak.

From Mt. Flora, head north along the ridge. Stay high until the descent is inevitable. Follow the ridge down to the saddle (5), where Bill Moore Lake is visible on the right. Follow the cairns up the hill to a second saddle, where Witter Peak, Slater Lake, Chinns Lake, and Sherwin Lake are visible on the right. On the left, the Winter Park Ski Resort is visible along with the town of Winter Park. Continue up the hill to the abandoned Common Carrier Telecommunications Site (6) and then to the top of Mt. Eva (7). A large tarn is visible between Mt. Eva and Parry Peak.

From Mt. Eva, head north toward Parry Peak. On the ascent to Parry Peak, there is a view of the Fall River Reservoir and Chinns Lake on the right (east). From the top of Parry Peak (8), looking north and clockwise are Longs Peak, Indian Peaks, the Continental Divide, James Peak, Mt. Bancroft, the Front Range Mountains, Fall River Reservoir, and Chinns Lake. Continuing from the south are Mt. Eva, Grays and Torreys Peaks, Mt. Flora, Englemann Peak, Colorado Mines Peaks, the Vasquez Mountains with the Gore Range in the background, Winter Park Ski Resort, the Troublesome Valley, the Fraser Valley, Lake Granby, and the Never Summer Range.

From Parry Peak, head east down into another saddle and up to Mt. Bancroft (9). From the top of Mt. Bancroft, looking south are the Fall River Reservoir, Grays and Torreys Peaks, Mt. Flora, Colorado Mines Peak, Mt. Eva, Vasquez Mountains, Parry Peak, Ptarmigan Peak, Winter Park Ski Resort, the Troublesome Valley, the town of Winter Park, the Fraser Valley, Lake Granby, and the Never Summer Range. To the north and clockwise are the mountains in Rocky Mountain National Park, Longs Peak, Indian Peaks, James Peak, Rollins Pass Road from the east side of the Continental Divide, and the Front Range Mountains.

On the descent from Mt. Bancroft both Lake Caroline and Loch Lomond are visible on the right. Continue east to the top of the next peak where there is a grassy meadow on the left. This is the easiest descent to the saddle en route to James Peak. On the right of the saddle is Ice Lake, which is a very deep lake. From the north side of the saddle, Loch Lomond, Stewart Lake, and Reynolds Lake are visible. The ascent up James Peak is very rocky and filled with giant boulders. Some bouldering is required, while following the cairns. Next is a flat open area with a clear view of James Peak ahead. Cross this shelf toward James Peak. The ground is again covered with rubble to the top of James Peak (10). Walk to the east edge of the peak to see James Peak Lake and Little Echo Lake. From here, turn left (north) at the fork (11) and descend through the switchbacks where there is a view of Heart Lake and Rogers Pass Lake on the right. At the next fork in the switchbacks (12), bear left and continue to descend. The hum from the East Portal is audible. At the bottom of the hill is an intersection (13) which is the Ute Trail. Turn left and follow this well-worn trail. Cross the aqueduct (14), continue straight (north), and follow the cairns to the fork (15) where the trail joins an old jeep road. The right fork leads to Rogers Pass.

For a short side trip to Rogers Pass, follow the jeep road to the right to the crest of the hill (15A). Both Heart Lake and Rogers Pass Lake are visible below. The East Portal of the railroad tunnel lies between the lakes in the distance to the northeast. Both Heart Lake and Rogers Pass Lake can be reached by continuing on a trail, which is just north of the pass. Return to the fork (15).

From the fork, follow the jeep road straight (north) and pass the fork for the CD Trail, which is on the right (16). Remain on the jeep road and gently descend. There are two long switchbacks near timberline. Once back into the Englemann spruce forest, it is a short distance to the railroad trestle (17).

Historical Note – Parry Peak was named by Charles Christopher Parry after himself. He was a botanist and physician who discovered several flowers in Grand County including the Parry Primrose and the Alpine Forget-Me-Not.

Mt. Flora was also named by Charles Christopher Parry for its abundance of alpine flora.

James Peak was named for Edwin C. James who was a naturalist and historian. He was also a member of the first party up Longs Peak and led the first party up Pikes Peak.

Mt. Bancroft was named after a naturalist who was mapping the flora in the area.

Mt. Flora (left) and the abandoned building on Mt. Eva (right)

Parry Peak, James Peak, and Mt. Bancroft

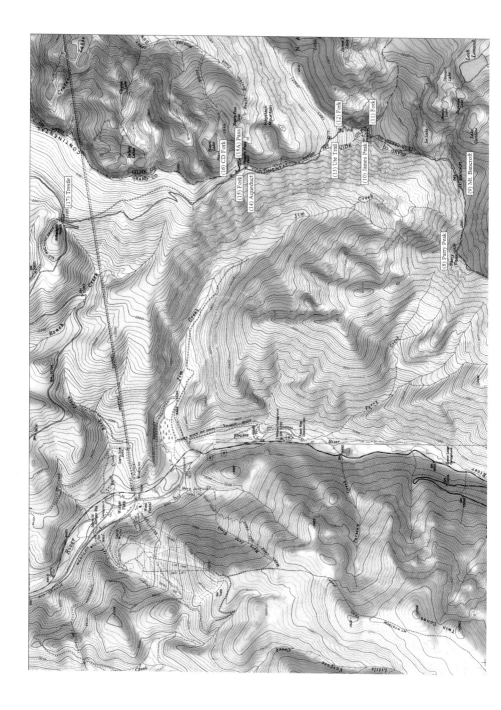

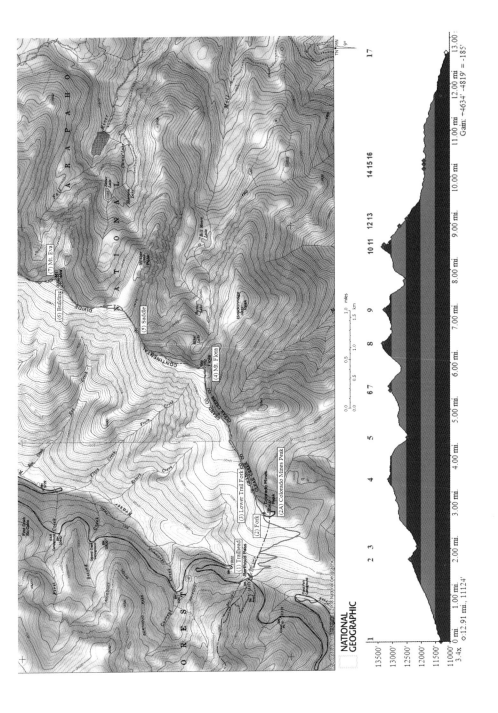

NATIONAL GEOGRAPHIC

(1) Trailhead
(2) Fork
(2A) Colorado Mines Peak
(3) Lower Trail Fork
(4) Mt. Flora
(5) Saddle
(6) Building
(7) Mt. Eva

ARAPAHO
NATIONAL
FOREST
CONTINENTAL DIVIDE

13500'
13000'
12500'
12000'
11500'
11000'
3.4x

0 mi.   1.00 mi.   2.00 mi.   3.00 mi.   4.00 mi.   5.00 mi.   6.00 mi.   7.00 mi.   8.00 mi.   9.00 mi.   10.00 mi.   11.00 mi.   12.00 mi.   13.00:

o:12.91 mi, 11124'   Gain: +4634 -4819 = -185'

1   2 3   4   5   67   8   9   10 11   12 13   14 15 16   17

51

9. JIM CREEK

Level of Difficulty - Moderate
One-way Mileage – 3.58 miles
One-way Hiking Time - 2 hours
Altitude, GPS Reading at Trailhead – 9224', 39°52'55"N, 105°45'17"W
Altitude, GPS Reading at Destination – 10,449', 39°51'38"N, 105°42'24"W
Trail Fee Required – No

🐾 <u>Yes,</u> 🐟 <u>Yes,</u> ▲ <u>Yes</u>, **WD** <u>JP</u>

Trailhead Location – On US Hwy 40, across from the Winter Park Ski Resort main entrance, between mile markers 232 and 233 is the Bonfils Stanton Foundation/Winter Park Outdoor Center. The trailhead is at the Outdoor Center sign (1).

Trail Description – From the sign, follow the trail to the right (south) along the "Discovery Trail". Cross the boardwalk over Jim Creek. At the end of the boardwalk, make a sharp left onto a vehicle access road. The first part of the hike passes a wheelchair accessible trail and disabled persons campground. Pass under the overhead viaduct (which transports water to Denver). The trail narrows to a single-track trail and leads to FSR 128 (Water Board Road) (2). Continue across FSR 128, to the right of Jim Creek on the trail through the tall willows. There are many alder trees and willows in this damp area. Parallel the creek and climb through a lodgepole pine forest. Large aspen stands are visible across the creek on the hillside to the left. These are brilliant in the fall. The trail nears the creek and the spruce and fir trees dot the landscape. James Peak looms ahead. The trail fades in the woods and marsh. Continue to parallel the creek and gradually climb through the woods past a boulder field, which is on the right. Head left, back to the creek. The creek runs through a canyon, which narrows, creating several spectacular waterfalls (3). Follow the creek a short distance further and remain to the right of the creek where possible. The trail reappears and the falls roar. The canyon narrows and the elevation gain increases further. Beyond the falls, the creek crosses onto private property. Please do not continue beyond the falls.

Note - This is a wonderful hike in the fall because the turning aspen leaves are brilliant against the hillside through the valley.

Historical Note – Jim Creek is the drainage from James Peak (named after Edwin C. James). The name Jim was diminutively used in place of James. Jim Creek was thought to be the headwaters of the Fraser River, originally called the James River.

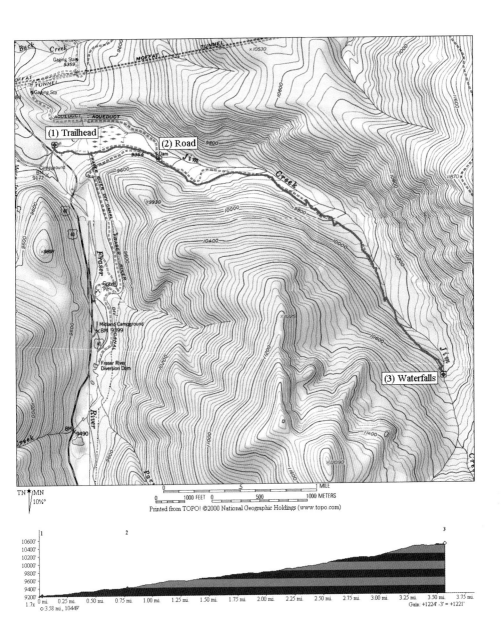

TN ★ MN
10½°

Printed from TOPO! ©2000 National Geographic Holdings (www.topo.com)

1.7x
○ 3.58 mi., 10449'

Gain: +1224' -3' = +1221'

10. ROGERS PASS AND JAMES PEAK

Level of Difficulty – Moderate (Pass), Difficult (Peak)
One-way Mileage - 2.52 miles (Pass), 4.57 miles (Peak)
One-way Hiking Time – 1 ½ hours (Pass), 3 hours (Peak)
Altitude, GPS Reading at Trailhead - 11, 081', 39°53'56"N, 105°42'28"W
Altitude, GPS Reading at Rogers Pass – 11,918', 39°52'18"N, 105°41'47"W
Altitude, GPS Reading at James Peak – 13,304', 39°51'07"N, 105°41'26"W
Trail Fee Required – No

🐕 Yes, 🚲 N/A, ⛰ Yes, WD JP

Trailhead Location – On US Hwy 40, north of the Winter Park Ski Resort main entrance, between mile markers 231 and 232, turn east onto CR 80 (FSR 149), also known as the Moffat Road to Corona Pass. Follow FSR 149 for 10.7 miles to the top of the railroad trestle. Park on the side of the road near the Rogers Pass Trail sign (1). The Moffat Road is a good dirt road. This road is the old railroad bed used by trains crossing the Continental Divide at Rollins Pass (near the town of Corona), traveling from Denver to Hot Sulphur Springs. (For an interpretive self-guided tour of the Moffat Road stop by the Winter Park Visitor's Center).

Trail Description – Begin below timberline through a spruce forest, but quickly climb through timberline into the alpine meadows. When the last tree is left behind, there is a great view of Parry Peak. Follow the trail across the tundra with views of the Winter Park Ski Resort on the right and the Vasquez Mountains behind it. Previous jeep travel is evident where the trail traverses the hillside across two switchbacks. It is a moderate climb to the Continental Divide ridgeline. On the right is an aqueduct (2) and on the left is a single-track trail that forks sharply and follows the CD Trail northward (3). Continue straight on the jeep road to the next fork (4). A faint trail with a cairn is on the right, while the jeep road continues on the left. Follow the jeep trail to Rogers Pass, which is just over the crest of the hill (5). Both Heart Lake and Rogers Pass Lake are visible below. The East Portal of the railroad tunnel lies between the lakes in the distance to the northeast. Heart Lake and Rogers Pass Lake can be reached by continuing on a trail just north of the pass.

To reach James Peak, return to the fork (4) and turn onto the faint Ute Trail. Cross the aqueduct (6) and follow the single-track trail. The trail is rockier and ascends steeply across the hillside. James Peak is ahead with Mt. Bancroft and Parry Peak towering above the Jim Creek drainage. When the trail approaches the ridgeline, James Peak is visible directly ahead (south). Cross over the Continental Divide ridgeline and where the trail begins to level off, a trail forks on the right (7) which begins the final ascent up to James Peak.. Turn right and climb through the long strenuous bouldered hillside. At the fork (8), bear right and continue through the switchbacks. Near the top of James Peak the trail comes to a "T" (9). Turn right and continue to the top of James Peak (10). The humm from the East Portal is clearly audible here. The peak is covered in scree and there are several rock shelters to hide from the wind. To the north are Heart Lake, Rogers Pass Lake, and the East Portal. Walk to the east edge of the peak to see James Peak Lake and Little Echo Lake. Further to the east are the Front Range Mountains with the Denver skyline in the distance. Looking south are Mount Bancroft, Mt. Eva, and Parry Peak. To the west are the Vasquez Mountains, the Winter Park Ski Resort, the Fraser Valley, the Troublesome Valley and the Never Summer Range in the distance, Lake Granby, the mountains in Rocky Mountain National Park, Longs Peak and Indian Peaks.

Historical Note – James Peak was named for Edwin C. James who was a naturalist and historian. He was a member of the first party up Longs Peak and led the first party up Pikes Peak.

Rogers Pass was named after Andrew P. Rogers. This was the proposed site of the Boulder Central and Utah Railroad and was originally used as an Indian trail.

James Peak ahead with Mt. Bancroft and Parry Peak on the right

Railroad Trestle on Corona Road near Rogers Pass Trailhead

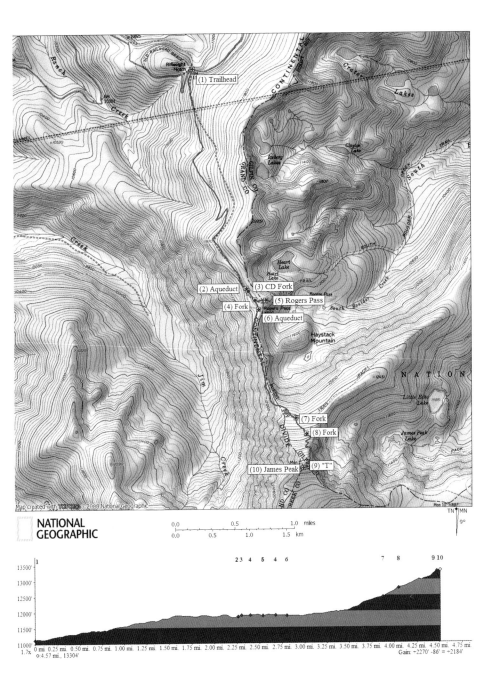

11. PUMPHOUSE, DEADMAN, AND CORONA LAKES

Level of Difficulty - Easy
One-way Mileage – 1.73 miles
One-way Hiking Time – 1 hour
Altitude, GPS Reading at Trailhead – 11,572', 39°55'21"N, 105°41'16"W
Altitude, GPS Reading at Destination – 11,213', 39°56'01"N, 105°41'43"W
Trail Fee Required – No

🐕 Yes, 🎣 Yes, ▲ Yes, **WD JP**

Trailhead Location – On US Hwy 40, north of the Winter Park Ski Resort main entrance, between mile markers 231 and 232, turn east onto CR 80 (FSR 149), also known as the Moffat Road to Corona Pass. Follow FSR 149 for 13 miles where the trail and all three lakes are visible on the left (1). There is no trailhead sign. Park at the wide spot in the road. The Moffat Road is a good dirt road. This road is the old railroad bed used by trains crossing the Continental Divide at Rollins Pass (near the town of Corona), traveling from Denver to Hot Sulphur Springs. (For an interpretive self-guided tour of the Moffat Road stop by the Winter Park Visitor's Center).

Trail Description – This trail is primarily at timberline. The barren tundra blends with the sparse Englemann spruce trees of the subalpine. From the trailhead, Deadman Lake is to the far left, Pumphouse Lake is slightly to the left, and Corona Lake is to the far right nestled in the trees. Follow the old wagon road down the hill. After a short distance, a distinct single-track trail turns to the left. Follow this single-track trail to Pumphouse Lake (2). A trail leads down to the water to the remains of the old pump house and coal pile. The pump house was used to provide water for the steam engines as they traveled over the pass. The mountain directly behind Pumphouse Lake is Mt. Epworth. To reach Deadman Lake, turn left (south), follow the shore of Pumphouse Lake, and continue up to the saddle. From the saddle, Deadman Lake (3) is visible and it is only a short distance to the water. To reach Corona Lake, return to Pumphouse Lake (2) and follow the old wagon road down to the creek, which is the Pumphouse Lake runoff. Cross the creek, continue up the hill, and pass a giant boulder field to Corona Lake (4). This deep lake sits in a cirque surrounded by Englemann spruce trees on both sides with a granite rock scree backdrop.

Historical Note – "Corona" is a Spanish word meaning "Crown". The town of Corona was referred to as the "Crown of the Continent". Corona Lake is the closest lake to the old town site.

Several stories surround Deadman Lake, many with tales of dead people. However, the most convincing story involves the construction of the railroad trestle and tracks. Boulders were needed to anchor the ties and tracks in place. These boulders were gathered from the spot where Deadman Lake now sits. These anchors were known as dead men (dead weight).

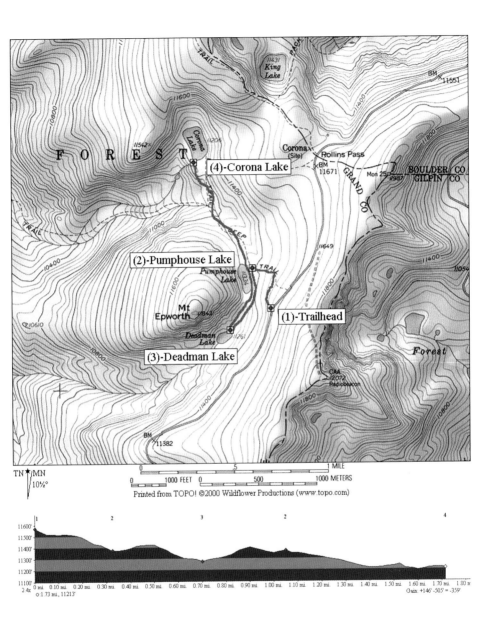

FOREST

(4)-Corona Lake

(2)-Pumphouse Lake

Mt Epworth

(3)-Deadman Lake

(1)-Trailhead

Corona (Site)
Rollins Pass
BM 11671
Mon 25
GRAND CO
BOULDER CO
GILPIN CO

Forest

King Lake

Printed from TOPO! ©2000 Wildflower Productions (www.topo.com)

TN MN
10½°

12. MT. EPWORTH

Level of Difficulty - Moderate
One-way Mileage - .85 miles
One-way Hiking Time – 1 hour
Altitude, GPS Reading at Trailhead – 11,574', 39°55'21"N, 105°41'16"W
Altitude, GPS Reading at Destination – 11,775', 39°55'21"N, 105°41'45"W
Trail Fee Required – No

🐾 Yes, 🚶 Yes, ▲ Yes, **WD** JP

Trailhead Location – See Pumphouse, Deadman, and Corona Lakes Trailhead (1), Hike #11, page 58.

Trail Description - This hike has one of the best views of Grand County. Follow the old wagon road down the hill through the tundra. After a short distance, a distinct single-track trail turns to the left. Follow this single-track trail to Pumphouse Lake (2). The mountain directly behind Pumphouse Lake is Mt. Epworth. Follow the lake around to the right (north) to the ridge. Follow the cairns up the ridgeline. Begin up Mt. Epworth through a hillside of small boulders, which quickly changes higher up to a field of much larger boulders. In this large boulder field, the cairns are more difficult to distinguish. From the top of Mt. Epworth (3), there are great 360° views. Looking south and clockwise along the Continental Divide are James and Parry Peaks, Berthoud Pass, the Continental Divide, Winter Park Ski Resort, Byers Peak, Bottle Peak, Sheep Mountain, the town of Fraser, White Cliffs, the towns of Tabernash and Granby, Lake Granby, the Never Summer Range, the mountains in Rocky Mountain National Park, the Continental Divide, and Rollins Pass.

Historical Note – Mt. Epworth was a named after a geologist who worked in the area looking for precious metals.

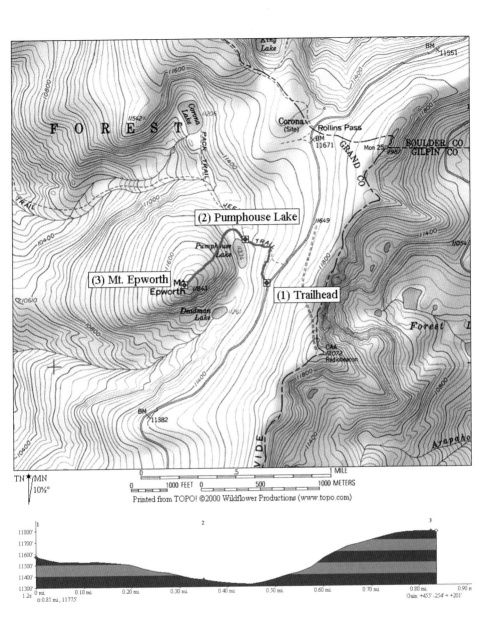

(2) Pumphouse Lake

(3) Mt. Epworth

(1) Trailhead

FOREST

King Lake

Corona Lake

Corona (Site)

Rollins Pass

BOULDER CO
GILPIN CO

Pumphouse Lake

Mt. Epworth

Deadman Lake

PACK TRAIL

GRAND CO

Mon 25

BM 11671

BM 11551

BM 11382

CAA Radiobeacon

Forest

Arapaho

DIVIDE

TN / MN
10½°

1 MILE

1000 FEET   500   1000 METERS

Printed from TOPO! ©2000 Wildflower Productions (www.topo.com)

61

13. ROLLINS PASS WAGON ROAD

Level of Difficulty - Moderate
One-way Mileage – 2.42 miles
One-way Hiking Time – 1 ½ hours
Altitude, GPS Reading at Trailhead – 11,575', 39°55'21"N, 105°41'16"W
Altitude, GPS Reading at Destination – 10,024', 39°55'52"N, 105°42'49"W
Trail Fee Required – No

🐾 Yes, 🐟 N/A, ▲ Yes, **WD** JP

Trailhead Location – See Pumphouse, Deadman, and Corona Lakes Trailhead (1), Hike #11, page 58.

Trail Description – This hike is the most challenging hike in the book from the standpoint of finding the trail and staying on it. John Quincy Adams Rollins built a toll road over Rollins Pass in 1873, which followed Ranch Creek all the way to the town of Tabernash. The road was eventually abandoned for wagon travel because the route was too rough, but pack animals and cattle drives ran this route for many years. The road was probably abandoned around 1938 when the railroad tracks from the Moffat Railroad were dismantled. Very little trail maintenance has been done through the years, but if one's imagination is free to return to the turn of the century, the wagon road is clearly visible.

Follow the old wagon road through the tundra. The trail gently rolls downhill with smooth wide turns. Pass Pumphouse Lake (2), which is on the left and continue into the valley toward Corona Lake. In the middle of the valley there is a creek. Cross this creek and count 26 paces along the trail. After 26 paces, look left (3). There is a clearing through the willows and no true sign of a trail. Turn left (west) into the willows and keep the creek on the left. The wagon road sits above the creek, is about 8' wide, and is relatively level with an even grade. Large pine trees have grown on the trail, which makes it almost indistinguishable for the first ¼ mile. Skirt around many large trees, until they thin and shorten in height. The trail looks more like a dry creek bed where erosion has taken its toll over the years. After ¼ mile from the turnoff at the clearing, this trail looks like a wagon road. Boulders are stacked along both sides of the trail's edge giving definition to the wagon road. Parallel the creek and travel deeper into the woods. In places the wagon road looks like it could still be used today. There are a few trail markers, along with a few cairns. Imagining a wagon traveling through the woods, over creeks, and through bogs, provides a mental picture for the old road. Keep the boulder lined edges in sight to identify the trail in overgrown areas. There are several campfire rings on the side of the trail. Guests of the Devil's Thumb Dude Ranch used these rings after the wagon road was abandoned. The switchback (4) is a good turn-around point. The trail continues and disappears into a wetland. Beyond the wetland the wagon road crosses onto private property. Please do not continue beyond the switchback.

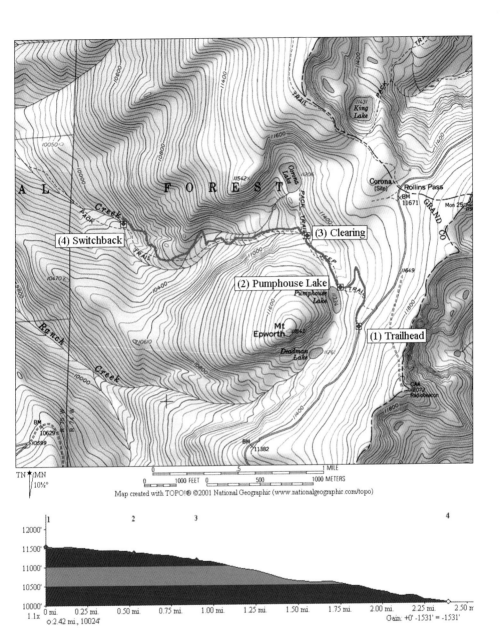

14. RADIO BEACON SITE

Level of Difficulty - Easy
One-way Mileage - .71 miles
One-way Hiking Time – ½ hour
Altitude, GPS Reading at Trailhead – 11,646', 39°55'36"N, 105°41'01"W
Altitude, GPS Reading at Destination – 11,942', 39°55'03"N, 105°40'56"W
Trail Fee Required – No

🐾 Yes, 🐴 N/A, ▲ Yes, **WD JP**

Trailhead Location – On US Hwy 40, north of the Winter Park Ski Resort main entrance, between mile markers 231 and 232, turn east onto CR 80 (FSR 149), also known as the Moffat Road to Corona Pass. Follow FSR 149 for 13.3 miles to a sign identifying the CD Trail (1). Park at the wide spot in the road. The Moffat Road is a good dirt road. This road is the old railroad bed used by trains crossing the Continental Divide at Rollins Pass (near the town of Corona), traveling from Denver to Hot Sulphur Springs. (For an interpretive self-guided tour of the Moffat Road stop by the Winter Park Visitor's Center).

Trail Description – This is a very short hike above timberline with the greatest reward being the fantastic view from the top. From the CD Trail sign, follow the trail up the old radio beacon service road. It is a gentle grade to the top. The concrete pad was the old radio beacon site, but the beacon has long since been removed. Turn left to the top of the hill (2). To the north is Corona Pass. To the northeast is the winding road of the east side of the Moffat Road and the Needle's Eye tunnel (now closed). To the east are Forest Lakes, the Moffat Railroad Tunnel, and the Front Range Mountains. To the south are the Arapaho Lakes and James Peak. Continuing clockwise are Berthoud Pass, Winter Park Ski Resort, the Vasquez Mountains, the Fraser Valley, the Never Summer Range, and Lake Granby.

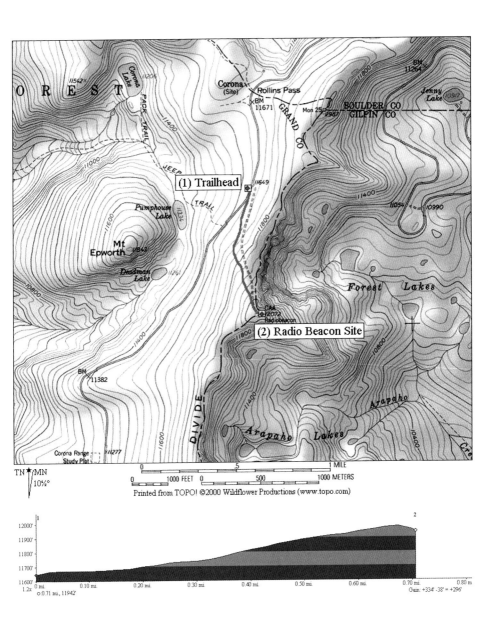

15. KING, BETTY, AND BOB LAKES

Level of Difficulty - Moderate
One-way Mileage – 1.98 miles
One-way Hiking Time – 1 hour
Altitude, GPS Reading at Trailhead – 11,604', 39°56'07"N, 105°40'55"W
Altitude, GPS Reading at Destination - 11,552', 39°57'06"N, 105°41'06"W
Trail Fee Required – No

🐕 Yes, 🚴 Yes, ⛺ Yes, **WD** JP

Trailhead Location – On US Hwy 40, north of the Winter Park Ski Resort main entrance, between mile markers 231 and 232, turn east onto CR 80 (FSR 149), also known as the Moffat Road to Corona Pass. Follow FSR 149 for 14 miles to a parking area and trailhead (1). The Moffat Road is a good dirt road. This road is the old railroad bed used by trains crossing the Continental Divide at Rollins Pass (near the town of Corona), traveling from Denver to Hot Sulphur Springs. (For an interpretive self-guided tour of the Moffat Road stop by the Winter Park Visitor's Center).

Trail Description – From Corona Pass and the billboard, follow the trail northwest. On the right, not far from the parking area are the ruins of the Corona Hotel built in 1913. Continue across the tundra to a fork and trail marker (2) identifying the High Lonesome Trail straight ahead and King Lake to the right. King Lake is visible below. Take the right fork down into the cirque to King Lake (3). This is a beautiful lake with great fishing. Snow generally remains on the hillside behind the lake year-round. Just past King Lake, a creek flows into the small tarn (4). Follow the main trail down to timberline. Pass the boulder field and several areas filled with wildflowers. Next is a creek (5) that flows from Betty and Bob Lakes. This creek creates a beautiful waterfall downstream, which is best viewed from the parking area. Cross the creek and at the fork, the trail marker identifies King Lake to the left and Betty and Bob Lakes to the right. This sign is slightly deceiving. The trail to the right leads to the town of Eldora. Betty and Bob Lakes are up the hill. Hike up the hill through the arctic willows and the stunted Englemann spruce trees. The stunted vegetation of timberline is clearly evident. The trail is faint and the brush is waist high in places. Hike uphill and keep the creek on the left to Betty Lake (6). This is a beautiful lake with a view of the Front Range Mountains below. Turn left (northwest) and follow the trail and cairns up past the creek to Bob Lake (7). There is generally snow on the scree hillside behind Bob Lake year-round. A summer snow skier is occasionally sited skiing through the narrow chute behind the lake to the water's edge.

Note - Although these three alpine lakes are not in Grand County, the hike is very popular and is accessed predominantly from Grand County.

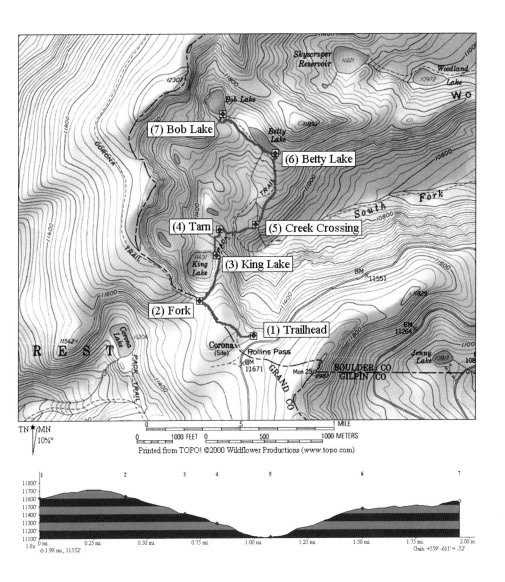

16. ROLLINS PASS (CORONA) TO DEVIL'S THUMB

Level of Difficulty - Moderate
One-way Mileage – 3.87 miles
One-way Hiking Time – 2 hours
Altitude, GPS Reading at Trailhead – 11,664', 39°56'05"N, 105°40'58"W
Altitude, GPS Reading at Destination - 12,235', 39°58'44"N, 105°41'09"W
Trail Fee Required – No

🐕 Leash, 🐟 N/A, ⛰ Permit, **WD** JP/IP

Trailhead Location – See King, Betty, and Bob Lakes Trailhead (1), Hike #15, page 66.

Trail Description – This entire hike is above timberline. Be aware of the ever-changing weather conditions. From Corona Pass and the billboard, follow the trail northwest. On the right, not far from the parking area are the ruins of the Corona Hotel built in 1913. Continue across the tundra to a fork and trail marker (2) identifying the High Lonesome Trail straight ahead and King Lake to the right. King Lake is visible below on the right and Winter Park Ski Resort is on the left. Continue straight along the well-worn High Lonesome Trail. The trail climbs a series of switchbacks and continues steeply along the Continental Divide ridgeline. This is the most difficult section of the hike. After the switchbacks, the trail levels off considerably and many cairns are visible. There is a high trail and a low trail. The low trail is the most direct route with terrific views to the west. Due to high winds, this is the suggested route. The high trail is a nice alternative for the return trip (weather permitting). Follow the low trail with view of the Vasquez Mountains on the left and the Fraser Valley below. Ahead are the towns of Fraser and Tabernash, Lake Granby, and the mountains in Rocky Mountain National Park. Make a gentle ascent and an equally gentle descent before rounding a bend where a saddle sits above the trail on the right. This is not the Devil's Thumb saddle; rather it is the cutoff route to Devil's Thumb Lake and Lake Jasper on the east side of the Continental Divide (see the High Trail Return Trip description below). Continue on the low trail up one more short climb. Around the next bend, on the right is Devil's Thumb Pass. Devil's Thumb is a unique finger (or thumb) shaped rock formation along the Continental Divide that is visible for miles from the valley below. However, it is barely distinguishable from this point and blends with the jagged cliff behind. Follow the trail down to the saddle, where the cairns and the worn trail disappear. Hike toward the CD Trail marker (3) and intersect the trail from Devil's Thumb Park (see Devil's Thumb, Hike #17, page 72). At the intersection, turn right (east) and climb to the top of the pass (4). The trail disappears, but turn left (north) from the top of the pass and head up the steep hill. Devil's Thumb from this perspective is difficult to see. Continue to hike uphill until the Thumb is obvious. Standing at the Thumb (5) looking east are Devil's Thumb Lake and the Front Range Mountains. Looking west below is the large meadow known as Devil's Thumb Park.

High Trail Return Trip - On the return from Devil's Thumb, either follow the low trail back to the trailhead or take a slightly longer more scenic route on the high trail. For the high trail, follow the ridgeline south from the Thumb down to the pass (4) and then up the opposite side. Looking up the hill (south) and slightly to the right are several cairns dotting the hillside. Follow these to the right of the peak below the Continental Divide ridgeline. The cairns loop to the backside of the hill. Head downhill to the saddle (6), where the cutoff to Devil's Thumb Lake and Lake Jasper are to the east. Both lakes are visible from this cutoff and the views are fabulous. Continue south along the ridgeline toward a boulder field. The cairns disappear, but remain near the ridgeline for the best route with the most spectacular views. Remain high on the boulder field where the trail reappears along the ridgeline. The views of the mountains on the Front Range are incredible. Betty, Bob, and King Lakes and the east side of the Moffat Road are visible. Intersect the inbound low trail (7), turn left, and return to the trailhead (1).

Historical Note – This route was one of many that was used to bring livestock over the Continental Divide at Rollins Pass from the Denver area to graze in the summer.

Devil's Thumb

69

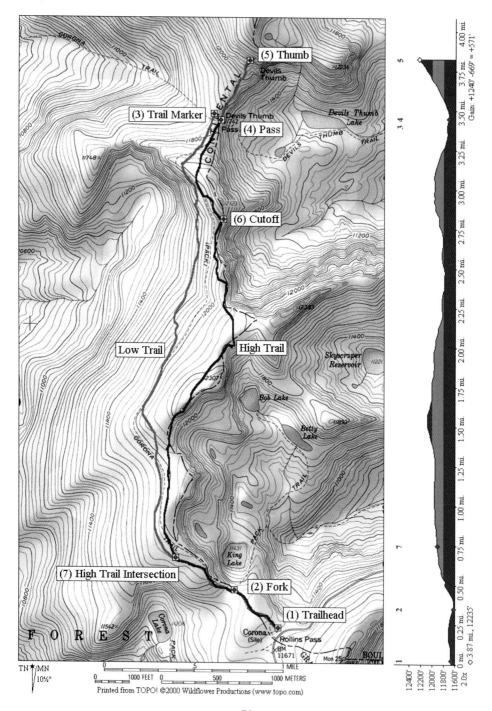

(5) Thumb

(3) Trail Marker

(4) Pass

(6) Cutoff

Low Trail

High Trail

(7) High Trail Intersection

(2) Fork

(1) Trailhead

Devils Thumb

Devils Thumb Lake

Skyscraper Reservoir

Bob Lake

Betty Lake

King Lake

Corona Lake

FOREST

Corona (Site)

Rollins Pass

CORONA TRAIL

CONTINENTAL

DEVILS THUMB TRAIL

(PACK)

TN / MN
10½°

1000 FEET   500   1000 METERS

Printed from TOPO! ©2000 Wildflower Productions (www.topo.com)

Gain: +1240' -669' = +571'

0 mi.   0.25 mi.   0.50 mi.   0.75 mi.   1.00 mi.   1.25 mi.   1.50 mi.   1.75 mi.   2.00 mi.   2.25 mi.   2.50 mi.   2.75 mi.   3.00 mi.   3.25 mi.   3.50 mi.   3.75 mi.   4.00 mi.

12400'   12200'   12000'   11800'   11600'

2.0x   @ 3.87 mi., 12235'

FRASER VALLEY

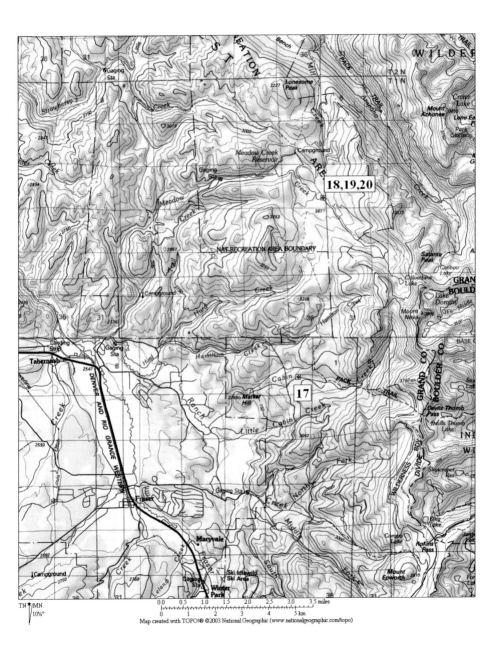

17. DEVIL'S THUMB

Level of Difficulty - Difficult
One-way Mileage – 3.93 miles
One-way Hiking Time – 3 ½ hours
Altitude, GPS Reading at Trailhead – 9609', 39°59'12"N, 105°44'35"W
Altitude, GPS Reading at Destination – 12,236', 39°58'44"N, 105°41'09"W
Trail Fee Required - No

🐕 Leash, 🐟 Yes, ▲ Permit, **WD** IP

Trailhead Location – At the north end of the town of Fraser on US Hwy 40, between mile markers 226 and 227 is County Road 8. Turn onto CR 8 and follow this road for 6.4 miles. CR 8 turns into a good single lane dirt road and becomes FSR 128 (Water Board Road). Turn left and continue for 1.1 miles. Turn right and continue for .3 miles where the road ends at a spillway. Park on the side of the road near the trailhead (1).

Trail Description – Hike along the left side of Cabin Creek through the montane forest and marsh. At a large meadow (Devil's Thumb Park), there are great views of Devil's Thumb Pass and the surrounding mountains. Cabin Creek skirts the right side of the Park while the trail continues around the left side. At a fork and trail marker (2), the sign identifies the High Lonesome Trail. Turn right. The trail is relatively flat until Devil's Thumb Park is out of view, when it rolls gently. The trail rejoins Cabin Creek. At the creek crossing is a fork. An old pack trail continues straight and a log foot bridge is on the right. Cross the foot bridge over Cabin Creek (3), where there is a nice place to sit with a beautiful view of Mt. Neva, Mt. Jasper, and an "unnamed" peak mirrored in the pond. Meet another creek, which has several cascading waterfalls (4) in early summer. Climb steadily uphill and cross into the Indian Peaks Wilderness. Next cross the creek (5) and the forest changes from the subalpine into timberline. The trees open up to an alpine meadow where the ascent is increasingly difficult. Above timberline, look back to see Devil's Thumb Park, the town of Tabernash, White Cliffs, and the Never Summer Range. Hike up across the tundra where Devil's Thumb takes shape on the left side of the saddle. The Thumb is a unique finger (or thumb) shaped rock formation along the Continental Divide ridgeline that is visible for miles from the valley below. Pass two CD markers to reach Devil's Thumb Pass (6). The worn trail to Devil's Thumb disappears, but turn left (north) and head up the steep hill. Devil's Thumb from this perspective is difficult to see. Climb until the Thumb is obvious. From Devil's Thumb (7) looking east are Devil's Thumb Lake and the Front Range Mountains. Looking south along the Continental Divide ridgeline are two large cairns in the distance above the old town of Corona. (Corona is where the Moffat Railroad originally came over at Rollins Pass.) To the southwest are great views of Winter Park Ski Resort, the Vasquez Mountains, and the Gore Range in the distance.

Side Trip – Unnamed Peak, 12,695' – From Devil's Thumb, continue north up this steep hill and bear left around the boulder field to the top of the peak (8). There are 360°

views from this point including Lake Granby, Columbine Lake, Mt. Neva, and the Indian Peaks Range.

Side Trip – Devil's Thumb Lake and Lake Jasper – From Devil's Thumb Pass (4), head south. Climb the hill and follow the cairns around the hill. On the back side of the hill is a saddle that follows the Continental Divide. From this saddle, a trail heads east to both Devil's Thumb Lake and Lake Jasper.

Historical Note – Devil's Thumb was named by the Ute Indians.

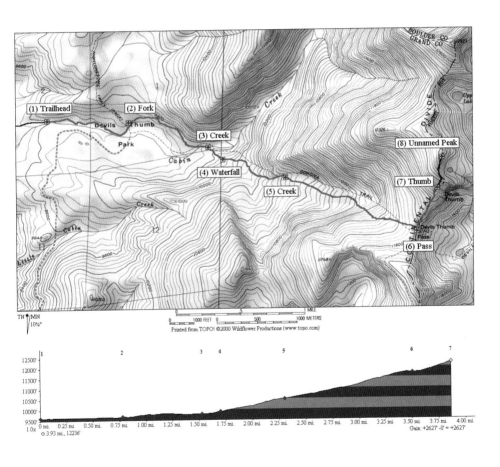

73

18. COLUMBINE LAKE

Level of Difficulty - Moderate
One-way Mileage – 2.86 miles
One-way Hiking Time – 1 ½ hours
Altitude, GPS Reading at Trailhead – 10,052', 40°02'40"N, 105°43'55"W
Altitude, GPS Reading at Destination – 11,067', 40°01'02"N, 105°41'56"W
Trail Fee Required – Yes

🐕 Leash, ⬤ Yes, ▲ Permit, WD IP

Trailhead Location – On US Hwy 40, east of Tabernash, between mile markers 224 and 225 (closer to 224), turn east on CR 83. Follow CR 83 for .4 miles to the fork. Turn left on CR 84, which turns into FSR 129. FSR 129 is a rough dirt road. Follow CR 84 (FSR 129) for 10.5 miles and then turn left on the road to the Junco Lake Trailhead (1).

Trail Description – Junco Lake Trailhead is the starting point for several hikes. Please sign in at the register box and follow the High Lonesome Trail to the Caribou Pass Trail, east of the parking area. There is a series of tank traps at the beginning of the trail. Not far from the trailhead is a fork (2), where the High Lonesome Trail turns to the right. Continue straight and follow an old jeep road through the montane forest. Cross several small creeks. The jeep road is fairly wide and in good condition, but one section is scattered with loose river rock and footing can be unstable here. Just beyond this area are the remains of an old cabin on the right (3). Continue to a clearing just before the Indian Peaks Wilderness boundary where there is a great view of Mt. Neva looming ahead. The clearing is filled with willows hiding the Columbine Lake creek. Dogs must be leashed when entering the Wilderness Area. Continue through the woods to a fork and trail marker (4). The Caribou Pass Trail is on the left and the Columbine Lake Trail is on the right. Head right and gradually climb. Cross several small meadows and large boulders. Weave through the boulders and approach the creek to a level area with several small ponds and marshes. Columbine Lake is ahead on the left (5) with the base of Mt. Neva as its backdrop. The lake is surrounded by trees and has a beautiful setting. Several small cascading streams flow into the lake lined with flowers.

Note - Because of all the standing water, mosquitoes can be bad in this area.

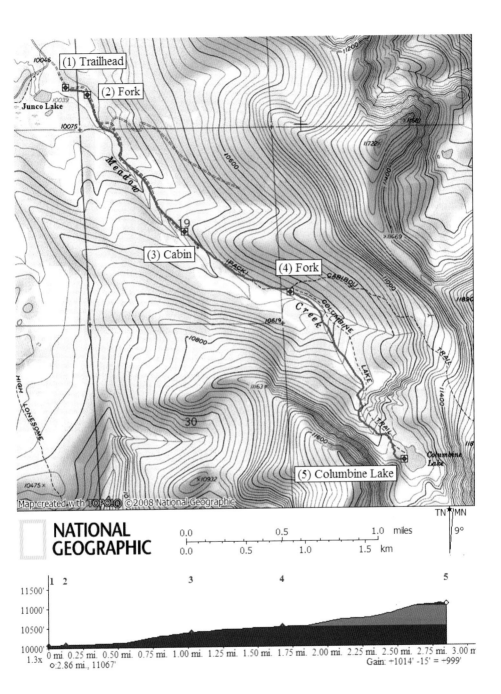

19. MT. NEVA

Level of Difficulty – More Difficult
One-way Mileage – 4.38 miles
One-way Hiking Time - 3 ½ hours
Altitude, GPS Reading at Trailhead – 10,052', 40°02'40"N, 105°43'55"W
Altitude, GPS Reading at Destination – 12,618', 40°00'24"N, 105°41'18"W
Trail Fee Required – Yes

🐕 Leash, 🦮 Yes, ▲ Permit, **WD** IP

Trailhead Location – See Columbine Lake Trail, Hike #18, page 74, Junco Lake Trailhead (1).

Trail Description – Follow the Columbine Lake Hike #18, page 74 description to (5). From Columbine Lake, follow the trail around to the south side of the lake. From the lake, head south where the trail is hard to find at first, but is visible on the approach to the saddle. This section of the trail is beautiful with all the large boulders throughout the marsh. Follow the trail up the switchbacks to the saddle (6). Turn left (east) up the ridgeline. The trail is faint and disappears frequently. The terrain is a mix of large boulders, loose rock, and scree. Quickly reach timberline. Along the ridgeline are a few windswept Englemann spruce trees. It is very steep, but the ridgeline is the easiest route to the top of Mt. Neva. The landscape begins with a few small boulders, but changes to short grasses, mosses, and low growing flowers. Follow the ridgeline southeast where the top of Mt. Neva is visible. Scramble over a few more large boulders to the top of Mt. Neva (7), where the views are terrific! Looking north and clockwise are Longs Peak, Lake Dorothy below, Mt. Achonee, Mt. George, Apache Peak, Navaho Peak, North and South Arapaho Peaks and the Front Range Mountains. Continuing clockwise are James Peak, Mt. Bancroft, and Parry Peaks, Winter Park Ski Resort, the Vasquez Mountains, the town of Winter Park, Byers Peak, the town of Fraser, Bottle Peak, the Gore Range, the Fraser Valley, Tabernash, Cottonwood Pass, Granby, the Troublesome Valley, Meadow Creek Reservoir, Lake Granby, Shadow Mountain Lake, the Never Summer Range, and Indian Peaks.

Historical Note - Mt. Neva was named by Ellsworth Bethel, a botany teacher from Denver, who was concerned over the naming of the mountains and thought it should be named for an Arapaho Indian.

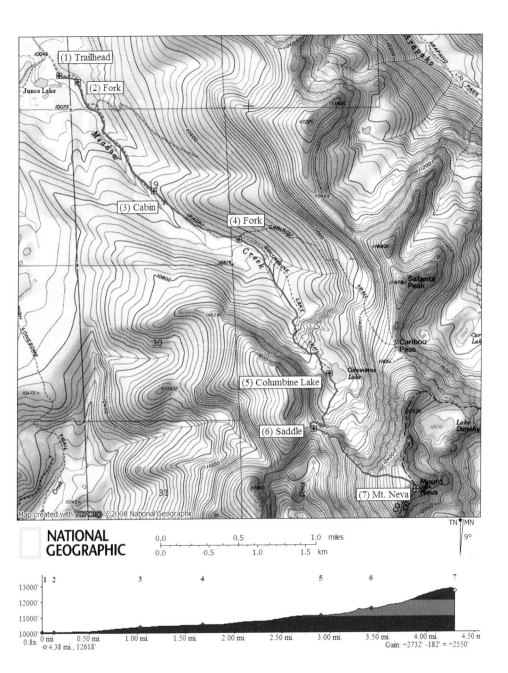

(1) Trailhead

Junco Lake

(2) Fork

Meadow

(3) Cabin

(4) Fork

CARIBOU

COLUMBINE

Creek

PACK

Satanta
Peak

Caribou
Pass

LAKE

TRAIL

(5) Columbine Lake

Columbine
Lake

Lake
Dorothy

(6) Saddle

HIGH
LONESOME

TRAIL

Creek

(7) Mt. Neva

Mount
Neva

Map created with TOPO!® ©2008 National Geographic

0.0   0.5   1.0   miles

0.0   0.5   1.0   1.5   km

TN ↑ MN

9°

13000'
12000'
11000'
10000'

0.8x

0 mi   0.50 mi.   1.00 mi.   1.50 mi.   2.00 mi.   2.50 mi.   3.00 mi.   3.50 mi.   4.00 mi.   4.50 n

○:4.38 mi., 12618'   Gain: +2732' -182' = +2550'

20. CARIBOU PASS AND LAKE DOROTHY

Level of Difficulty – Moderate (Pass), Difficult (Lake)
One-way Mileage – 3.26 miles (Pass), 4.14 miles (Lake)
One-way Hiking Time – 2 hours (Pass), 2 ½ hours (Lake)
Altitude, GPS Reading at Trailhead – 10,052', 40°02'40"N, 105°43'55"W
Altitude, GPS Reading at Pass – 11,819', 40°01'10"N, 105°41'27"W
Altitude, GPS Reading at Lake – 12,065', 40°00'47"N, 105°41'02"W
Trail Fee Required – No

🐾 Leash, ✒ Yes, ▲ Permit, WD IP

Trailhead Location – See Columbine Lake Trail, Hike #18, page 74, Junco Lake Trailhead (1).

Trail Description – Follow the Columbine Lake Hike #18, page 74 description to (4). Take the left fork toward Caribou Pass. The grade of the trail is more difficult. Pass through several meadows and climb steeply from the montane to the subalpine forest. The spruce trees thin to timberline. To the right, although not visible, are Columbine Lake and a peek-a-boo view of Byers Peak through the saddle above Columbine Lake. To the left is the Indian Peaks Range. To the west are White Cliffs and Cottonwood Pass. Continuing clockwise are Meadow Creek Reservoir, Lake Granby, and Shadow Mountain Lake. At the crest of the hill is Caribou Pass (5). Over the ridge is a great view of Caribou Lake below and Arapaho Pass at the top of the switchbacks. Due north is Santanta Peak. Turn right (south) and follow the old pack trail that hugs the side of the mountain directly ahead. Along the trail are fantastic views of the Indian Peaks Range on the left and the Front Range Mountains ahead. The Arapaho Peaks are to the east and Navaho and Apache Peaks are further north. After clearing the side of the hill, turn right (south) at the fork (6) to Lake Dorothy (7). This is a beautiful lake with Mt. Neva as its backdrop. (See Mt. Neva Hike #19, page 76 for peak access).

Side Trip – For a great overnight trip, continue to Caribou Lake. Refer to Arapaho, Caribou, and High Lonesome Loop, Hike #45, page 148 for more details.

Historical Note – Caribou Pass was one of the routes considered as a road over the Continental Divide into the Fraser Valley. Tremendous money and effort were spent to build the road, but by the time the road reached Caribou Pass from the east, the money was gone.

Lake Dorothy was named for Dorothy Lehman. She was the daughter of a Grand County rancher, who used this route frequently on his trips to Denver.

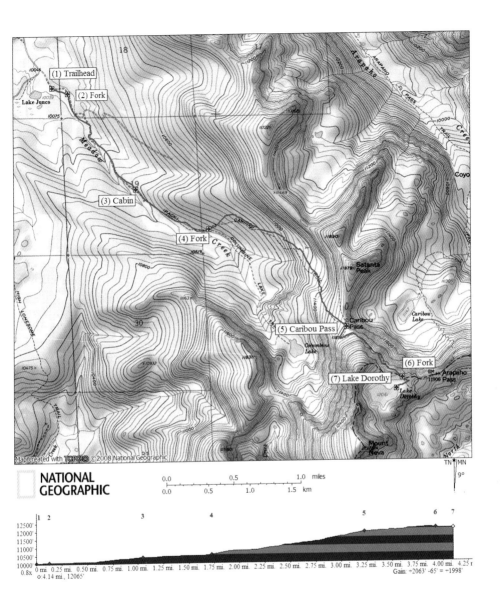

79

VASQUEZ MOUNTAINS

The most popular access to the Vasquez Mountains is from the east through the Fraser Valley from US Hwy 40. However, these same mountains and most of the trails can be accessed from the west via CR 3 and from the south via Jones Pass Road.

Fraser Experimental Forest

Several trailheads in the Fraser Experimental Forest have been relocated from their original location. Many factors have driven these changes including insufficient parking and environmental disturbances of the on-going experiments within the forest. To allow for easier access to the destinations, these trails are now recommended as bike and hike combination trips. It is suggested to bike the road and then hike the trail. The maps emphasize the hike portion and the profile reflects only the hike portion. However directions, distances, elevations, and waypoints are given for the road portion.

Warning:

Hikes 22, 23, 24 – The USDA Forest Service identified that a section of the mountain between points (0) and (1) is starting to slide down to that section of trail/old road bed. It is anticipated that when it does fail, this section may no longer be passable.

Hikes 25, 26, 27, 28 – Per the USDA Forest Service, the St Louis Creek Road (FSR 160) is washed out where St. Louis Creek crosses underneath it (about 1 mile from the hike trailhead (1)). It is impassable to motor vehicles & is not scheduled to be repaired. St. Louis Creek at the wash-out can still be crossed on foot with Caution.

Please contact the USDA Forest Service (970) 887-4100 for details.

VASQUEZ MOUNTAINS
East Access through Fraser Experimental Forest

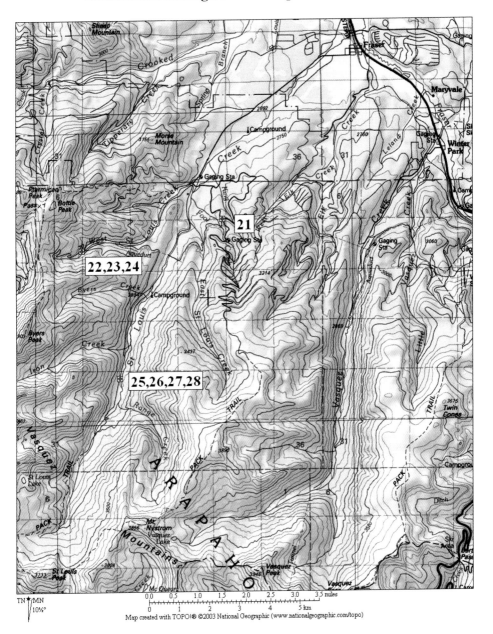

21. MT. NYSTROM 🚵 + 🥾
(map and profile begin at hike trailhead)

Level of Difficulty – Most Difficult
One-way Mileage – bike (5.80 miles) + hike (5.67 miles)
One-way Hike/Bike Time – bike (2 hours) + hike (3 hours)
Altitude, GPS Reading at Bike Trailhead (0) – 9491', 39°53'52"N, 105°52'12"W
Altitude, GPS Reading at Hike Trailhead (1) – 11,367', 39°51'49"N, 105°51'51"W
Altitude, GPS Reading at Destination – 12,653', 39°48'32"N, 105°54'07"W
Trail Fee Required - No

🐕 Yes, 🐟 N/A, ⛰ Yes, WD VQ

Trailhead Location – On US Hwy 40 in the town of Fraser, at the Fraser Valley Shopping Center, turn south on CR 72 for .3 miles. Turn right onto Fraser Pkwy for .8 miles. Turn left on CR 73 for 4.2 miles. Turn left at Vasquez Creek FSR 159 for .4 miles. Turn right onto Fool Creek Road (FSR) USFS 162 for 1.0 mile to King Creek Road FSR 163. At the 4-way intersection, park on the side of the road (0).

Trail Description –
Bike – Begin straight ahead on Fool Creek Road FSR 162. Pass around the gate and climb toward the Mt. Nystrom trail. This is a long steady ascent on a service road. Several side roads lead to various experimental areas, but remain on the main road. When the road degrades, several roads cross each other, but they all lead to the top. At the buck and rail fence, bear left to the gate (1). Park bikes near the gate. Bikes are not permitted beyond this point.
Hike - This is a wonderful trail that is almost entirely above timberline. Be aware of the ever-changing weather conditions. Pass around the gate. Begin in a mature forest, which is rare for this area since it was logged extensively in the 1950's. The forest quickly opens into grassy meadows where the fir and spruce trees are sparse. Follow the faint trail above timberline. Over the crest of the hill are three Experimental Forest stations. The first outbuilding measures water flow, while the other two measure weather conditions. **Please stay away from these stations as they are in operation.** Follow the cairns through the grassy meadow and pass the second station. The trail is visible on the ridgeline. At the large cairn (2), Byers and Bill's Peaks are on the right and Colorado Mines Peak is on the left. Continue up the hill and slightly to the right. The trail is faint, but hike up to the saddle (3) where there are views of Vasquez Peak and several tarns on the left. The Gore Range is visible in the distance on the right and an unnamed peak is on the left. The St. Louis Divide is the next ridge to the right with Ute Peak behind it. Hike up the hill to the top of the unnamed peak (4). Looking north and clockwise are Lake Granby, the mountains in Rocky Mountain National Park, Longs Peak, Indian Peaks, James Peak area, Winter Park Ski Resort, Colorado Mines Peak, Stanley Mountain, Vasquez Peak, Jones Pass Road, and Mt. Nystrom. Many tarns dot the valley below.

Leave the unnamed peak and head southwest down the hill and bear right. Hike down to the grassy saddle and up through a boulder field to the top of this peak (5). This could very well have been called "Boulder" peak because of the numerous boulders. Follow the rocky hillside down to the next saddle. Vasquez Peak is clearly in view on the left with Vasquez Lake below. Hike up the ridge to the large cairn (6). Turning left leads to Vasquez Lake and continuing straight leads to Mt. Nystrom (see below for Vasquez Lake Side Trip description).

From the cairn, continue up the ridge toward Mt. Nystrom. Ascend rapidly to the summit of Mt. Nystrom (7). Looking southeast and clockwise are McQueary Lake, Pettingell Peak (the tallest in the foreground), Hagar Mountain, and the mountains of the South Fork area. Continuing from the west are the Gore Range, St. Louis Peak, St. Louis Divide, Ute Peak, Williams Fork Mountains, Bill's Peak, Byers Peak, Ptarmigan Peak, and Bottle Peak.

Vasquez Lake Side Trip – From the cairn (6) at the saddle, head south. Before descending, get a good bearing on the lake, tarns and the cairns. The cairns are very difficult to find from down in the valley. The cairns follow a counter-clockwise semi-circle around the tarns to the lake. Descend the hillside to a meadow and a beautiful creek. Cross the creek at the gigantic boulder, continue through the meadow, and keep the tarns on the left. Find an opening through the stunted Englemann spruce trees to reach Vasquez Lake (6A). This is a wonderful lake with water flowing from the snow melt above. The terrain in marshy in spots allowing arctic willows and abundant wildflowers to grow. This side trip is .63 miles one-way and the elevation at the lake is 11,791'.

Monument Side Trip – Follow the same return route to the saddle between the "Boulder" peak (5) and the unnamed peak (4). There is a faint trail on the left that bypasses the climb back up the unnamed peak (4) and heads toward the Monument. Follow the faint trail across the grassy alpine meadow hillside and maintain the same elevation from the saddle to the Monument (5A). The Monument is perched on a pinnacle and is visible from miles away. It is believed that the monument was erected in memory of a sheepherder who died during a snow storm while tending his sheep.

From the Monument, head due east toward the large cairn (2) on the ridgeline above the experimental weather station. Maintain the same elevation from the Monument to the large cairn. From the large cairn (2), turn left and follow the inbound trail back to the trailhead (1). This return trip is only slightly longer and eliminates the elevation gain over the unnamed peak (4).

Historical Note – Mt. Nystrom was named after a naturalist who worked in the area.

This trail was originally called the "High Line Trail".

Vasquez Lake

Sheepherder's Monument

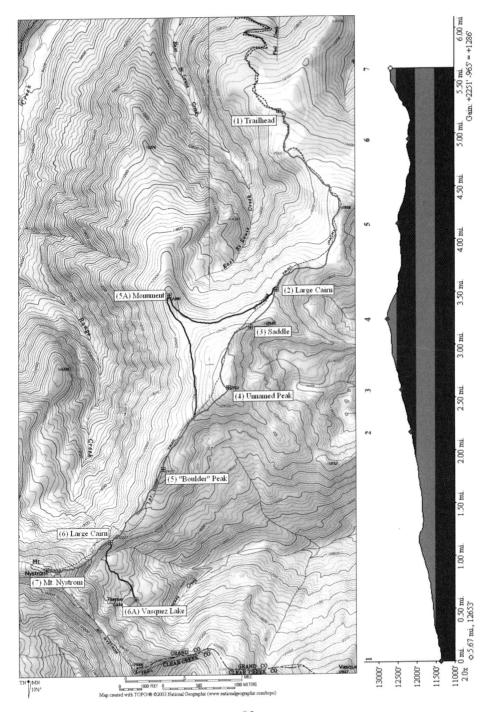

(1) Trailhead
(2) Large Cairn
(3) Saddle
(4) Unnamed Peak
(5) "Boulder" Peak
(5A) Monument
(6) Large Cairn
(6A) Vasquez Lake
(7) Mt. Nystrom
Mt Nystrom

GRAND CO
CLEAR CREEK CO

Map created with TOPO!® ©2003 National Geographic (www.nationalgeographic.com/topo)

◇5.67 mi, 12653'

2.0x   Gain: +2251'-965' = +1286'

85

22. BYERS PEAK LOOP 🚲 + 🥾
(profile begins at hike trailhead)

Level of Difficulty –Difficult
Round-trip Mileage – bike (3.20 miles) + hike (5.60 miles)
Round-trip Hike/Bike Time – bike (1/2 hour) + hike (4 hours)
Altitude, GPS Reading at Bike Trailhead (0) – 9809', 39°53'19"N, 105°55'31"W
Altitude, GPS Reading at Hike Trailhead (1) – 10,545', 39°53'01"N, 105°56'06"W
Altitude, GPS Reading at Destination – 12,804', 39°51'53"N, 105°56'50"W
Trail Fee Required - No

🐕 Yes, 🚣 N/A, ▲ Yes, WD BP

Trailhead Location – On US Hwy 40 in the town of Fraser, at the Fraser Valley Shopping Center, turn south on CR 72 for .3 miles. Turn right onto Fraser Pkwy for .8 miles. Turn left on CR 73 for 7.0 miles. Make a sharp right turn and follow the Byers Peak Trailhead road for another 3.0 miles to the gate (0) and parking area. CR 73 is a good dirt road and the Byers Peak Trailhead road is a good dirt road with a few potholes.

Trail Description -
Bike - Pass around the gate and climb this steady ascent through several switchbacks on a service road. On the right is the Bottle Pass Trailhead (5). Park bikes here. Bikes are not permitted on the Bottle Pass or Byers Peak Trails.
Hike – Continue to the end of the service road to the Byers Peak Trailhead (1). Begin on a relatively steep grade through a lush subalpine forest. There are several opportunities to view Bottle Peak, the mountains in Rocky Mountain National Park, and Indian Peaks through the trees. This grade continues to timberline where there is a great view of Byers Peak. At timberline, pass the B & B Trail (Bottle Pass/Byers Peak Trail) fork (2), which is on the right and climb up the ridgeline. Below on the right is Keyser Creek. Alpine Buttercups and Mountain Bluebells dot this alpine landscape in June and July. The trail is rocky in places and a short section of bouldering is required. Continue up the steep trail and pass several false pinnacles to the Byers Peak summit (3). From the summit, the 360° views are incredible. Looking north and clockwise are the Never Summer Range, the mountains in Rocky Mountain National Park, Ptarmigan Peak, Bottle Peak, Indian Peaks, the Continental Divide, Mt. Nystrom, St. Louis Peak, Bill's Peak, the Gore Range, Williams Fork Mountains, and the Williams Fork Reservoir. The landscape below offers a good example of the glacial carving from thousands of years ago.

On the descent from Byers Peak, return to the B & B Trail fork (2) at timberline and turn left. Follow the clear-cut and cairns down the hill. There is a cairn on the far right where a worn trail appears in the mature lodgepole pine forest. Descend through the forest on this beautiful trail away from the busy trail to the peak. At the end of this descent, follow the trail up a small hill and switchback to a meadow. Continue up through the meadow to the Byers Peak/Bottle Pass marker (4). Turn around to see the great view of Byers Peak on the left and Bill's Peak straight ahead. The magnitude of the massive Byers

Peak is obvious from this view and gives perspective to its enormous size. Follow the trail on the right and descend to the Bottle Pass Trailhead (5). Return to the bikes and turn left and descend on the service road to the Bike Trailhead (0).

Historical Note – Byers Peak, originally called Mt. Byers, was named after William Newton Byers. He is remembered for founding the Rocky Mountain News (newspaper), and owning/developing the town of Hot Sulphur Springs and the resort.

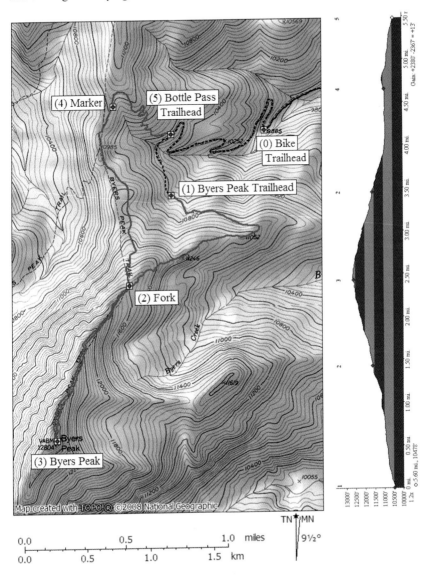

23. BYERS PEAK TO BILL'S PEAK LOOP 🚲 + 🚶
(profile begins at hike trailhead)

Level of Difficulty – Most Difficult
Round-trip Mileage – bike (3.20 miles) + hike (9.88 miles)
Round-trip Hike/Bike Time – bike (1/2 hour) + hike (8 hours)
Altitude, GPS Reading at Bike Trailhead (0) - 9809', 39°53'19"N, 105°55'31"W
Altitude, GPS Reading at Hike Trailhead (1) – 10,545', 39°53'01"N, 105°56'05"W
Altitude, GPS Reading at Byers Peak – 12,804', 39°51'52"N, 105°56'50"W
Altitude, GPS Reading at Bill's Peak – 12,703', 39°51'21"N, 105°57'45"W
Trail Fee Required - No

🐈 Yes, 🐟 N/A, ▲ Yes, WD BP

Trailhead Location – See Byers Peak Loop Trailheads (0) and (1), Hike #22, page 86.

Trail Description – Follow the Byers Peak Loop Hike #22, page 86 description to (3). To reach Bill's Peak, continue southwest past the summit down the back ridgeline. The trail is sometimes faint and very rocky. This leads to a small saddle (4) between Byers and Bill's Peaks. Continue west up the ridgeline of Bill's Peak. The trail disappears frequently and the grade and terrain are very difficult in places. Below on the left are several beautiful tarns. At the top of Bill's Peak (5), Byers Peak has a different appearance than what is viewed from the Fraser valley. Keyser Ridge is visible to the west.

From Bill's Peak, head north and follow the faint trail down the grassy ridgeline. Several cairns mark the way. On the left are Ute Peak and Ute Pass in the distance and a tarn in the valley below. Ahead is a dramatic craggy rock formation along the ridgeline, evidence of the severe wind and weather that occurs at this altitude. At the unidentified fork, remain right up the hill and continue to hug the ridgeline. The left fork leads to Keyser Ridge and Lake Evelyn. Up the hill is a trail marker identifying the St. Louis Divide Trail with Bottle Peak straight (6). Left also leads to Keyser Ridge and Lake Evelyn nestled in the trees below. Follow the trail toward Bottle Peak, but watch for a trail to fork sharply right down into the valley below. At this switchback (7), the trail now heads in the opposite direction and looks straight at the majestic Bill's Peak with Byers Peak on the left. Descend below timberline into the cirque with its Alp-like setting. The trail is faint with cairns along the edge of the trees to Keyser creek below. Cross a creek at the cairn (8) and then cross a second creek at the next cairn. Follow the marshy meadow into the valley and keep Keyser Creek and its tributaries on the left. Move away from the creek through the open marsh and forest to a huge boulder field. Skirt the edge of the boulders and cross the creek. Continue on the well worn trail and cross the creek one last time. At the intersection and trail marker, Keyser Creek Road is on the left and Byers Peak Trail is up the hill (9). Follow the Byers Peak Trail through the woods. This is a moderate ascent with one switchback (10) to the Bottle Pass marker

(11). Follow the trail sign toward the Bottle Pass Trailhead and return to the bikes at the Bottle Pass Trailhead (12). Turn left and descend on the service road to the Bike Trailhead (0).

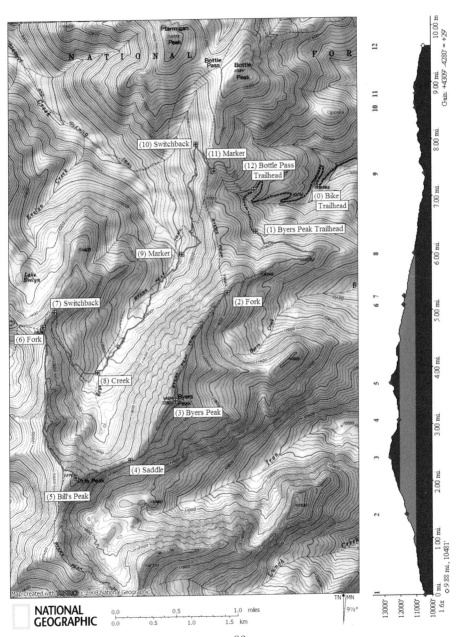

24. BOTTLE PEAK, BOTTLE PASS, AND PTARMIGAN PEAK

🚲 + 🚶 (profile begins at hike trailhead)

Level of Difficulty – Moderate
One-way Mileage – bike (1.4 miles) + hike (2.24 miles)
One-way Hike/Bike Time – bike (15 minutes) + hike (2 hours)
Altitude, GPS Reading at Bike Trailhead (0) - - 9809', 39°53'19"N, 105°55'31"W
Altitude, GPS Reading at Hike Trailhead (1) – 10,523', 39°53'18"N, 105°56'06"W
Altitude, GPS Reading at Ptarmigan Peak – 11,736', 39°54'22"N, 105°56'53"W
Trail Fee Required - No

🐕 Yes, 🐟 N/A, ▲ Yes, **WD** BP

Trailhead Location – See Byers Peak Loop Trailhead (0), Hike #22, page 86.

Trail Description –

Bike – Pass around the gate and climb this steady ascent through several switchbacks on the service road. On the right is the Bottle Pass Trailhead (1). Park bikes here. Bikes are not permitted on the Bottle Pass Trail.

Hike - The lower portion of this trail is through a mostly coniferous subalpine forest with a few marshes along the way. Climb up several switchbacks and quickly gain elevation. At timberline the trail forks. Looking north, the bare peak on the left is Ptarmigan Peak and on the right is the base of Bottle Peak. The environment at this altitude is brutal on flora because of the extreme cold, fierce winds, and strong sun's rays. The plant life consists mostly of forbs and lichens, which grow low to the ground. Most of the plants have a cushion appearance and flower usually in June and July. Take the right fork onto the tundra and bear right up the hill to the top of Bottle Peak (2) where the views are terrific. Looking north and clockwise are the Never Summer Range, the mountains in Rocky Mountain National Park, Indian Peaks, and the James Peak area. Continuing south and clockwise are Colorado Mines Peak, Berthoud Pass, Byers Peak, Bill's Peak, the Gore Range, and Ptarmigan Peak.

To reach Bottle Pass, head west down to the saddle (3). The scenery is impressive and is reminiscent of scenes from "The Sound Of Music". The trees are stunted and wind beaten, but the alpine meadow has great flowers and terrific views of Byers and Bill's Peaks.

To reach Ptarmigan Peak, leave Bottle Pass and bear right up the hill. The hike up to Ptarmigan Peak is enjoyable because of the abundance of alpine flowers. The hillside is covered in both tundra grasses and marsh resulting in a diverse and plentiful display of flowers. The clusters of Alpine Forget-Me-Nots are indeed unforgettable with their brilliant periwinkle petals. From the top of Ptarmigan Peak (4), looking west are great views of the Williams Fork Mountains and valley and northwest below is the Church Park area.

Note - There are two Ptarmigan Peaks in Grand County. The other is in the Williams Fork Mountains. Refer to the Ptarmigan Pass and Peak Hike #83, page 276 for trail access.

Historical Note - Bottle Pass was named long before Bottle Peak and was originally further south near the "Trail Marker" between Bottle Peak and Byers Peak.

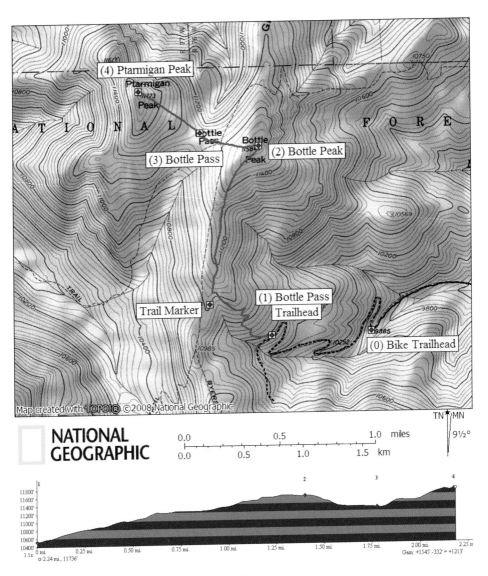

25. ST. LOUIS LAKE 🚲 + 🚶
(map and profile begin at hike trailhead)

Level of Difficulty – Difficult
One-way Mileage – bike (3.01 miles) + hike (2.82 miles)
One-way Hike/Bike Time – bike (½ hour) + hike (1 ½ hours)
Altitude, GPS Reading at Bike Trailhead (0) – 9520', 39°51'06"N, 105°54'37"W
Altitude, GPS Reading at Hike Trailhead (1) – 10,287', 39°48'53"N, 105°55'51"W
Altitude, GPS Reading at Destination - 11,532', 39°49'20"N, 105°56'54"W
Trail Fee Required - No

🐕 Yes, 🐎 Yes, ▲ Yes, WD None

Trailhead Location – On US Hwy 40 in the town of Fraser, at the Fraser Valley
Shopping Center turn south on CR 72 for .3 miles. Turn right onto Fraser Pkwy for .8
miles. Turn left on CR 73 for 8.7 miles to the Bike Trailhead (0). CR 73 is a rough dirt
road.

Trail Description –

Bike – Pass around the gate and follow the service road beside St. Louis Creek to the end
of the road to the St. Louis Lake Trailhead (1). Park bikes here. Bikes are not permitted
on the St. Louis Lake Trail.

Hike - This is a wonderful wildflower hike in late June and July. Cross the bridge over
St. Louis Creek and with the creek on the left. Hike through the coniferous forest of
spruce and pine trees. Follow the trail through marshes with a multitude of marsh
marigolds carpeting the forest floor in June. Cross the creek two more times on log foot
bridges and parallel St. Louis Creek. The trail opens up to a wonderful meadow that is
blanketed with wildflowers in July. From the meadow, the St. Louis Divide is directly in
view. Cross the meadow and follow the creek up to a fork and trail marker (2) identifying
the St. Louis Peak Trail on the left and the St. Louis Lake Trail on the right. Take the
right fork up a short hillside through the woods. Hike through the forest, open treed
areas, meadows, and cross several creeks. There are great views of the St. Louis Divide
on the left and St. Louis Peak and Mt. Nystrom on the right. Level off slightly and reach
St. Louis Lake (3), which sits in a bowl with a dramatic rocky mountain backdrop.
Water flows into the lake from the snow melt on the steep hillside behind the lake. The
fishing is excellent and the wildflowers are abundant on the grassy hillsides. The views
are great from anywhere around the lake.

Historical Note – the St. Louis area was named for St. Louis, Missouri, the home of
many of the early explorers.

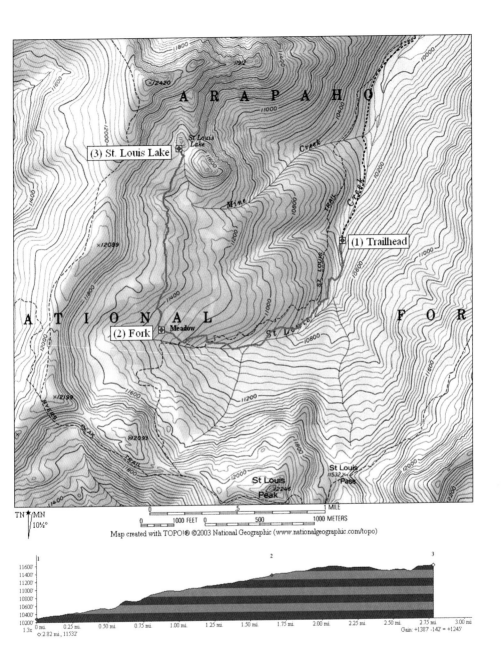

(3) St. Louis Lake

(1) Trailhead

(2) Fork

Meadow

St Louis Lake

ARAPAHO

NATIONAL FOR

St Louis Peak

St Louis Pass

Map created with TOPO!® ©2003 National Geographic (www.nationalgeographic.com/topo)

TN/MN
10½°

26. ST. LOUIS PEAK 🚲 + 🚶
(map and profile begin at hike trailhead)

Level of Difficulty –Difficult
One-way Mileage – bike (3.01 miles) + hike (3.76 miles)
One-way Hike/Bike Time – bike (1/2 hour) + hike (2 hours)
Altitude, GPS Reading at Bike Trailhead (0) – 9520', 39°51'06"N, 105°54'37"W
Altitude, GPS Reading at Hike Trailhead (1) – 10,287', 39°48'53"N, 105°55'51"W
Altitude, GPS Reading at Destination - 12,261', 39°47'42"N, 105°56'19"W
Trail Fee Required - No

🐾 Yes, 🐟 Yes, ▲ Yes, **WD** None

Trailhead Location – See St. Louis Lake Trailheads (0) and (1), Hike #25, page 92.
Park bikes at the St. Louis Lake Trailhead (1). Bikes are not permitted beyond this point.

Trail Description – This is a wonderful wildflower hike in late June and July. Cross the bridge over St. Louis Creek and with the creek on the left. Hike through the coniferous forest of spruce and pine trees. Follow the trail through marshes with a multitude of marsh marigolds carpeting the forest floor in June. Cross the creek two more times on log foot bridges and parallel St. Louis Creek. The trail opens up to a wonderful meadow that is blanketed with wildflowers in July. From the meadow the St. Louis Divide is directly in view. Cross the meadow and follow the creek up to a fork and trail marker (2) identifying the St. Louis Pass Trail on the left and the St. Louis Lake Trail on the right. Take the left fork and cross St. Louis Creek. Hike through the marsh and subalpine forest where the trees thin and the forest gives way to the tundra. At timberline, the St. Louis Divide is immediately ahead with St. Louis Peak, Mt. Nystrom, and an unnamed peak on the left. Follow the trail up the hill and to the left into the alpine. At the top of the small saddle (3) is another trail marker, where the St. Louis Pass Trail intersects the St. Louis Divide Trail. The views from the saddle looking north are of Bill's and Byers Peaks. Continuing clockwise are the mountains in Rocky Mountain National Park, Longs Peak and Indian Peaks. Looking south are the Williams Fork Mountains and the Jones Pass Road. The trail to the right leads to Bill's and Byers Peaks and the trail to the left leads to St. Louis Peak. Turn left and head up the left side of the hill where Alpine Forget-Me-Nots abound. Cross the St. Louis Divide ridgeline where there are great views of the Williams Fork Mountains. Follow the cairns down a short hill and then climb again. The trail forks at the bottom of the St. Louis Peak ridgeline. Follow the faint trail on the right along the ridgeline to the top of St. Louis Peak (4). Additional views from the peak looking southeast and clockwise are of Jones Pass, Pettingell Peak (the tallest in the foreground), Hagar Mountain, Coon Hill, and the Williams Fork Mountains.

Side Trip – Mt. Nystrom – From St. Louis Peak, continue northeast on the St. Louis Divide Trail to St. Louis Pass and then to Mt. Nystrom. Also see Mt. Nystrom Hike #21, page 82 and Jones Pass to Mt. Nystrom Hike #40, page 132 for peak access.

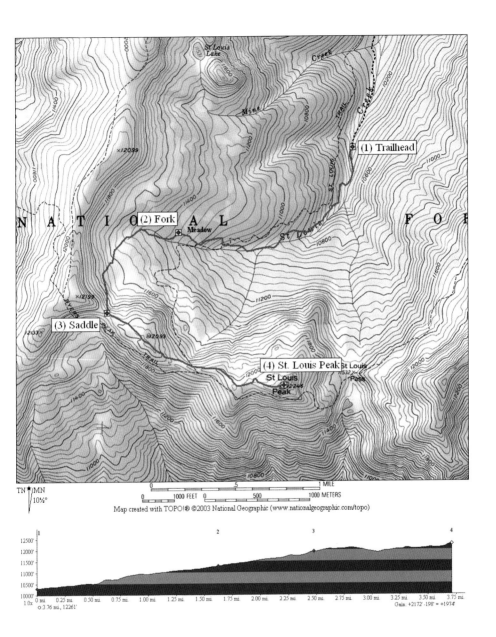

(1) Trailhead

(2) Fork
Meadow

(3) Saddle

(4) St. Louis Peak
St Louis
Pass
St Louis
Peak

St Louis
Lake

Creek

Mine

St Louis Creek

TRAIL

PEAK

TRAIL

N A T I O N A L   F O

TN   MN
10½°

0   .5   1 MILE

1000 FEET 0   500   1000 METERS

Map created with TOPO!® ©2003 National Geographic (www.nationalgeographic.com/topo)

12500'
12000'
11500'
11000'
10500'
10000'
1.0x

0 mi.   0.25 mi.   0.50 mi.   0.75 mi.   1.00 mi.   1.25 mi.   1.50 mi.   1.75 mi.   2.00 mi.   2.25 mi.   2.50 mi.   2.75 mi.   3.00 mi.   3.25 mi.   3.50 mi.   3.75 mi.

3.76 mi., 12261'
Gain: +2172' -198' = +1974'

27. ST. LOUIS DIVIDE LOOP 🚲 + 🚶
(map and profile begin at hike trailhead)

Level of Difficulty – Difficult
Round-trip Mileage – bike (6.02 miles) + hike (7.60 miles)
Round-trip Hike/Bike Time – bike (1 hour) + hike (4 hours)
Altitude, GPS Reading at Bike Trailhead (0) - 9520', 39°51'06"N, 105°54'37"W
Altitude, GPS Reading at Hike Trailhead (1) – 10,295', 39°48'53"N, 105°55'51"W
Altitude, GPS Reading at Divide – 12,221', 39°48'09"N, 105°57'42"W
Altitude, GPS Reading at Lake – 11,532', 39°49'22"N, 105°56'55"W
Trail Fee Required - No

🐕 Yes, 🎣 Yes, ▲ Yes, WD BP

Trailhead Location – See St. Louis Lake Trailheads (0) and (1), Hike #25, page 92. Park bikes at the St. Louis Lake Trailhead (1). Bikes are not permitted beyond this point.

Trail Description – This loop combines part of the St. Louis Peak Trail and the St. Louis Lake Trail connecting the two by the St. Louis Divide. It is a great way to hike along the St. Louis Divide for fantastic views while spending minimal time above timberline and without backtracking. Follow the trail description for St. Louis Peak, Hike 26, page 94, description to (3) to the St. Louis Divide Trail. From the saddle, turn right and follow the trail toward Bill's and Byers Peaks. A second trail marker (4) at the top of the hill identifies Bill's Peak to the north and Darling Creek/Williams Fork River to the west. Hike to the top of the small knoll for a great 360° view of the Vasquez Mountains and valleys. Looking north and clockwise are Bill's Peak, Byers Peak, the St. Louis Divide, St. Louis Lake nestled in the trees, Longs Peak, the mountains in Rocky Mountain National Park, Indian Peaks, Mt. Nystrom, St. Louis Peak, Jones Pass Road, Pettingell Peak, Hagar Mountain, Coon Hill, Ptarmigan Peak, the Gore Range, Ute Peak, Williams Peak, Williams Fork Reservoir, and the Never Summer Range.

Continue toward Bill's Peak along the St. Louis Divide and follow the cairns where the trail is faint. The St. Louis Divide is in an alpine zone and the ground cover varies from grasses and forbs to moss covered rocks. At the next small saddle, head right (east) toward St. Louis Lake. There is no visible trail to the lake, but hike down through the loose rocky scree, to the marsh and meadow above the lake. St. Louis Lake (5) is a wonderful mountain lake and is appreciated from anywhere around the lake.

To return to the trailhead, continue to the south end of the lake. Cross several creeks and hike through several meadows and open treed areas. The views on the left are of an unnamed peak, Mt. Nystrom, a second unnamed peak, and St. Louis Peak. On the right is the St. Louis Divide. Continue through a small forest and down a short hill to the fork and trail marker (2). Turn left at the fork and follow the inbound trail through the wonderful wildflower meadow back to the St. Louis Lake Trailhead (1). Return to the bikes and descend on the service road to the Bike Trailhead (0).

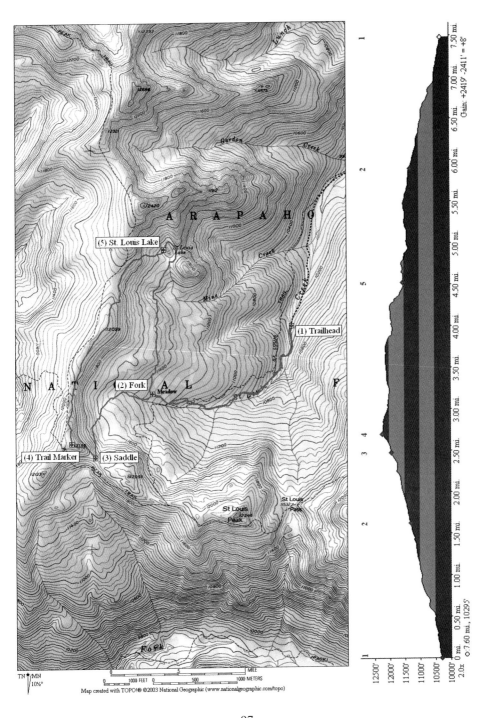

(5) St. Louis Lake

(1) Trailhead

(2) Fork

(4) Trail Marker

(3) Saddle

St Louis Peak

Map created with TOPO!® ©2003 National Geographic (www.nationalgeographic.com/topo)

28. MINE CREEK 🚲 + 🚶
(map and profile begin at hike trailhead)

Level of Difficulty - Moderate
One-way Mileage – bike (3.01 miles) + hike (.91 miles)
One-way Hike/Bike Time – bike (1/2 hour) + hike (1 hour)
Altitude, GPS Reading at Bike Trailhead (0) - 9520', 39°51'06"N, 105°54'37"W
Altitude, GPS Reading at Hike Trailhead (1) – 10,046', 39°49'25"N, 105°55'43"W
Altitude, GPS Reading at Destination – 11,067', 39°49'31"N, 105°56'26"W
Trail Fee Required – No

🐾 Yes, 🐟 N/A, ▲ No, WD None

Trailhead Location – On US Hwy 40 in the town of Fraser, at the Fraser Valley Shopping Center turn south on CR 72 for .3 miles. Turn right onto Fraser Pkwy for .8 miles. Turn left on CR 73 for 8.7 miles to the trailhead (0). CR 73 is a rough dirt road.

Trail Description –
Bike – Pass around the gate and follow the service road beside St. Louis Creek for .6 miles. Park bikes here. Bikes are not permitted on the Mine Creek Trail. The trailhead is not marked, but begin on the side road on the right (1).
Trail Description – Follow this side road that was originally used for access to the mine. Mine Creek is audible on the left not far from the trailhead and parallels the trail part of the way to the mine. The trail is fairly steep for a road. Begin in a dense montane forest with lodgepole pine, spruce, and fir trees, but ascend quickly to a sub-alpine forest. The wide road abruptly changes into a single-track trail (2). Continue upward to an avalanche clearing, where there is a good view of St. Louis Peak. In the avalanche clearing above, mountain goats occasionally graze on the hillside. Follow the trail through the woods to a small collapsed cabin (3). The mine is immediately on the right (north) up the hill (4).

Beyond the cabin and mine to the west, the trail disappears into a beautiful cirque with tall spruce trees on both sides of the valley. The stunted trees near the scree are short due to avalanche damage. The views to the east of Mt. Nystrom and its divide are unmatched. West of the cirque, over the saddle is St. Louis Lake.

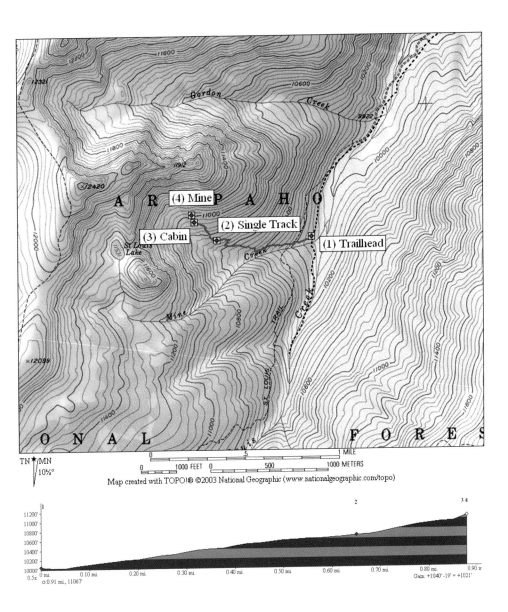

Nine Mile Mountain Trail in Fall

VASQUEZ MOUNTAINS
East Access

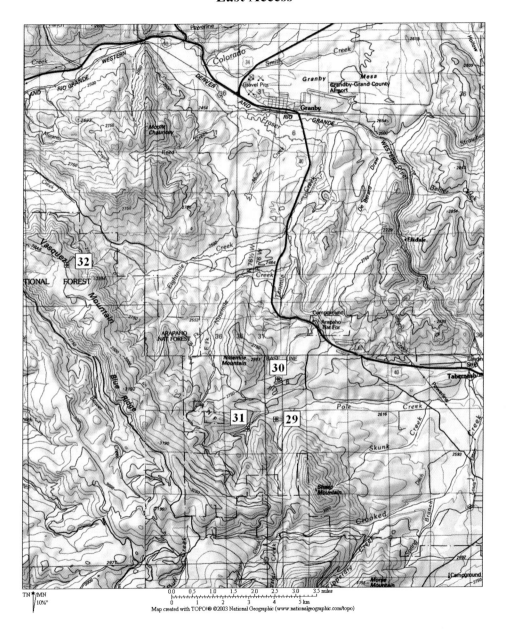

TN /MN
10¾°

0.0   0.5   1.0   1.5   2.0   2.5   3.0   3.5 miles
0   1   2   3   4   5 km

Map created with TOPO!® ©2003 National Geographic (www.nationalgeographic.com/topo)

29. SHEEP (SNOW) MOUNTAIN

Level of Difficulty – Difficult
One-way Mileage – 2.81 miles
One-way Hiking Time – 2 hours
Altitude, GPS Reading at Trailhead – 8863', 39°58'40"N, 105°56'25"W
Altitude, GPS Reading at Destination – 10,646', 39°57'12"N, 105°55'18"W
Trail Fee Required - Yes

🐕 Leash, 🐟 Yes, ▲ Yes, WD None

Trailhead Location – On US Hwy 40, between Tabernash and Granby, at mile marker 219, turn southwest into the Snow Mountain Ranch -YMCA of the Rockies entrance (CR 53) and follow this for 1.1 miles. Stop at the Program Building on the right for a day pass and then return to CR 53 and continue for another .3 miles where the road forks. Take the right fork and remain on CR 53 for another 1.3 miles where the road splits three ways. Take the middle road toward Columbine Point. Park at the top of the hill (1). These are good dirt roads off US Hwy 40.

Trail Description – Pass around the gate and follow the service road counter-clockwise around the reservoir. After the road crosses over a creek, there is a large billboard on the right that identifies the Sheep (Snow) Mountain Trail (2). This trail begins on Snow Mountain Ranch property and crosses into both Bureau of Land Management and US Forest Service lands. The journey up Sheep Mountain requires hiking up four separate peaks. Begin in a beautiful lodgepole pine forest and gradually climb up through an equally beautiful aspen forest to 1st Peak (3). From 1st Peak there are several opportunities to enjoy the terrific views. Looking north and clockwise are the town of Granby, Lake Granby, and the mountains in Rocky Mountain National Park in the background. Counter-clockwise of Granby are Nine Mile Mountain, Cottonwood Pass, Little White Cliffs, White Cliffs, Blue Ridge, Bottle Peak, and Byers Peak. Continue beyond 1st Peak, where there is very little shade and the views to the left of the trail are limited due to the tall trees. Hike up to 2nd Peak (4), where the views of the valley below are fabulous. Second Peak is mostly in the trees and the views are the best off the trail. Continue up to 3rd Peak (5), which is a false summit. To reach the top of Sheep Mountain, descend to a saddle and then climb to the 4th Peak (6). From the top looking left (east) through the trees are peek-a-boo views of the Indian Peaks Range and the Continental Divide. Looking right (west) are fantastic views of Byers Peak, Bill's Peak and Ptarmigan Peak.

Historical Note - Sheep Mountain was given its name because sheep grazed on the mountain many years ago when ranching was a way of life in the Fraser Valley. At one time, ranching sheep was more popular than cattle in Grand County. Sheep Mountain has since been locally renamed Snow Mountain after Snow Mountain Ranch.

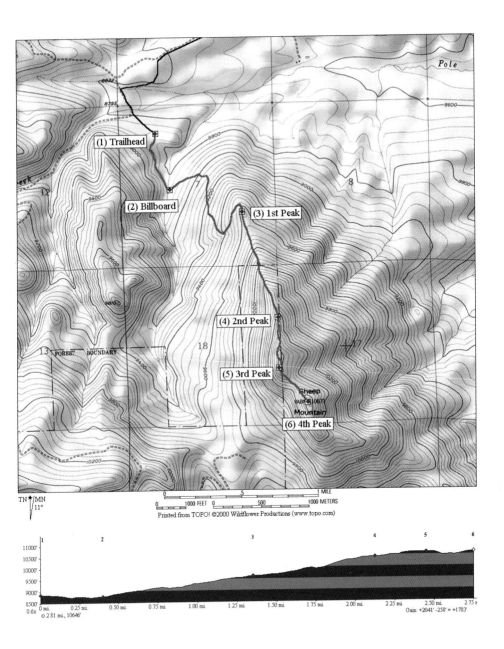

(1) Trailhead

(2) Billboard

(3) 1st Peak

(4) 2nd Peak

(5) 3rd Peak

Sheep
Mountain

(6) 4th Peak

Pole

FOREST BOUNDARY

TN ★ /MN
11°

Printed from TOPO! ©2000 Wildflower Productions (www.topo.com)

Gain: +2041' -258' = +1783'

○ 2.81 mi., 10646'

30. NINE MILE MOUNTAIN

Level of Difficulty - Moderate
One-way Mileage – 1.70 miles
One-way Hiking Time – 1 hour
Altitude, GPS Reading at Trailhead – 8727', 39°59'30"N, 105°56'22"W
Altitude, GPS Reading at Destination – 9697', 39°59'53"N, 105°57'10"W
Trail Fee Required - Yes

🐕 Leash, 🐟 N/A, ▲ No, WD None

Trailhead Location – On US Hwy 40, between Tabernash and Granby, at mile marker 219, turn southwest at the Snow Mountain Ranch – YMCA of the Rockies entrance (CR53) and follow this for 1.1 miles. Turn right onto CR 531 (Association Drive) and stop at the Program Building for a day pass. Continue on CR 531 for .7 miles to Geronimo Campground, which is on the right. Turn right at the campground and park immediately on the right side of the road. The trailhead marker is visible (1) ahead. CR 53 and CR531 are good roads, but CR 531 has a few pot holes.

Trail Description - Hike through a coniferous forest to a mature aspen stand. This stand is especially great in the fall with the yellow and gold foliage. Near the end of the aspen stand are two benches. Pass these benches and ascend to the fork (2). Turn right, leave the aspens and ascend steeply through the lodgepole pine forest to a clearing where there is a rock outcropping on the right (3) and a horse tie up area on the left. This is not the top, however this is the best location to enjoy the views. To reach the top of Nine Mile Mountain, continue on the trail to the next clearing. Stop as soon as the highway and the town of Tabernash are visible on the right. The bushes hide the trail. Turn left through the bushes where the trail appears. Follow this trail to a small rock outcropping with peek-a-boo views of Lake Granby and the Continental Divide. From this point, the summit of Nine Mile Mountain is visible to the left at the top of the small knoll. There is no trail, but a cairn identifies the peak (4). Return to the first rock outcropping (3) where the views to the east are of the Continental Divide, the town of Tabernash below, Pole Creek Golf Course on the right, Snow Mountain Ranch below, Winter Park Ski Resort in the distance, and Sheep (Snow) Mountain on the far right.

Note - For a shorter hike up Nine Mile Mountain, inquire at the Program Building for directions to the alternate trailhead.

Historical Note – Frequently, landmarks such as creeks or mountains were named for their distance from the nearest town. Nine Mile Mountain was named because of it distance from the town of Hot Sulphur Springs.

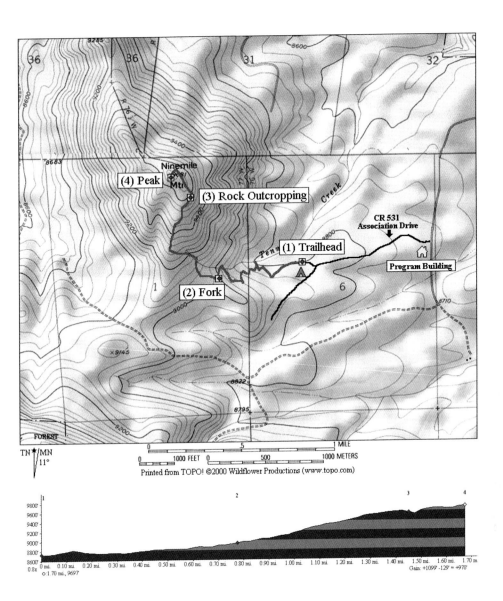

31. SNOW MOUNTAIN RANCH WATERFALL

Level of Difficulty - Easy
One-way Mileage – 1.05 miles
One-way Hiking Time – ½ hour
Altitude, GPS Reading at Trailhead – 8893', 39°58'28"N, 105°57'11"W
Altitude, GPS Reading at Destination – 9269', 39°58'06"N, 105°58'04"W
Trail Fee Required – Yes

🐕 Leash, ➤ N/A, ▲ No, **WD** None

Trailhead Location – On US Hwy 40, between Tabernash and Granby, at mile marker 219, turn southwest into the Snow Mountain Ranch – YMCA of the Rockies entrance (CR 53) and follow this for 1.1 miles. Stop at the Program Building on the right for a day pass and then return to CR 53 and continue for another .3 miles where the road forks. Take the right fork and remain on CR 53, for another 1.3 miles where the road forks three ways. Take the right fork and continue .7 miles to the Waterfalls Trailhead. Park on the left side of the road across from the trailhead (1). These are good dirt roads, but the last .7 miles is rough with several pot holes. This last road is not suitable for trailer turnaround.

Trail Description – Begin this hike parallel to Pole Creek. The creek is hidden in the willows on the left side, but several beaver ponds are visible along the way. On the right is a great stand of aspens that is brilliant in the fall. Climb gradually through the montane forest. The remains of a couple of old cabins are near the edge of the trail. The willows disappear and the open valley narrows where the hillsides on both sides of the creek merge. Follow the trail up a slightly steeper grade. The trees form a thick canopy where the forest is damp and cool. The trail ends at the waterfall (2). The waterfall is about 25' high and in early summer the flow is quite heavy. Mosses grow thick on the rocks and logs.

Historical Note – Snow Mountain Ranch was previously owned by the Just family, who homesteaded and ranched it until the YMCA of the Rockies purchased it. The original ranch still remains on the Snow Mountain Ranch property.

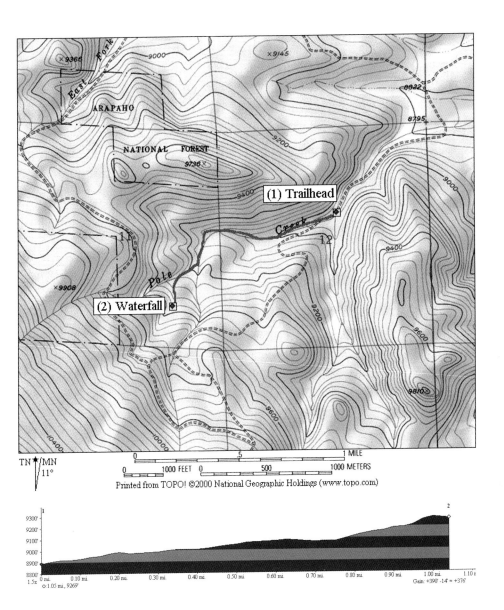

32. WHITE CLIFFS 🚲 + 🚶

(CR 555 and this bike/hike are scheduled for logging - contact USDA Forest Service 970-887-4100 for details)

Level of Difficulty - Moderate
One-way Mileage – bike (5.06 miles) + hike (.42 miles)
One-way Hiking/Biking Time – bike (1 ½ hours) + hike (½ hour)
Altitude, GPS Reading at Trailhead – 9721', 40°01'53"N, 106°02'13"W
Altitude, GPS Reading at Destination – 10,533', 39°58'32"N, 106°00'01"W
Trail Fee Required - No

🐕 Yes, 🛶 N/A, ▲ Yes, WD None

Trailhead Location – On US Hwy 40, between Tabernash and Granby, between mile markers 216 and 217, head west on CR 55. Follow this dirt road for 5.4 miles to the top of Cottonwood Pass and turn left onto CR 555. Continue on this road for 3.1 miles where the road forks three ways. Park on the left side of the road. There is no trailhead sign. The trailhead is at the gated road on the left (1). These are good dirt roads.

Trail Description –
Bike - Pass around the gate and follow the logging road until a road forks to the left (2). Turn left here and follow the road around the east side of Blue Ridge. This trail is primarily in a lodgepole pine forest. Evidence remains of many clear-cut areas. Follow the road to the next fork (3). Turn right and continue on this road to the next fork (4). Again, turn right. There are two more forks and at each fork turn right (5) and (6). Next, cross from the left (east) side of Blue Ridge over a slight pass to the right (west) side of Blue Ridge and descend for a short distance. There is a cairn on the right side of the road at the dip in the hill (7). Park bikes here.
Hike - Follow the trail beside the cairn. The trail is not well worn, but is easy to follow up the ridgeline of the hill. Continue through more lodgepole pine forest to a clear-cut. Hike up the hill. There are cairns most of the way to the top. From the top of White Cliffs (8), on the left are the severely eroded white cliff sandstone formations. From up close, they have the appearance of stacked rocks. Looking north and clockwise are the Never Summer Range, the mountains in Rocky Mountain National Park, Indian Peaks, the James Peak area, Winter Park Ski Resort, Ptarmigan Peak, Byers and Bill's Peaks, the Gore Range, Williams Fork Reservoir, and the Troublesome Valley.

Note – White Cliffs is visible from almost anywhere in the Fraser Valley. No trees or shrubs grow on this sandstone formation, thus the white face of these cliffs is appropriately named.

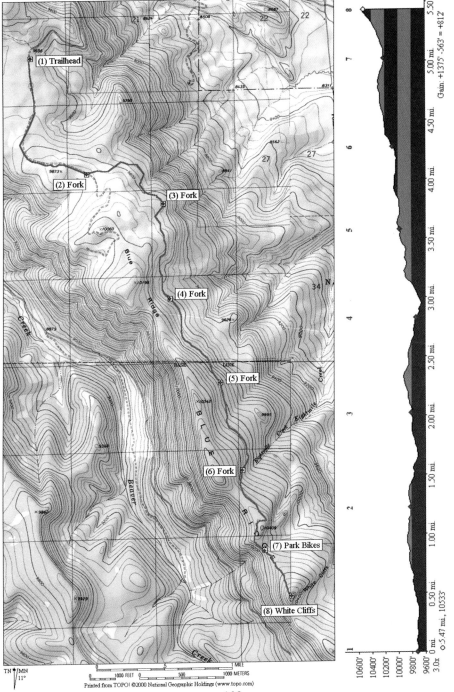

(1) Trailhead
(2) Fork
(3) Fork
(4) Fork
(5) Fork
(6) Fork
(7) Park Bikes
(8) White Cliffs

TN MN
11°

0   1000 FEET   1 MILE
0   500   1000 METERS

Printed from TOPO! ©2000 National Geographic Holdings (www.topo.com)

Gain: +1375' -563' = +812'
◇ 5.47 mi, 10533'
3.0x

Approaching Bottle Pass and Ptarmigan Peak

VASQUEZ MOUNTAINS
West Access

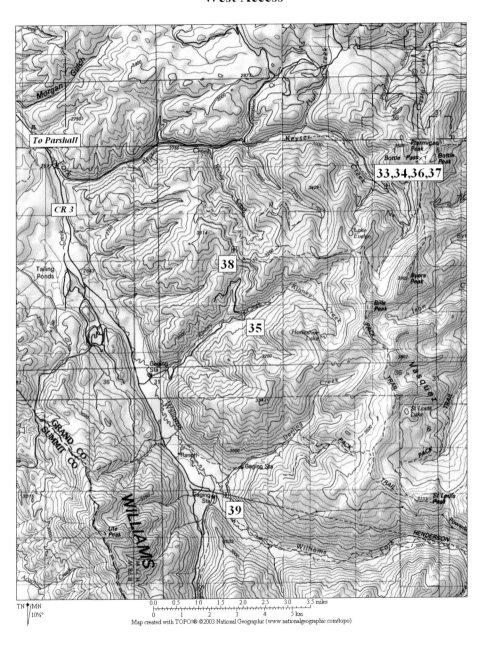

33. BILL'S PEAK TO BYERS PEAK LOOP

Level of Difficulty –Most Difficult
Round-trip Mileage - 12.19 miles
Round-trip Hiking Time – 8 hours
Altitude, GPS Reading at Trailhead – 10,043', 39°53'37"N, 105°57'23"W
Altitude, GPS Reading at Bill's Peak – 12,637', 39°51'21"N, 105°57'45"W
Altitude, GPS Reading at Byers Peak – 12,643', 39°51'52"N, 105°56'50"W
Trail Fee Required - No

🐕 Yes, 🐎 N/A, ▲ Yes, WD BP

Trailhead Location – On US Hwy 40, just east of Parshall, between mile markers 197 and 198, turn south onto CR 3. On CR 3, between mile markers 15 and 16, head left (east) onto CR 32 (FSR 139). Follow CR 32 for 4.7 miles. Turn right at the sign for the Lake Evelyn Trail and Bottle Pass Trail, FSR 136. Follow this single lane rough dirt road for 3.9 miles to the trailhead (1). Both CR 3 and CR 32 are good dirt roads.

Trail Description – Begin at the Bottle Pass Trailhead. Follow the old Keyser Creek logging road and climb up the switchbacks. Pass the fork and trail marker, which is on the left identifying the Bottle Pass Trail. Continue on the old logging road through the lodgepole pine forest to another fork and trail marker (2) identifying Byers Peak to the left up the hill. Remain straight and cross Keyser Creek. Follow the trail and cross the creek again. Skirt the edge of the boulder field and move away from the creek through open marsh and forest. The forest changes from montane to subalpine with spruce and fir trees surrounding the meadow. Keep Keyser Creek on the right up through the valley. Byers Peak is on the left and Bill's Peak is straight ahead. This cirque has an alp-like setting with beautiful peaks and meadows. There are several cairns to identify the direction of the trail through the marsh. When the trees thin, head west across Keyser Creek and its tributaries at the cairn (3). After crossing the creeks, hike uphill to the west away from Bill's Peak. The trail is faint, but there are cairns along the edge of the trees and the worn trail reappears above. Hike through timberline into the alpine and out of the cirque. At the ridgeline (4), make a sharp left (south) toward Bill's Peak. At the trail marker identifying the St. Louis Divide Trail with St. Louis Peak ahead (5), continue straight (south) along the ridgeline. On the right (west) are Keyser Ridge and Lake Evelyn nestled in the trees below. At the next fork, right also leads to Keyser Ridge and Lake Evelyn. Remain straight (south) toward Bill's Peak and hug the ridgeline. On the left is a dramatic craggy rock formation, evidence of the severe wind and weather that occurs at this altitude. To the right of the trail lies a tarn with Ute Peak and Ute Pass in the background. The trail is faint along the grassy ridgeline, but several cairns mark the way to the top of Bill's Peak (6). From the top of Bill's Peak looking north and clockwise are the Never Summer Range, the mountains in Rocky Mountain National Park, Ptarmigan Peak, Bottle Peak, Byers Peak, the Vasquez Mountains, St. Louis Divide, the Gore Range, Ute Peak, the Kinney Creek valley below, and Keyser Ridge.

From the Bill's Peak summit, head east down the ridgeline toward Byers Peak. Below on the right are several beautiful tarns. The grade and terrain are difficult here and the trail disappears frequently to the saddle (7). From the saddle, continue northeast up the ridgeline to Byers Peak. The trail is faint and rocky to the top of Byers Peak (8). Additional views looking east and clockwise include Indian Peaks and the Continental Divide, Mt. Nystrom and St. Louis Peak. Next are Bill's Peak, the Gore Range, St. Louis Divide, the Williams Fork Mountains, and the Williams Fork Reservoir. Inspecting the landscape below offers a good example of the glacial carvings from thousands of years ago.

Continue north from the Byers Peak summit. On the descent from Byers Peak at timberline, there is a fork (9) for the B & B Trail (Bottle Pass/Byers Peak Trail) to the left. Turn left and follow the clear-cut and cairns down the hill. There is a cairn on the far right where a worn trail appears in the mature lodgepole pine forest. Descend through the forest on this beautiful trail. At the end of this descent, follow the trail up a small hill and switchback to a meadow. Continue up through the meadow to the Byers Peak/Bottle Pass marker (10). Turn around to see the great view of Byers Peaks on the left and Bill's Peak straight ahead. The magnitude of the massive Byers Peak is apparent from this view and gives perspective to its enormous size. Head west (left) toward Keyser Creek Road. Follow this trail through the subalpine forest, make one switchback (11) and continue to the old Keyser Creek logging road (2). Turn right and follow the inbound trail back to the Bottle Pass Trailhead (1).

The West Side of Byers Peak

Bill's Peak Ridge

Byers and Bill's Peaks

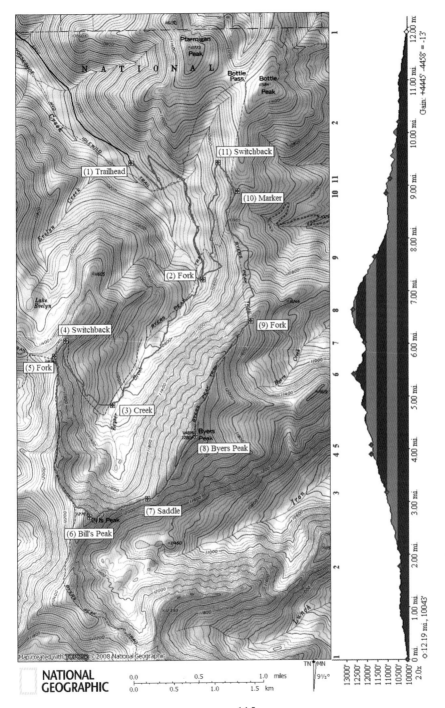

NATIONAL
GEOGRAPHIC

115

34. LAKE EVELYN AND HORSESHOE LAKE

Level of Difficulty – Moderate (Lake Evelyn), Most Difficult (Horseshoe Lake)
One-way Mileage – 2.49 miles (Lake Evelyn), 6.10 miles (Horseshoe Lake)
One-way Hiking Time – 1 ½ hours (Lake Evelyn), 3 ½ hours (Horseshoe Lake)
Altitude, GPS Reading at Trailhead – 10,023', 39°53'37"N, 105°57'23"W
Altitude, GPS Reading at Lake Evelyn – 11,158', 39°52'46"N, 105°58'17"W
Altitude, GPS Reading at Horseshoe Lake – 11,245', 39°50'50"N, 105°58'55"W
Trail Fee Required - No

🐕 Yes, 🚵 Yes, ▲ Yes, WD BP

Trailhead Location – See Bill's Peak to Byers Peak Loop Trailhead (1), Hike #33, page 112.

Lake Evelyn Trail Description – The Bottle Pass Trailhead and the Lake Evelyn Trailhead begin in the same parking area. Begin at the Lake Evelyn Trailhead. Cross Keyser Creek soon after the trailhead and head toward Evelyn Creek. The creek creates rapids, moves briskly, and cascades over the rocks. Gradually move away from the creek where the terrain changes from a montane forest to a beautiful subalpine forest. It is a moderate climb with a short switchback near the end. Lake Evelyn (2) is a charming mountain lake surrounded by trees and is great for fishing.

Horseshoe Lake Trail Description – From Lake Evelyn, follow the trail around the right side of the lake and up the hill to the left. Follow the cairns through the marsh up to the saddle of Keyser Ridge (3). Look back at the mountains in Rocky Mountain National Park in the distance, Ptarmigan Peak in the foreground, Lake Granby, the Never Summer Range, and Lake Evelyn below. At the saddle, the trail marker identifies Keyser Ridge, with the St. Louis Divide Trail to the left, and the Kinney Creek Trail straight. Follow the Kinney Creek Trail straight (south) down into the valley through the open trees with views of the St. Louis Divide on the left. Occasional views of the Gore Range are visible in the distance. Approach Kinney Creek where the forest is dense. Kinney Creek is a beautiful creek lined with flowers in June and July. The water flows swiftly over the rocks of this beautiful mountain stream. Next is a fork and trail marker (4) identifying Kinney Creek Trail to the right and Horseshoe Lake Trail to the left. Right leads to the trailhead of the Horseshoe Lake Hike #35, page 118 and left leads to Horseshoe Lake. Turn left and immediately cross Kinney Creek. Gently climb through this beautiful subalpine forest and cross several more creeks. Pass two boulder fields, which are on the left and then cross a short meadow with continued views of the cirque surrounding Horseshoe Lake. Follow the cairns into the trees and arrive at Horseshoe Lake (5). The fishing is good here and worth the hike.

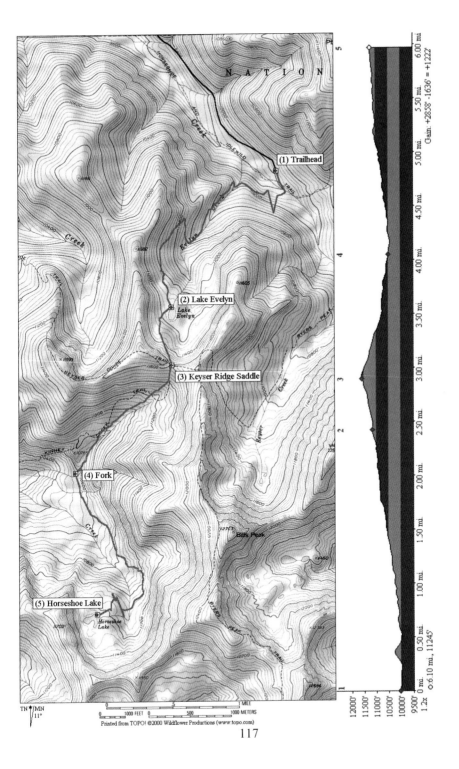

(1) Trailhead

(2) Lake Evelyn

(3) Keyser Ridge Saddle

(4) Fork

(5) Horseshoe Lake

N A T I O N

Byers Peak

Bills Peak

Horseshoe Lake

Lake Evelyn

TN ★ MN
11°

0   1000 FEET   5
0   500   1000 METERS   1 MILE

Printed from TOPO! ©2000 Wildflower Productions (www.topo.com)

0: 6.10 mi., 11245'   1.2x

Gain: +2858'-1636' = +1222'

0 mi.   0.50 mi.   1.00 mi.   1.50 mi.   2.00 mi.   2.50 mi.   3.00 mi.   3.50 mi.   4.00 mi.   4.50 mi.   5.00 mi.   5.50 mi.   6.00 mi.

9500'   10000'   10500'   11000'   11500'   12000'

117

35. HORSESHOE LAKE

Level of Difficulty - Moderate
One-way Mileage – 4.29 miles
One-way Hiking Time – 2 ½ hours
Altitude, GPS Reading at Trailhead – 9723', 39°51'14"N, 106°01'00"W
Altitude, GPS Reading at Destination – 11,245', 39°50'50"N, 105°58'55"W
Trail Fee Required - No

🐕 Yes, 🚲 Yes, ▲ Yes, **WD** BP

Trailhead Location – On US Hwy 40, just east of Parshall, between mile markers 197 and 198, turn south onto CR 3. On CR 3, drive 17.9 miles, between mile markers 18 and 19 and head south onto CR 30 toward South Fork and Sugar Loaf Campgrounds. Follow CR 30 for 2.6 miles and turn left onto CR 302. Follow this road for 3.6 miles to the Kinney Creek Trailhead (1). These are good dirt roads.

Trail Description – Begin along Kinney Creek through a young lodgepole pine forest. Gradually move away from the creek and climb slowly through a beautiful montane forest of spruce and fir trees. Cross several small creeks, which flow into Kinney Creek. Climb up the switchbacks to a fork and trail marker (2) identifying Horseshoe Lake to the right and Kinney Creek Trail and Lake Evelyn to the left. Take the right fork and immediately cross Kinney Creek. Gently climb through this beautiful subalpine forest and cross several more creeks. Pass two boulder fields, which are on the left, and eventually cross the short meadow with views of the cirque surrounding Horseshoe Lake. Follow the cairns into the trees and arrive at Horseshoe Lake (3). The fishing is good here and worth the hike.

Note - Horseshoe Lake can also be accessed from the Lake Evelyn and Horseshoe Lake Hike #34, page 116.

Note - Horseshoe Lake is in the shape of a horseshoe.

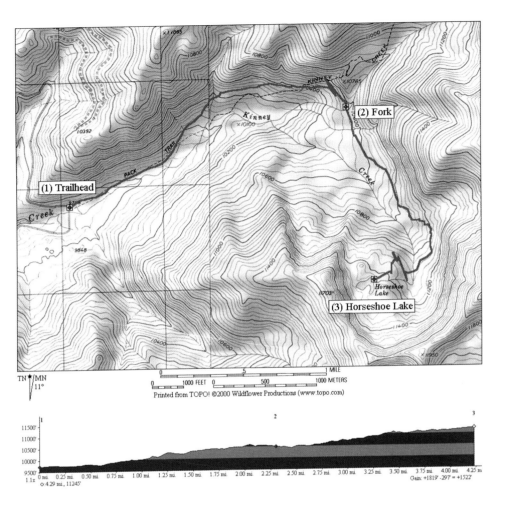

(1) Trailhead

(2) Fork

(3) Horseshoe Lake

Printed from TOPO! ©2000 Wildflower Productions (www.topo.com)

36. BILL'S PEAK LOOP

Level of Difficulty – More Difficult
Round-trip Mileage – 10.06 miles
Round-trip Hiking Time – 6 ½ hours
Altitude, GPS Reading at Trailhead – 10,057', 39°53'37"N, 105°57'23"W
Altitude, GPS Reading at Destination – 12,637', 39°51'21"N, 105°57'45"W
Trail Fee Required - No

🐾 Yes, 🐟 Yes, ▲ Yes, WD BP

Trailhead Location – See Bill's Peak to Byers Peak Loop Trailhead (1), Hike #33, page 112.

Trail Description – This is a wonderful hike that is made up partly from the Bill's Peak to Byers Peak Loop Hike #33, page 112 and partly from the Lake Evelyn and Horseshoe Lake Hike #34, page 116. Follow the Lake Evelyn and Horseshoe Lake Hike #34, page 116 description to (3) the saddle of Keyser Ridge. At the intersection and trail marker, turn left (east) toward the St. Louis Divide Trail. Not far from the saddle and marker is a cairn on the right (4) off the main trail. Turn right toward the cairn to a clearing. Continue to timberline and head south (right). There are several cairns that lead to a well worn trail and fork (5) just below the ridgeline. At this fork, continue straight (south). On the left is a dramatic craggy rock formation along the ridgeline, evidence of the severe wind and weather that occurs at this altitude. On the right of the trail lies a tarn with Ute Peak and Ute Pass in the background. Follow the cairns along the faint grassy trail to the top of Bill's Peak (6). From the top of Bill's Peak looking north and clockwise are the Never Summer Range, the mountains in Rocky Mountain National Park in the background, Ptarmigan Peak, Bottle Peak, Byers Peak, the Vasquez Mountains, St. Louis Divide, the Gore Range, Ute Peak, the Kinney Creek valley below, and Keyser Ridge.

From the Bill's Peak summit, return along the ridgeline to the fork (5). At the fork, bear right instead of returning to the Keyser Ridge saddle. Continue along the ridgeline to the fork and trail marker (7) on the top of the hill. The trail marker identifies the St. Louis Divide Trail with Bottle Peak ahead. To the left are Keyser Ridge and Lake Evelyn nestled in the trees below. Follow the trail toward Bottle Peak, but watch for a trail to fork sharply to the right into the valley below. Follow this switchback (8), where the trail now heads in the opposite direction and looks straight at the majestic Bill's Peak with Byers Peak to the left. Descend below timberline into the cirque with its Alp-like setting. The trail is faint with cairns along the edge of the trees to Keyser Creek below. Cross a creek at the cairn (9) and then cross a second creek at the next cairn. Follow the marshy meadow into the valley and keep Keyser Creek and its tributaries on the left. Move away from the creek and through the open marsh and forest to a huge boulder field. Skirt the edge of the boulders and cross the creek again. Continue on the well worn trail and cross the creek one last time. At the intersection, the trail marker identifies Keyser Creek Road on the left and Byers Peak Trail up the hill (10). Follow the old Keyser Creek logging road and descend through the lodgepole pine forest and switchbacks to the Lake Evelyn Trailhead (1).

Historical Note – Bill's Peak was originally called Eclipse Peak. A Frenchman used this peak as a mountaineering training ground in winter in the early days. Some local historians believe the peak was later renamed after a local miner and prospector.

Bill's Peak and Cirque

Little Red Elephant flower

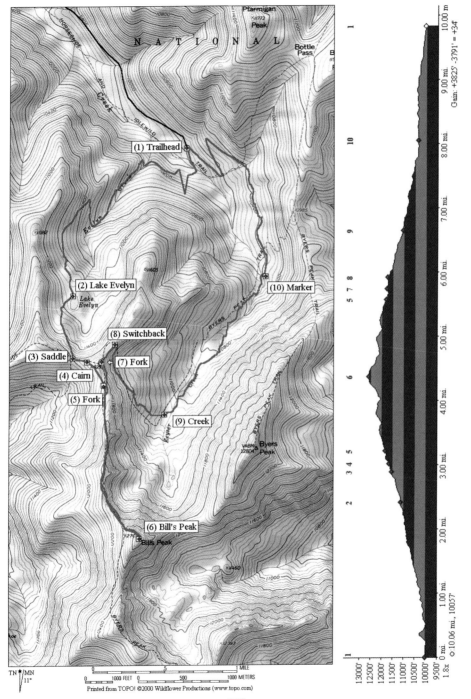

TN MN
11°

0   1000 FEET   0   500   1000 METERS
0   5   1 MILE

Printed from TOPO! ©2000 Wildflower Productions (www.topo.com)

37. BOTTLE PASS, BOTTLE PEAK, AND PTARMIGAN PEAK

Level of Difficulty – Difficult
One-way Mileage – 3.35 miles
One-way Hiking Time – 3 hours
Altitude, GPS Reading Trailhead – 10,019', 39°53'37"N, 105°57'23"W
Altitude, GPS Reading at Bottle Peak – 11,602', 39°54'08"N, 105°56'11"W
Altitude, GPS Reading at Ptarmigan Peak – 11,723', 39°54'22"N, 105°56'53"W
Trail Fee Required – No

🐕 Yes, 🚲 N/A, ▲ Yes, WD BP

Trailhead Location – See Bill's Peak to Byers Peak Loop Trailhead (1), Hike #33, page 112.

Trail Description – Begin at the Bottle Pass Trailhead. Follow the old Keyser Creek logging road and climb up the switchbacks to the trail marker on the left identifying Bottle Pass (2). The trail to Byers Peak continues on the logging road. Turn left at the sign and climb uphill through the montane forest. The trail is steep with very few switchbacks. The lodgepole pine trees give way to the Englemann spruce trees. The forest is dense in this subalpine region. The trail is faint and virtually disappears. Continue up the hill through timberline and across the tundra to Bottle Pass (3). From the pass, the scenery is impressive and is reminiscent of scenes from "The Sound Of Music". The trees are stunted and wind beaten, but the alpine meadow has wonderful flowers and terrific views of Byers and Bill's Peaks. The elevation at the pass is 11,299'.

From the pass, Bottle Peak is on the right (east) and Ptarmigan Peak is on the left (west). Turn right and hike toward Bottle Peak. The plant life consists mostly of mosses and lichens, which grow low to the ground. Most of the plants have a cushion appearance and flower usually in June and July. From the top of Bottle Peak (4) there are terrific views. Looking north and clockwise are the Never Summer Range, the mountains in Rocky Mountain National Park, Indian Peaks, and the Continental Divide. In the distance toward Berthoud Pass are the communications stations on top of Colorado Mines Peak. Continuing south and clockwise are Byers and Bill's Peaks, the Gore Range, and Ptarmigan Peak.

To reach Bottle Peak, return to Bottle Pass (3) and bear right up the hill. The hillside up to Ptarmigan Peak is enjoyable because of the abundance of alpine flowers. The hillside is covered in both tundra grasses and marsh resulting in a diverse and plentiful display of flowers. The clusters of Alpine Forget-Me-Nots are indeed unforgettable with their brilliant periwinkle petals. From the top of Ptarmigan Peak (5), looking west are great views of the Williams Fork Mountains and valley and northwest below is the Church Park area.

Note - The one-way mileage for this hike is described from the trailhead to Bottle Pass, continuing to Bottle Peak, returning to Bottle Pass, and ending at Ptarmigan Peak.

Note - There are two Ptarmigan Peaks in Grand County. The other is in the Williams Fork Mountains. Refer to the Ptarmigan Pass and Peak Hike #83, page 276 for trail access.

Historical Note - The section of trail from the trailhead (1) to Bottle Pass (3) was part of the old "Horseshoe and Idlewild" Trail that connected the Williams Fork River to the Fraser River.

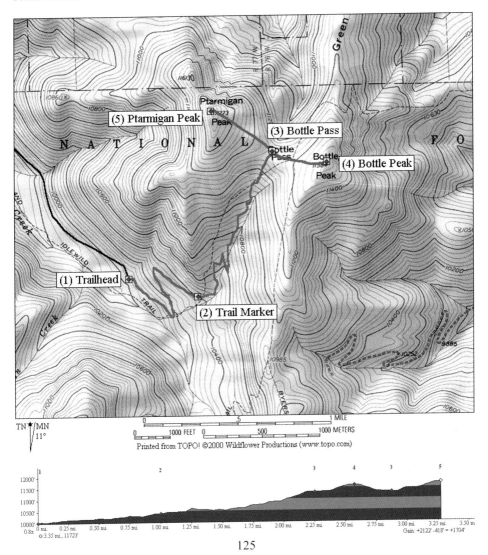

125

38. KEYSER RIDGE

Level of Difficulty – Moderate
One-way Mileage – 3.58 miles
One-way Hiking Time – 2 ½ hours
Altitude, GPS Reading at Trailhead – 10561', 39°52'26"N, 106°01'15"W
Altitude, GPS Reading at Destination – 11,806', 39°52'22"N, 105°58'03'W
Trail Fee Required – No

🐾 Yes, 🐟 N/A, ▲ Yes, WD BP

Trailhead Location – On US Hwy 40, just east of Parshall, between mile markers 197 and 198, turn south onto CR 3. On CR 3, between mile markers 15 and 16 head left (east) onto CR 32 (FSR 139) for .9 miles. Turn right onto FSR 140. FSR 140 forks after 5.5 miles. From this fork, the road loops back making a circle. Take the right fork, which is the better route. Continue on FSR 140 for another 2.1 miles to the trailhead (1). CR3 and FSR 139 are good dirt roads and FSR 140 is a rough dirt road.

Trail Description – This is a great hike to the top of Keyser Ridge and to the St. Louis Divide Trail with very little elevation gain and very little exposure above timberline. The views from the top of the St. Louis Divide Trail are unmatched. The trail to Keyser Ridge begins as a common trailhead with Kinney Creek Trail for motorized vehicles. However, not far from the parking area the two trails split (2). Take the right fork toward Keyser Ridge and follow the old logging road through the forest of lodgepole pine, aspen, spruce, and fir trees. Continue on the logging road to the fork and trail marker on the left (3) where the single-track trail leads to Lake Evelyn and Keyser Ridge. Turn left and follow the single-track trail. This is a very pleasant hike through the forest. When the forest opens up on the right side of the trail, there are peek-a-boo views of Byers Peak on the left, Bill's Peak in the center, and the St. Louis Divide on the right. Keyser Ridge is visible on the left side of the trail. The trail meets Keyser Ridge at the saddle. At the saddle is an intersection and trail marker (4) identifying Keyser Ridge, the St. Louis Divide Trail ahead (east) at the top of the ridgeline, the Lake Evelyn Trail to the left (north), and the Kinney Creek Trail to the right (south). Looking north and clockwise are Lake Evelyn below nested in the trees, Lake Granby in the distance, Ptarmigan Peak, Longs Peak, Bottle Peak, Byers Peak, Bill's Peak, St. Louis Divide, the Kinney Creek valley, the Gore Range in the distance, Keyser Ridge, and the Never Summer Range.

Follow the trail up the grassy hillside above timberline toward the St. Louis Divide Trail. At the top of the ridgeline is an intersection and trail marker (5) identifying the St. Louis Divide Trail with Bottle Peak to the left (north) and St. Louis Peak to the right (south). Just over the ridge are fantastic views of the glacially carved Keyser valley below with the massive Byers Peak as the backdrop. To the left of Byers Peak are the Continental Divide and the town of Fraser.

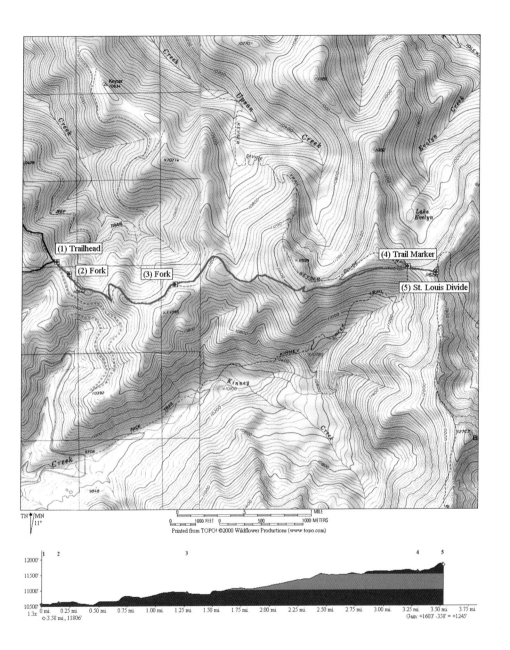

(1) Trailhead
(2) Fork
(3) Fork
(4) Trail Marker
(5) St. Louis Divide

TN ★ /MN
/11°

0   1000 FEET   0   1000 METERS
0   500

1 MILE

Printed from TOPO! ©2000 Wildflower Productions (www.topo.com)

12000'
11500'
11000'
10500'
1.3x

1   2   3   4   5

0 mi.   0.25 mi.   0.50 mi.   0.75 mi.   1.00 mi.   1.25 mi.   1.50 mi.   1.75 mi.   2.00 mi.   2.25 mi.   2.50 mi.   2.75 mi.   3.00 mi.   3.25 mi.   3.50 mi.   3.75 mi.
○ 3.58 mi., 11806'   Gain: +1603' -358' = +1245'

127

39. DARLING CREEK

Level of Difficulty – More Difficult
One-way Mileage – 6.02 miles
One-way Hiking Time – 4 hours
Altitude, GPS Reading at Trailhead – 8946', 39°47'48"N, 106°01'29"W
Altitude, GPS Reading at Destination – 12,162', 39°48'10"N, 105°57'41"W
Trail Fee Required – No

🐎 Yes, 🐕 Yes, ▲ Yes, WD None

Trailhead Location – On US Hwy 40, just east of Parshall, between mile markers 197 and 198, turn south onto CR 3. On CR 3, drive 17.9 miles, between mile markers 18 and 19 and head south onto CR 30 toward South Fork and Sugar Loaf Campgrounds. Follow CR 30 for 5.5 miles through the tunnel under the conveyor. Turn left to Darling Creek Road and parallel the conveyor for .4 miles to the trailhead (1). Both CR 3 and CR 30 are well-maintained dirt roads.

Trail Description – Begin near the entrance to the Henderson Tunnel. This tunnel transports molybdenum ore from the mine on the east side of the Continental Divide to the mill on the west side.

From the chain link fence, head south, away from the tunnel around to the Williams Fork Creek. Follow the bank of the creek and pass several beaver ponds. A fork and trail marker (2) identifies the South Fork Trail on the right and Darling Creek Trail on the left. Take the left fork up the hill. Cross over the tunnel into a beautiful aspen forest and then into a lodgepole pine forest. Cross Darling Creek (3) and continue through the forest with only a moderate elevation gain. Cross over Darling Creek (4) again. Pass a boulder field, which is on the left and follow the creek, which is on the right. The elevation increases more rapidly. The trail intersects a logging road (5). Cross straight over the road back onto the trail. The Englemann spruce and subalpine fir trees appear and the forest opens up. The St. Louis Divide is visible above the trees. A large cairn (6) is in the grassy meadow where the trail disappears. Another cairn is across the meadow. This crossing may be marshy. Stay high and keep the cairn in view. In the meadow, the St. Louis Divide is visible ahead, the Gore Range is to the right, and Ute Peak is in the foreground. Follow the cairns above timberline and at the last visible cairn (7) across the hillside, look up to the top of the ridge to the next cairn. Follow the faint trail to the top of the St. Louis Divide where there is another marker (8) and head left (north) along the ridge to a trail marker identifying Darling Creek/Williams Fork River to the west, St. Louis Pass to the east and Bill's Peak to the north. Hike to the top of the small knoll (9) for 360° views. Looking north and clockwise are Bill's and Byers Peaks, the St. Louis Divide, St. Louis Lake nestled in the trees, Longs Peak and the mountains in Rocky Mountain National Park, Indian Peaks, Mt. Nystrom, St. Louis Peak, Jones Pass, Pettingell Peak, Hagar Mountain, Coon Hill, Ptarmigan Peak, the Gore Range, Ute Peak, Williams Peak, Williams Fork Reservoir, and the Never Summer Range.

Historical Note – Darling was a bachelor and trapper who lived in a cabin near the Darling Creek Trailhead. His cabin was destroyed when the Henderson Tunnel was built. The Darling Creek Trail was built by the Forest Service to provide easier access from the Williams Fork Valley to the Fraser Valley.

St. Louis drainage from the top of the St. Louis Divide

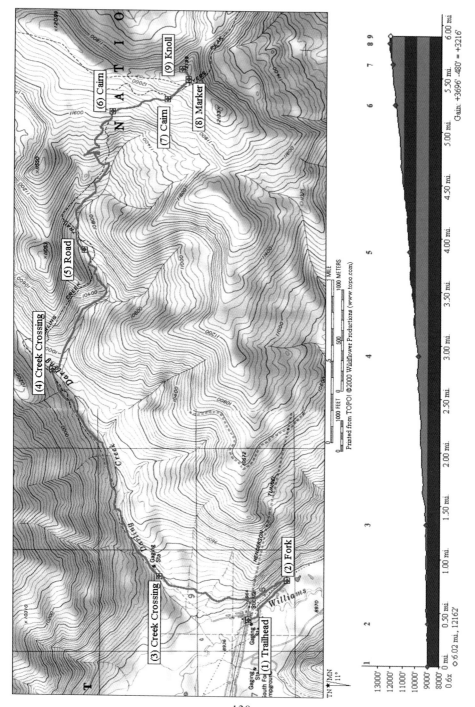

TN/MN
11°

(1) Trailhead
(2) Fork
(3) Creek Crossing
(4) Creek Crossing
(5) Road
(6) Cairn
(7) Cairn
(8) Marker
(9) Knoll

Williams

Darling Creek

South Fork
Campground
Gaging Sta.

1000 FEET   0   1000 METERS
0   500   1   MILE
Printed from TOPO! ©2000 Wildflower Productions (www.topo.com)

13000'
12000'
11000'
10000'
9000'
8000'

0.6x   0 mi.   0.50 mi.   1.00 mi.   1.50 mi.   2.00 mi.   2.50 mi.   3.00 mi.   3.50 mi.   4.00 mi.   4.50 mi.   5.00 mi.   5.50 mi.   6.00 mi.
◇6.02 mi, 12162'   Gain: +3696' -480' = +3216'

130

VASQUEZ MOUNTAINS
South Access

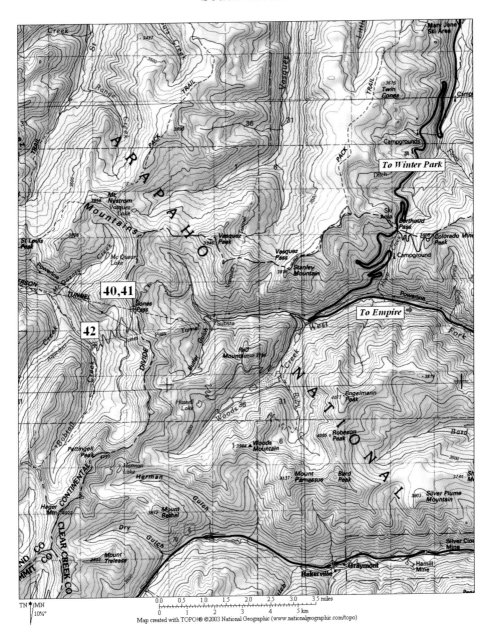

40. JONES PASS TO MT. NYSTROM

Level of Difficulty – Moderate
One-way Mileage – 3.09 miles
One-way Hiking Time – 1 ½ hours
Altitude, GPS Reading at Trailhead – 12,498', 39°46'26"N, 105°53'22"W
Altitude, GPS Reading at Destination – 12,659', 39°48'32"N, 105°54'07"W
Trail Fee Required – No

🐾 Yes, 🐟 N/A, ▲ Yes, WD VQ

Trailhead Location – On US Hwy 40, west of Berthoud Falls in Clear Creek County at the switchback between mile markers 248 and 249, turn west toward the Henderson Mine. From US Hwy 40 to Jones Pass is 5.6 miles. Follow signs for the mine and then to Jones Pass. Take the side road to the right that bypasses the mine and just after the bypass at the entrance to the woods is a register box. Register here and continue. This is a good dirt road, but it is narrow. Four-wheel drive is helpful at the switchbacks for traction. The road up to the pass is a single lane with room for passing at the switchbacks. Park at the top of the pass on the left side of the road. Begin the hike at the CD Trail marker on the right (north) side of the road (1).

Trail Description – This hike is entirely above timberline. Be aware of the ever-changing weather conditions. From the trailhead, looking south are Pettingell Peak and Hagar Mountain along the Continental Divide, Coon Hill along the Williams Fork Mountains, and the Bobtail Valley below. Continuing clockwise are the Gore Range, the East Fork of the Williams Fork Valley, Ute Peak, and Williams Peak. Looking northeast and clockwise are Longs Peak, the Indian Peaks Range, Vasquez Peak, the Henderson Mine and valley, and Englemann Peak. The hum of the Henderson Mine is audible below.

Follow the trail north across the tundra and pass a small tarn on the left. The landscape is barren and consists mostly of gravel and spotty tundra grasses. Cross into the Vasquez Peak Wilderness. Looking west and clockwise are the Williams Fork Mountains, the St. Louis Divide, McQueary Lake below, Bills Peak, Byers Peak, the Troublesome Valley in the distance, Mt. Nystrom and the Never Summer Range in the distance. Continuing from the north are Lake Granby, the mountains in Rocky Mountain National Park, Longs Peak, and the Indian Peaks Range. On the right is a clear view of Vasquez Peak and Red Mountain behind the Henderson Mine.

The Henderson Mine produces Molybdenum, a lubricant and an additive to tool steels. Molybdenum is excavated from the mine through tunnels below Red Mountain. The result is that Red Mountain is caving in on itself from the center, which is visible from this location.

Continue to traverse the hillside along the CD Trail through several gentle ascents and descents. At a bend, Vasquez Lake is visible ahead. Upon seeing Vasquez Lake, the trail to Mt. Nystrom splits away from the CD Trail at the trail marker (2). The Mt. Nystrom Trail goes both right and left. Right descends rapidly and continues to Vasqzez Pass and left leads to Mt. Nystrom. Turn left and head northwest on the faint trail. Follow the ridgeline where the trail reappears. Continue across the tundra where the landscape changes slightly with boulders and more tundra grasses. Vasquez Lake is again visible below on the right and McQueary Lake is visible below on the left. Pass several boulder fields. The peaks and valleys are more pronounced on this section, but the trail is still a relatively moderate grade. There is a trail marker on the right (3) just off the ridgeline of the hill. The marker identifies Vasquez Creek to the east and St. Louis Creek to the west. Continue a short distance up the hill where there is a post visible on top of a rocky knoll. This is the peak of Mt. Nystrom (4).

The views from the top of Mt. Nystrom are spectacular. Looking north and clockwise are the Never Summer Mountains in the distance, Lake Granby, the mountains in Rocky Mountain National Park, Longs Peak, the Indian Peaks Range, Unnamed Peak, Twin Cones at Winter Park Ski Resort, James Peak, Parry Peak, Mt. Bancroft, Mt. Eva, Mt. Flora, and Colorado Mines Peak. Next are Vasquez Peak and Englemann Peak. In the valley below is a glimpse of McQueary Lake, Pettingell Peak, Hagar Mountain, a small tarn below, the Gore Range in the distance, the dome shaped St. Louis Peak, Ute Peak, and the St. Louis Valley below. Continuing from the west are Williams Peak, Bill's Peak, Byers Peak, the Troublesome Valley in the distance, and Sheep Mountain.

Side Trip – St. Louis Peak – from Mt. Nystrom, continue southwest along the ridgeline to St. Louis Pass and then to St. Louis Peak. Also refer to St. Louis Peak Hike #26, page 94 for peak access.

Side Trip – Vasquez Lake – from Mt. Nystrom, follow the trail to the northeast down into the valley. Refer to the Mt. Nystrom Hike #21, page 82 for a detailed description to Vasquez Lake.

Historical Note – Jones Pass is named after John S. Jones. He built a wagon road over Jones Pass from the Clear Creek Valley to the Williams Fork Valley. He hoped this road would provide easier access to Grand County over the Continental Divide. His dream never materialized.

A view of Vasquez Peak on the way to Mt. Nystrom

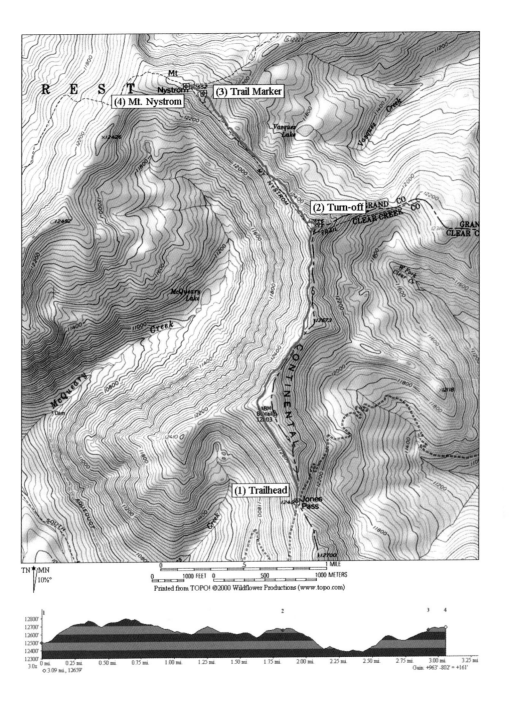

41. JONES PASS TO VASQUEZ PEAK

Level of Difficulty – More Difficult
One-way Mileage – 4.35 miles
One-way Hiking Time – 2 ½ hours
Altitude, GPS Reading at Trailhead – 12,474', 39°46'26"N, 105°53'22"W
Altitude, GPS Reading at Destination – 12,879', 39°47'46"N, 105°51'18"W
Trail Fee Required – No

🐾 Yes, 🔌 N/A, ▲ Yes, WD VQ

Trailhead Location – See Jones Pass to Mt. Nystrom Trailhead (1), Hike #40, page 132.

Trail Description – Follow the Jones Pass to Mt. Nystrom Hike #40, page 132 description to (2). Upon seeing Vasquez Lake, continue right on the worn CD Trail and descend rapidly down the switchbacks. The Henderson Mine and Red Mountain are clearly visible. At the bottom of the switchbacks the trail levels off and traverses around the next hill. To the left is a great view of the Vasquez Valley. The landscape is covered in short tundra grasses and scree. Mt. Nystrom is visible above Vasquez Lake and an unnamed peak is to the north. Ahead is Vasquez Peak and to the east and clockwise are James Peak, Parry Peak, Mt. Bancroft, Mt. Eva, and Mt. Flora. Descend from the hill to a saddle. At the saddle (3) leave the well worn CD Trail and head left up the ridgeline leading to Vasquez Peak. A faint trail appears on the ridgeline along with a few cairns, but they both eventually disappear. Continue to climb up the steep hillside and pass the last of the stunted Englemann spruce trees and Arctic Willows. Alpine wildflowers dot the landscape, but boulders take over the tundra. There are only boulders and scree up to the Vasquez Peak summit (4). The views from Vasquez Peak are unbelievable. Looking north and clockwise are Lake Granby, the mountains in Rocky Mountain National Park, Longs Peak, the Indian Peaks Range, Rollins Pass Road, Twin Cones at Winter Park Ski Resort, James Peak, Parry Peak, Mt. Bancroft, Mt. Eva, Mt. Flora, Colorado Mines Peak, Stanley Mountain, Englemann Peak, Robeson Peak, Bard Peak, and Woods Mountain. Continuing clockwise from the south are Pettingell Peak, Jones Pass Road, the Gore Range, Ute Peak, Williams Peak, Mt. Nystrom, Vasquez Lake below, Bill's Peak, Byers Peak, Ptarmigan Peak, Bottle Peak, the Troublesome Valley in the distance, an unnamed peak, and the Never Summer Range in the distance.

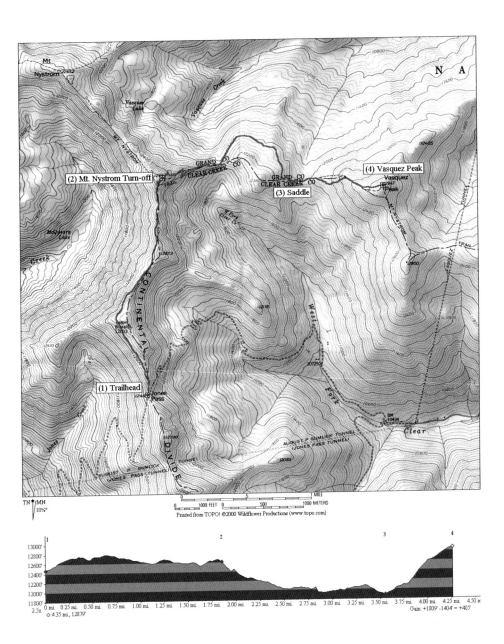

42. McQUEARY LAKE

Level of Difficulty – Moderate
One-way Mileage – 2.83 miles
One-way Hiking Time – 1 ½ hours
Altitude, GPS Reading at Trailhead – 10,383', 39°45'46"N, 105°54'21"W
Altitude, GPS Reading at Destination – 11,018', 39°47'27"N, 105°53'58"W
Trail Fee Required – No

🐾 Yes, 🐾 Yes, ▲ Yes, WD VQ

Trailhead Location – On US Hwy 40, west of Berthoud Falls in Clear Creek County at the switchback between mile markers 248 and 249, turn west toward the Henderson Mine. From US Hwy 40 to the trailhead is 8.4 miles. Follow signs for the mine and then to Jones Pass. Take the side road to the right that bypasses the mine and just after the bypass at the entrance to the woods is a register box. Register here and continue. This is a good dirt road to the top of Jones Pass, but both 4-wheel drive and high clearance are suggested beyond the pass down to the trailhead. The road is narrow and is a single lane with little room to pass except at the switchbacks. Once at the bottom of the hill, there is a "T". The trailhead is at the gate on the right (1). Park on the side of the road. Do not park in front of the gate.

Trail Description – This is a short hike to a remote destination. The first half of the trail is along a service road, while the second half follows a faint trail to the lake parallel to the creek. Pass around the gate and follow the service road used by the Denver Water Board. Just beyond the trailhead are several USDA Forest Service buildings and Denver Water Board facilities. On the left is a data collection site to measure snow, rain, and temperature for forecasting water supplies. Follow the road through a subalpine forest across a hillside with a great view of the Williams Fork Creek valley. Ute Peak is at the end of the valley and St. Louis Peak is the dome shaped peak on the right. The road bends to the right and forks (2). At the fork continue straight to the dam (3). At the dam the trail is faint. Pass the dam on the right and parallel the creek. Travel through forest, marsh, willows, and avalanche scree. McQueary Lake (4) sits in an open meadow surrounded by mountains. The Continental Divide towers above to the right (east) and the ridge leading to Mt. Nystrom is ahead (north). Many trees circle the lake, but the backdrop of the surrounding scree covered mountains is stark in contrast. The lake is very shallow and elk frequent this area.

Historical Note – Eight McQueary brothers came to Grand County from Missouri and between them, several creeks and lakes have taken their name.

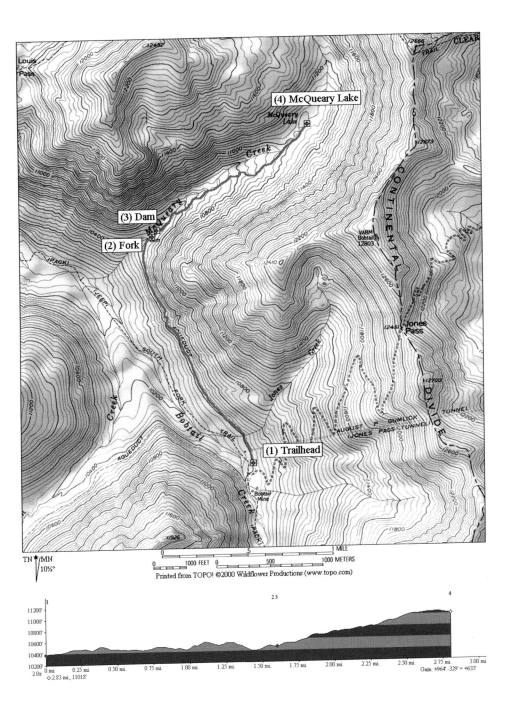

Monarch Lake

INDIAN PEAKS

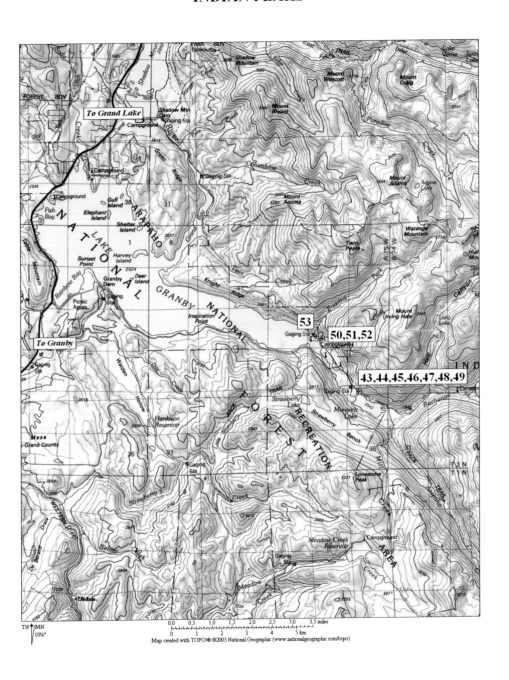

43. MONARCH LAKE LOOP

Level of Difficulty – Easy
Round-trip Mileage – 4.07 miles
Round-trip Hiking Time – 2 hours
Altitude, GPS Reading at Trailhead – 8345', 40°06'39"N, 105°44'48"W
Altitude, GPS Reading at Highest Point – 8459', 40°06'24"N, 105°44'09"W
Trail Fee Required – Yes

🐕 Leash, 🦴 Yes, ▲ Permit, WD IP

Trailhead Location – On US Hwy 34, between Granby and Grand Lake, between mile markers 5 and 6, turn east on CR 6 (FSR 125). From US Hwy 34 to the trailhead is 9.8 miles. Cross the Granby Dam and follow all signs to Monarch Lake. This is a good dirt road. Trailhead parking is at the end of the road at the Road Closed gate.

Trail Description – Pass around the gate, walk to the Forest Service cabin, and register. The trailhead sign is next to the cabin (1). The Arapaho Pass Trail is on the right. Turn right toward the west side of Monarch Lake. The view across the lake with the mountain backdrop is beautiful, especially with the early morning reflection off the water. Cross over a dam and pass a picnic area in the woods. In the woods, the view of Monarch Lake disappears. Climb above the lake to the remains of four cabins – three on the left and one on the right. These cabins housed workers from the Monarch Lumber Company that once occupied this area. Next is an old boiler on the left side of the trail (2) probably used to run the sawmill. This is a spruce-fir forest and is shaded by the canopy of the trees. At the fork and trail marker (3), the High Lonesome Trail is on the right where there are the remains of several old cabins. Continue straight on the Arapaho Pass Trail where there are more old cabins on the right and an outhouse on the left. Cross Arapaho Creek where there is another fork and trail marker (4). The Arapaho Pass Trail continues to the right, but take the left fork and follow the Arapahoe Pass Spur Trail. The trees open slightly with small meadows leading to lake level. Climb gently through the forest. Cross Buchanan Creek on the wooden bridge. This is a beautiful wide creek. At a fork and trail marker (5), the Cascade Creek Trail turns to the right leading to the Pawnee Pass Trail, Cascade Creek Trail, and the Buchanan Pass Trail. Take the left fork and continue around the lake. The creek runs near the trail hidden behind the thick tall willows. There are several short ascents and descents and a clear view of the creek beside the trail. Pass through a field of boulders, which have fallen from the stone cliffs above. The trail is well maintained through this area. When Monarch Lake is again visible, hug the lake back to the trailhead (1).

Historical Note – Monarch Lake was built by the Rocky Mountain Lumber Company (formerly the Monarch Gold and Copper Mining and Smelting Company) to transport lumber from the hillsides to the mills.

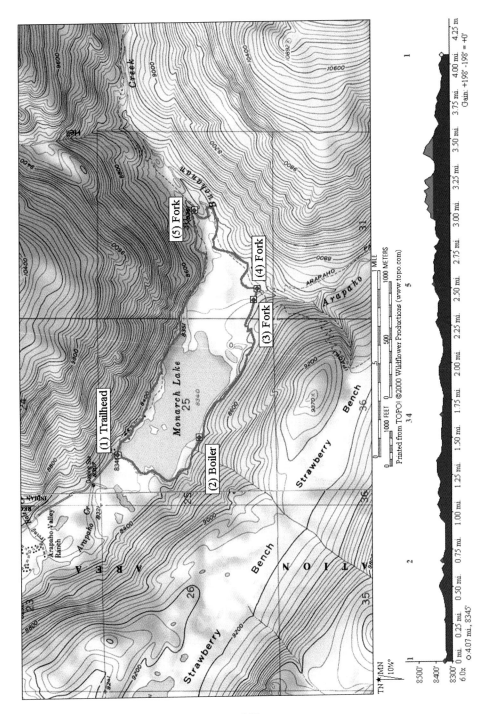

(1) Trailhead
(2) Boiler
(3) Fork
(4) Fork
(5) Fork

Monarch Lake

Strawberry Bench

Arapaho Valley Ranch

Printed from TOPO! ©2000 Wildflower Productions (www.topo.com)

8500'
8400'
8300'

0 mi.   0.25 mi.   0.50 mi.   0.75 mi.   1.00 mi.   1.25 mi.   1.50 mi.   1.75 mi.   2.00 mi.   2.25 mi.   2.50 mi.   2.75 mi.   3.00 mi.   3.25 mi.   3.50 mi.   3.75 mi.   4.00 mi.   4.25 m

6.0x   0.407 mi., 8345'   Gain: +198' -198' = +0'

TN
MN
10½°

44. HIGH LONESOME, CARIBOU, and STRAWBERRY CREEK LOOP 🌙

Level of Difficulty – Difficult
Round-trip Mileage – 20.99 miles
Round-trip Hiking Time – 2-3 days
Altitude, GPS Reading at Trailhead – 8345', 40°06'39"N, 105°44'47"W
Altitude, GPS Reading at Highest Point – 10,321', 40°04'01"N, 105°44'31"W
Trail Fee Required – Yes

🐾 Leash, 🎣 Yes, ▲ Permit, WD IP

Trailhead Location – See Monarch Lake Loop Trailhead (1), Hike #43, page 142.

Trail Description – A small portion of this trail lies in the Indian Peaks Wilderness. Please consult a map identifying the boundary to determine if a camping permit is required. Pass around the gate, walk to the Forest Service cabin, and register. The trailhead sign is next to the cabin (1). The Arapaho Pass Trail is on the right. Turn right toward the west side of Monarch Lake. The view across the lake with the mountain backdrop is beautiful, especially with the early morning reflection off the water. Cross over a dam and pass a picnic area in the woods. In the woods, the view of Monarch Lake disappears. Climb above the lake to the remains of four cabins – three on the left and one on the right. These cabins housed workers from the Monarch Lumber Company that once occupied this area. Next is an old boiler on the left side of the trail (2) probably used to run the sawmill. This is a spruce-fir forest and is shaded by the canopy of the trees. At the fork and trail marker (3), the High Lonesome Trail is to the right where there are the remains of several old cabins, many with wood burning stoves still remaining. Leave the Arapaho Pass Trail and turn right (south) onto the High Lonesome Trail. Ascend steeply through several switchbacks, and parallel Mill Creek, which flows into Arapaho Creek. At an intersection and trail marker (4), Strawberry Bench Trail is on the right, but continue straight (south) on the High Lonesome Trail. The CD Trail also runs along the High Lonesome Trail. Cross Mill Creek where there is a steep uphill climb with several switchbacks. Cross Mill Creek again. Continue to climb to the High Lonesome Mining Camp on the right (5). There is an old cabin and outhouse located here.

There is no visible trail to the High Lonesome Mine, but it is .2 mile northwest from the cabin. The High Lonesome Mine was once a source for the gem aquamarine. All that remains is rubble and a deep open shaft (6). From the mine looking east is a great view of Mt. Achonee. Return to the mining camp (5). From the mining camp, continue south on the trail. Follow the cairns through a small meadow, hike uphill a short distance further and reach a low pass with a view of Meadow Creek Reservoir ahead and Indian Peaks to the left. Follow the trail downhill and cross an old road to a fork and trail marker (7). The sign identifies the Strawberry Creek Trail to the right and the High Lonesome Trail continuing to the left. Follow the trail to the right and count 50 paces.

There is a small "Trail" sign on the left. Turn left and follow this trail through the woods to the meadow. FSR 129 is visible ahead, which leads to Junco Lake and Meadow Creek Reservoir. At the front edge of the meadow, leave the worn trail, turn right, and cross the meadow (8). Head west along the edge of the willows parallel to the road. There is no visible trail here and the meadow can be wet in spring. At the far west end of the meadow is an "i" marking blazed on a tree leading into the woods. Cross the old road and continue along this trail through the woods (9). On the left is a marshy wetland, which is the headwater to Strawberry Creek. Descend slowly and parallel the marsh, which widens as the trail winds along. Follow the "Trail" sign (10) and arrow to the right, which detours around the marsh. Hug the forest, pass over boulders, and head back into the forest. Continue to descend until there is a significant uphill climb that detours around the marsh. Remain high on the hillside until the wetland below is cleared. Follow the trail down the hill and continue to parallel the creek and marsh. Follow the meadow's edge into the forest. There is another "Trail" sign (11) pointing right around another marsh. Follow the sign and trail to a small meadow. Cross through the meadow (west) on the right side. The trail reappears at the far end of the meadow. Continue to a fork (12) and trail marker. This sign identifies the Caribou Trail to the left and Strawberry Creek Trail to the right. Take the left fork along the Caribou Trail alongside Strawberry Creek. The remains of an old cabin (13) are on the right of the trail beside the creek. The creek is quite rapid and twists its way down the valley. Mature aspen trees line this creek valley. At the horse corral and meadow is a fork (14). A road on the left leads to the High Lonesome Hut and the Caribou Trail continues right. Remain on the Caribou Trail and follow the double-rut road parallel to Strawberry Creek. At the next fork, there are two trail markers (15). The first identifies Meadow Creek Reservoir and Strawberry Creek Trail up the hill to the right. The second identifies Doe Creek and Strawberry West Trail straight ahead. Little Strawberry Creek flows into Strawberry Creek here. Continue straight through the willows, cross Little Strawberry Creek, and follow the large meadow. The meadow is on private property, but follow the fence, which is to the left of the meadow. At the next fork and trail marker (16) are the remains of an old cabin in the meadow. Doe Creek and Lake Granby are to the left. Continue straight up the hill. Pass several beaver ponds to another fork and trail marker (17) again showing Strawberry Creek Trail to the right. Continue straight through the woods and descend. At the next fork and trail marker (18), left (north) leads to Lake Granby and straight (east) leads to the High Lonesome Trail and the Indian Peaks Wilderness. Continue straight and cross the creek and head back into the woods. The trail skirts the large meadow, known as Strawberry Bench. The trail is fairly level through a beautiful lodgepole pine forest. There is a park bench (19) along the trail with a great view of the Buchanan Creek draw and Thunderbolt Peak. If the light is right, Monarch Lake is visible through the trees shimmering below. Pass a few ponds, which are on the right and cross several small creeks with Strawberry Bench again on the right. Cross into the Indian Peaks Wilderness and enjoy the views of Indian Peaks.

At an intersection and trail marker (4) Monarch Lake is to the left. Turn left and descend steeply through several switchbacks. At the fork and trail marker (3), turn left and follow the inbound trail around Monarch Lake back to the trailhead (1).

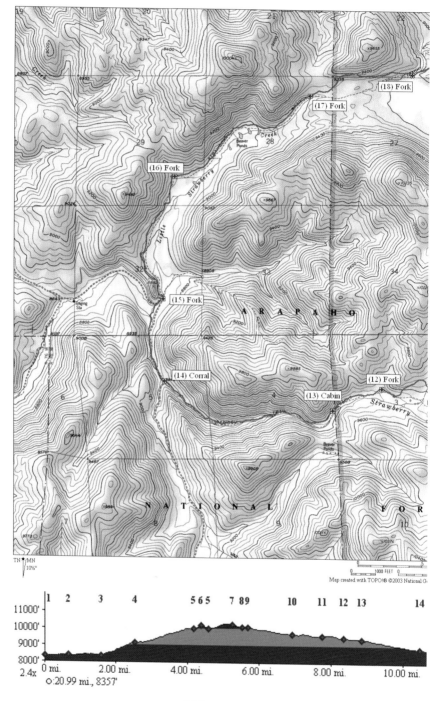

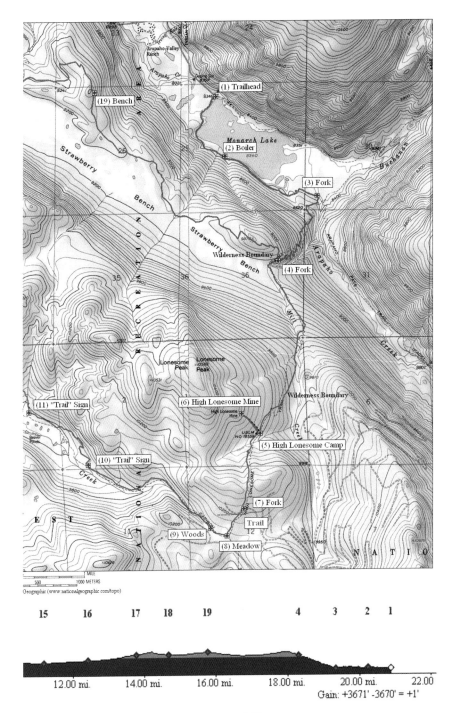

(1) Trailhead
(19) Bench
(2) Boiler
Monarch Lake
(3) Fork
Wilderness Boundary
(4) Fork
Lonesome Peak
(6) High Lonesome Mine
(11) "Trail" Sign
(5) High Lonesome Camp
(10) "Trail" Sign
(7) Fork
Trail 12
(9) Woods
(8) Meadow

500   1000 METERS
MILE

Geographic (www.nationalgeographic.com/topo)

15   16   17   18   19   4   3   2   1

12.00 mi.   14.00 mi.   16.00 mi.   18.00 mi.   20.00 mi.   22.00

Gain: +3671' -3670' = +1'

147

45. ARAPAHO, CARIBOU, AND HIGH LONESOME LOOP

Level of Difficulty – More Difficult
Round-trip Mileage – 22.56 miles
Round-trip Hiking Time – 2-3 days
Altitude, GPS Reading at Trailhead – 8357', 40°06'39"N, 105°44'47"W
Altitude, GPS Reading at Arapaho Pass – 11,914, 40°00'52"N, 105°40'41"W
Altitude, GPS Reading at Caribou Pass – 11,813, 40°01'10"N, 105°41'27"W
Trail Fee Required – Yes

🐕 Leash, ⬥ Yes, ▲ Permit, WD IP

Trailhead Location – See Monarch Lake Loop Trailhead (1), Hike #43, page 142.

Trail Description – Pass around the gate, walk to the Forest Service cabin, and register. The trailhead sign is next to the cabin (1). The Arapaho Pass Trail is on the right. Follow this trail around the west side of Monarch Lake. Cross over a dam and pass a picnic area in the woods. In the woods, the view of Monarch Lake disappears. Climb above the lake to the remains of four cabins – three on the left and one on the right. These cabins housed workers from the Monarch Lumber Company that once occupied this area. Next is an old boiler on the left side of the trail (2) probably used to run the sawmill. This is a spruce-fir forest and is shaded by the canopy of the trees. At the fork and trail marker (3), the High Lonesome Trail is on the right where there are the remains of several old cabins. Continue straight on the Arapaho Pass Trail where there are more old cabins on the right and an outhouse on the left. Cross Arapaho Creek where there is another fork and trail marker (4). The Arapahoe Pass Spur Trail continues straight, but turn right along the creek and follow the Arapaho Pass Trail. Quickly climb above the creek through many switchbacks. The forest is dense. Parallel the creek and wind up the valley. Meet the creek where the valley narrows and the hillside is steep with scree. Gently ascend through a primarily spruce-fir forest, which is lush with many flowers and low growing ground covers. The water flow increases and the valley continues to narrow. The rocks are covered with mosses due to the shade and moisture. Continue to wind along the creek up the valley where there is a giant boulder field on the left. Beyond the boulder field is a long boulder wall on the left. Continue through the forest to a small clearing with a view of Mount George on the left. Cross the creek at a conveniently fallen tree on the right of the trail, where there are remains of an old bridge. Continue up to a clearing on top of a large boulder with a view of Mount George, Apache Peak, Navaho Peak, Arikaree Peak, and North Arapaho Peak. The trees thin slightly and the meadows widen to Coyote Park (5). This is a beautiful park loaded with wildflowers and surrounded by a cirque made up of North Arapaho Peak, South Arapaho Peak, and the base of the north ridgeline of Mt. Neva. Arapaho Creek runs through the center of the meadow, making this a beautiful spot to spend time.

Continue into the woods and climb over boulders. Many of these boulders have drill and chisel marks, evidence of clearing the forest for passage for pack animals. Many of the drills still remain in the stone. The boulders are numerous and the water rushes over the large rocks providing a picture perfect setting. Follow the trail uphill through the switchbacks where the spruce trees thin and the meadows widen. There is a clearing with a view of Santanta Peak straight ahead and Mt. Neva looming to the left (south). Hike uphill to a shelf where the trail is level and there is a glimpse of Caribou Lake through the trees. The trail does not lead to the lake, but a short side trip will reveal the shallow lake (6).

Between Santanta Peak and Mt. Neva is Caribou Pass above to the southwest. Looking southeast, the steep climb up to Arapaho Pass is visible across the hillside. From Caribou Lake, ascend out of the subalpine through timberline. The meadow grasses quickly change to scree and tundra grasses near the ridgeline (7) to Arapaho Pass (8). At the pass there is a fork and trail marker. Left leads to the town of Hessie, the 4th of July Mine, and Arapaho Glacier in Boulder County. Take the right fork toward Caribou Pass. Hike across the scree, loose rock and mosses on the ridge. The next two forks lead to Lake Dorothy (9 & 10). This is a beautiful deep lake with the majestic Mt. Neva as its backdrop. Hike across the hillside on an old pack trail around the edge of Mt. Neva. Ahead is a view of Meadow Creek Reservoir, Lake Granby, and Shadow Mountain Lake. The Troublesome Valley and the Never Summer Range are also visible in the distance. At the bend are views of Cottonwood Pass and the Vasquez Mountains. The next fork and trail marker (11) identifies Caribou Pass. There is a faint trail ahead and slightly down. This is a continuation of the pack trail down the hill. Santanta Peak (11A) is .5 miles ahead (north) along the ridgeline. This is a nice side trip with incredible views of Indian Peaks and Coyote Park. Return to Caribou Pass.

From Caribou Pass, turn left down the steep trail. The trail consists of loose rock, making travel slow. The tundra turns into meadow and the spruce trees reappear. The wildflowers are beyond belief. There is a small tarn on the right side of the trail. Wind down the steep hill where the meadow is even more beautiful. At the next fork and trail marker (12), Columbine Lake is to the left. Remain straight and continue down the hill. The grade is not nearly as steep and the single-track trail widens as evidence of an old jeep road appears. Return to a montane forest with spruce, fir and lodgepole pine trees. There is an old cabin on the left (13). Next, the trail is filled with loose river rock for a short distance making footing unstable. There are several tank traps and at the fork and trail marker (14), the High Lonesome Trail is on the left. Continue straight to the Junco Lake Trailhead (15). At the Junco Lake Trailhead billboard turn right onto the High Lonesome Trail. This is also combined with the CD Trail. Follow the trail through the woods and pass several meadows to a road (16). Turn right onto the road and then turn left at the next road (17). Not far from this turn, the trail forks to the right. Follow this trail up the hill. There is a sharp right turn, which is identified clearly (18). Head downhill to another road (19). Turn left on this road and follow it up to the next fork and trail marker (20). The trail marker identifies the Strawberry Creek Trail on the left and the High Lonesome Trail on the right up the hill. Follow the High Lonesome Trail up the hill, over a low pass, and down the other side. Hike through the forest to a small meadow. Just beyond the meadow on the left are the remains of the High Lonesome Mine Camp (21). There is an old cabin and outhouse located here. For a side trip to the High Lonesome Mine, leave the main trail and head northwest .2 miles. There is not a visible trail, but it is easy to find. The High Lonesome Mine was once a source for the gem aquamarine. All that remains is rubble and a deep open shaft (21A). From the mine looking east is a great view of Mt. Achonee. Return to the mining camp (21).

From the mining camp, continue north. Cross Mill Creek (22) and descend through several switchbacks. Cross Mill Creek a second time and arrive at an intersection and trail marker (23) identifying Strawberry Bench to the left and both the High Lonesome Trail and Arapaho Pass Trail straight ahead. Continue straight along the CD Trail toward Monarch Lake. Descend steeply through several switchbacks, where Mill Creek flows into Arapaho Creek. At the bottom of the hill are the ruins of several old cabins, many with wood burning stoves still remaining. At the fork and trail marker (3), turn left and follow the inbound trail around Monarch Lake back to the trailhead (1).

Historical Note – Arapaho Pass was one of the original routes over the Continental Divide used by the Indians.

Santanta Peak was named after a Kiowa Indian warrior.

Flowers in Coyote Park

Coyote Park

Caribou Lake

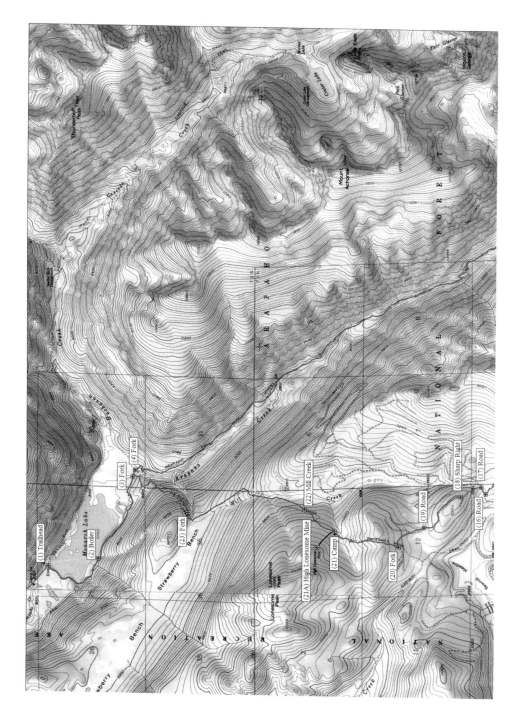

152

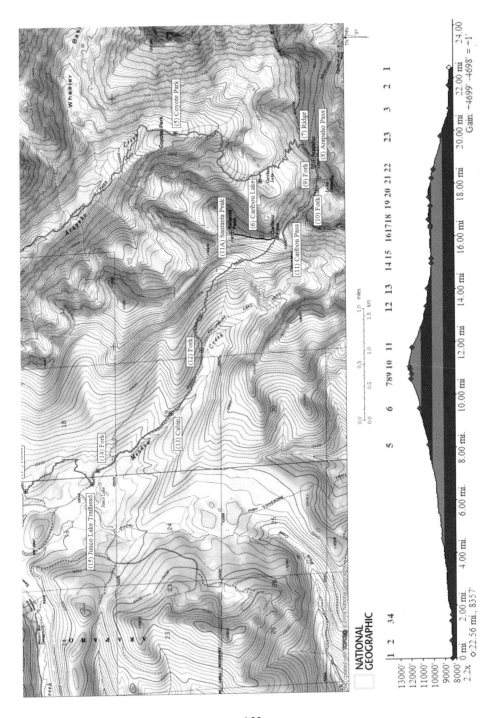

46. CASCADE CREEK TO MIRROR LAKE, CRATER LAKE, AND LONE EAGLE PEAK

Level of Difficulty – Difficult
One-way Mileage – 7.43 miles
One-way Hiking Time – 4 ½ hours
Altitude, GPS Reading at Trailhead – 8349', 40°06'39"N, 105°44'48"W
Altitude, GPS Reading at Crater Lake – 10,322', 40°04'38"N, 105°39'45"W
Trail Fee Required – Yes

🐾 Leash, 🐟 Yes, ▲ Permit, WD IP

Trailhead Location – See Monarch Lake Loop Trailhead (1), Hike #43, page 142.

Trail Description – Pass around the gate, walk to the Forest Service cabin and register. The trailhead sign is next to the cabin (1). The Cascade Creek Trail is to the left. Follow this trail around the north side of Monarch Lake with views of the lake through the trees on the right. Pass over several sections of fallen boulders from the hillside above. The lake disappears behind the tall willows, which hides Cascade Creek. The willows thin and the creek runs next to the trail. Cross into the Indian Peaks Wilderness and reach a fork and trail marker (2). The Arapaho Pass Spur Trail is to the right and the Cascade Trail is to the left. Take the left fork and approach Cascade Creek where the water roars and crashes over the boulders. Ascend through several switchbacks and cross Hell Canyon Creek over a sturdy bridge. Continue to climb through the montane forest. Pass large boulders, which are on the left and parallel Cascade Creek, which is on the right. At a fork and trail marker (3) the Buchanan Pass Trail is on the left and the Cascade Creek Trail is straight. Continue straight and parallel Cascade Creek.

Cross Buchanan Creek on another sturdy bridge and climb up the steep switchbacks. From the bottom switchback is a great view of a great cascading waterfall (4). This is just the beginning of a long series of waterfalls. The trail levels off for a short distance through a beautiful dense forest with carpet-like groundcover. Continue uphill where there is a small aspen meadow. Thunderbolt Peak is visible on the left and Mt. Achonee is ahead on the right. Cross Cascade Creek on a foot bridge and pass an old beaver pond. Just beyond the pond is one of the more spectacular cascading falls (5). There are numerous side trails from which to view the falls. Continue climbing and cross another foot bridge over Cascade Creek. The landscape is filled with giant boulders and more cascading falls (6). Move away from the creek where there is a view across a marsh of shear rock cathedral shaped pinnacles. Follow the trail through the meadows and forest and continue to climb moderately in elevation. Cross Cascade Creek again and at the next fork and trail marker (7) the Cascade Creek Trail (Pawnee Pass Trail) is on the left and Crater Lake Trail is on the right. Take the right fork toward Crater Lake. This is the first glimpse of Lone Eagle Peak with Fair Glacier on the left and Peck Glacier on the right. Hike over the giant boulders that are part of the trail. Approach Triangle Lake

154

creek, which is on the right and soon cross over it. The boulders are monstrous in size on the left with sheer rock face spires looming along the massive ridge above.

Parallel the creek and turn right, away from the creek. At this turn, there is a faint trail that follows the creek (8). This is the return route from the Triangle Lake Side Trip (see below). Continue to the top of the hill to Mirror Lake (9). Mirror Lake is beautiful and is surrounded by boulders and trees. The spire of Lone Eagle Peak is on the left, and Peck Glacier and Mt. Achonee are on the right. There is a massive awe-inspiring wall of spires to the east (far left) that deserves a name, but has none. The wall has a Gothic appearance. Continue around the right side of Mirror Lake to Crater Lake (10). The sheer granite walls behind the lake form an amphitheater. Peck Glacier is hanging on to Mt. George, which is barely visible behind Lone Eagle Peak. Trees are delicately perched on the cliff ledges above the lake between the scree.

Triangle Lake Side Trip – For a closer look at Lone Eagle Peak and to visit Triangle Lake and Fair Glacier, follow Crater Lake around to the left (east). Pass several camp sites to the gully. From the gully, turn right (south) toward Lone Eagle Peak where the trail is faint. Follow the gully uphill to the boulders where small cairns identify the trail. The trail is tight against the base of Lone Eagle Peak and is covered in boulders. Climb steeply in elevation where the boulders increase in size. Be cautious of both fallen rock and falling rock from above. Descend along the faint trail to a mass of stunted Englemann spruce trees perched in a saddle. Pass through the saddle where Fair Glacier lies high above and Triangle Lake sits down in the valley. Scramble over boulders the size of cars to reach Triangle Lake (10A). The triangle shape and aquamarine color are pronounced. (The aquamarine color is common for glacial lakes and is a result of finely ground up rock suspended in the water reflecting and refracting light). Apache Peak is on the left of Fair Glacier and Mt. George is on the right. To return to Mirror Lake, follow the creek from Triangle Lake through the valley. The creek disappears under the boulders, but continue down the drainage into the valley. There are two cliffs ahead, with a boulder field (10B) between them that is easy to hike down. Beyond the boulder field is a beautiful meadow filled with flowers. The creek runs through the center of the meadow and is surrounded by spruce trees. The meadow narrows and the forest takes over. Follow the creek to the fork (8) near Mirror Lake. This side trip is 2.30 miles round-trip.

Historical Note – Lone Eagle Peak (originally Lindbergh Peak) was named by Fred Fair in honor of Charles A. Lindbergh for promotional reasons. Fair needed publicity to raise funds to build a road to view the peak. Lindbergh occasionally came to Grand County and visited his friend Harry Knight – refer to Historical Note on Knight Ridge Hike #53, page 179.

Fred Fair discovered Fair Glacier and Isabelle Glacier. Isabelle Glacier is nearby on the east side of the Continental Divide and is named for Fred's wife.

The name "Crater Lake" is misleading because a glacier created it, not a volcano.

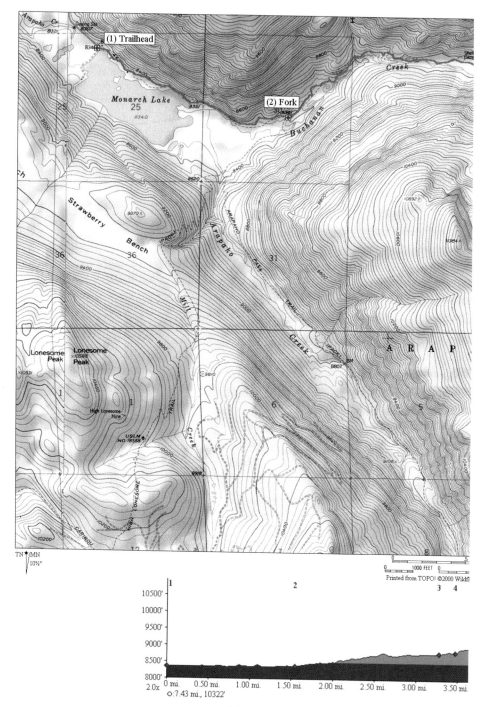

(1) Trailhead

Monarch Lake
25
8340

(2) Fork

Creek

9000

Buchanan

25

10400

Strawberry

9870

10892

11384

Bench
36

9400

36

Arapaho

31

8600

Mill

8800

Creek

ARAP

Lonesome
Peak

Lonesome
Peak

9810

8807

BM

TRAIL

6

5

High Lonesome
Mine

USLM
NO. 18558

Creek

9918

LONESOME

CARIBOU

10200

10200

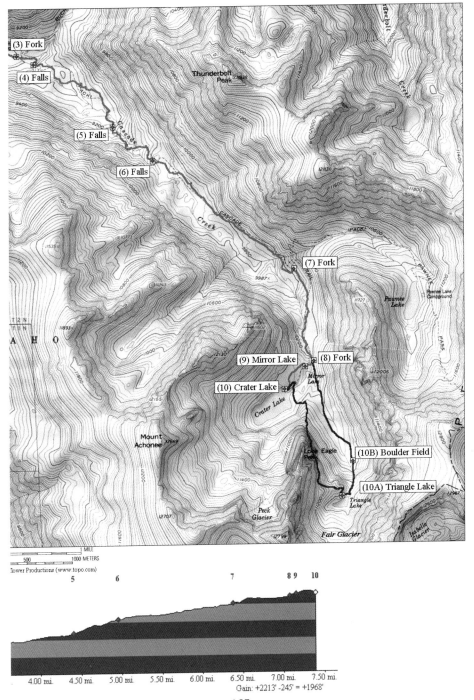

(3) Fork

(4) Falls

(5) Falls

(6) Falls

Thunderbolt Peak

(7) Fork

(9) Mirror Lake

(8) Fork

(10) Crater Lake

Pawnee Lake

Pawnee Lake Campground

Mount Achonee

Crater Lake

Lone Eagle

(10B) Boulder Field

(10A) Triangle Lake

Triangle Lake

Peck Glacier

Fair Glacier

Isabelle Glacier

MILE
500   1000 METERS

lower Productions (www.topo.com)

5   6   7   8 9   10

4.00 mi.   4.50 mi.   5.00 mi.   5.50 mi.   6.00 mi.   6.50 mi.   7.00 mi.   7.50 mi.

Gain: +2213' -245' = +1968'

47. CASCADE CREEK TO PAWNEE LAKE AND PASS

Level of Difficulty – More Difficult (Lake), Most Difficult (Pass)
One-way Mileage – 8.04 (Lake), 9.81 miles (Viewpoint)
One-way Hiking Time – 4 hours (Lake), 6 hours (Viewpoint)
Altitude, GPS Reading at Trailhead – 8347', 40°06'39"N, 105°44'48"W
Altitude, GPS Reading at Lake – 10,866', 40°05'14"N, 105°38'43"W
Altitude, GPS Reading at Pass – 12,536', 40°04'34"N, 105°38'07"W
Trail Fee Required – Yes

🐾 Leash, 🦴 Yes, ▲ Permit, WD IP

Trailhead Location – See Monarch Lake Loop Trailhead (1), Hike #43, page 142.

Trail Description – Follow the Cascade Creek to Mirror Lake, Crater Lake, and Lone Eagle Peak Hike #46, page 154 description to (7). At the fork and trail marker, Cascade Creek Trail is on the right and Pawnee Pass Trail is on the left. Take the left fork. Cross Cascade Creek at a safe location and follow the switchbacks and ascend the hill. At a clearing near the top of the switchbacks is a view of Lone Eagle Peak and the valley below. From left to right are Apache Peak, Fair Glacier, Lone Eagle Peak, Mount George, Peck Glacier, and Mt. Achonee. Continue through the woods. At both the next scree field and the meadow is a view of Mt. Toll ahead. (The silhouette of Mt. Toll resembles Abraham Lincoln's head with the cone shaped peak in the middle being his nose. From CO 125, west of Lake Granby, these mountains not only resemble Lincoln's head, but also extend to include his upper torso.)

The landscape is filled with boulders, meadows, and marsh. Follow the creek, which is on the left and parallel the Indian Peaks Range to Pawnee Lake (8). The trail does not directly lead to the lake, so take a side trip to enjoy the view before continuing up to the pass. Pawnee Lake is surrounded on the north by trees and boulders and on the far south by scree and rock.

Leave the lake and continue on the trail. The Englemann spruce trees quickly stunt and the meadows widen. The boulders increase in number and size and the meadows are filled with wildflowers. The trail up to the pass is not visible from timberline, but there is a double-notched arrowhead image high above. The pass is just above in the slot to the right. Follow the trail up through the boulders. This was a well traveled pack trail years ago. Many large boulders have fallen onto the trail over time, but the trail is still negotiable with a minimum of bouldering. Follow the numerous switchbacks and ascend steeply toward the pass. A few stone walls still remain on the edge of the trail up to Pawnee Pass (9). Unlike most passes, this is a large flat area. At the pass is a trail marker identifying the Continental Divide with the Arapaho National Forest to the west and the Roosevelt National Forest to the east. To appreciate the view to the east, continue a short distance on the east side of the Continental Divide (10). Looking east and clockwise is a view of Brainard Lake, Long Lake, Left Hand Reservoir, the Front

Range Mountains, Barker Hut on top of Niwot Mountain, Kiowa Peak, Niwot Ridge, and Shoshoni Peak. To the northeast are Pawnee Peak and Mount Audubon.

The view to the west is best appreciated on the descent from the pass. Looking south is the unnamed ridge that separates the Crater Lake valley from the Pawnee Lake valley. In the distance is the Troublesome Valley, Lake Granby, Mount Irving Hale and the Never Summer Range.

Historical Note – Pawnee Lake and Pass were named by Ellsworth Bethel, a botany teacher from Denver, who was concerned over the naming of the mountains and thought it should be named for an Indian tribe.

Pawnee Lake

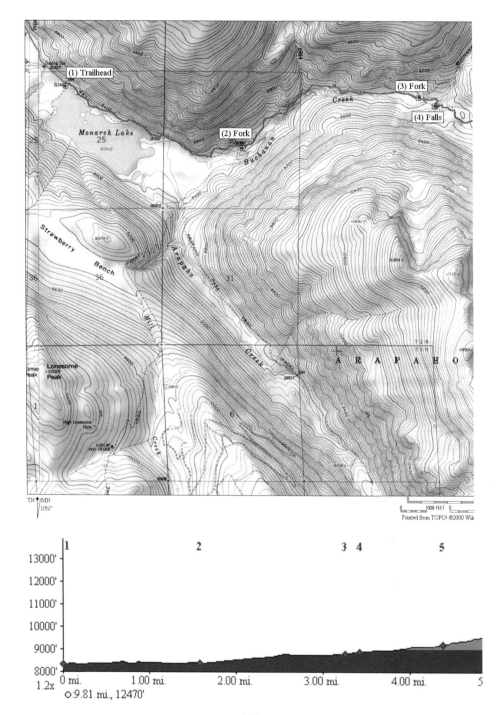

160

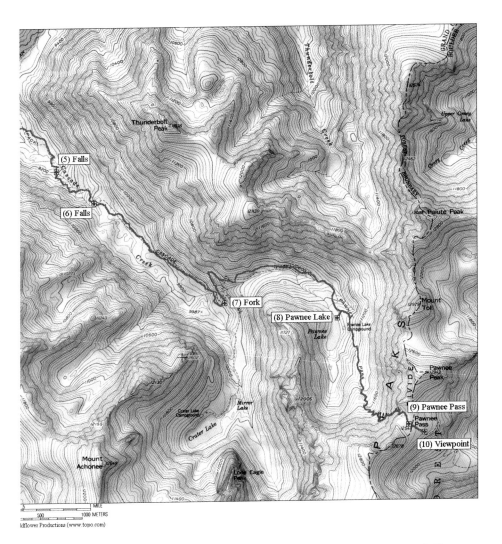

(5) Falls

(6) Falls

(7) Fork

(8) Pawnee Lake

(9) Pawnee Pass

(10) Viewpoint

Thunderbolt Peak

Upper Coney Lake

Paiute Peak

Mount Toll

Pawnee Peak

Pawnee Pass

Pawnee Lake Campground

Pawnee Lake

Mirror Lake

Crater Lake Campground

Crater Lake

Mount Achonee

Lone Eagle Peak

5   MILE
500   1000 METERS

ldflower Productions (www.topo.com)

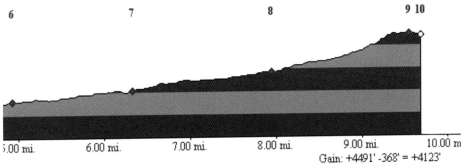

Gain: +4491' -368' = +4123'

161

48. GOURD LAKE

Level of Difficulty – More Difficult
One-way Mileage – 8.16 Miles
One-way Hiking Time - 4 hours
Altitude, GPS Reading at Trailhead – 8338', 40°06'39"N, 105°44'48"W
Altitude, GPS Reading at Destination – 10,835', 40°08'07"N, 105°40'14"W
Trail Fee Required – Yes

🐕 Leash, 🐾 Yes, ▲ Permit, **WD** IP

Trailhead Location – See Monarch Lake Loop Trailhead (1), Hike #43, page 142.

Trail Description – Pass around the gate, walk to the Forest Service cabin and register. The trailhead sign is next to the cabin (1). The Cascade Creek Trail is to the left. Follow this trail around the north side of Monarch Lake with views of the lake through the trees on the right. Pass over several sections of fallen boulders from the hillside above. The lake disappears behind the tall willows, which hides Cascade Creek. The willows thin and the creek runs next to the trail. Cross into the Indian Peaks Wilderness and reach a fork and trail marker (2). The Arapaho Pass Spur Trail is to the right and the Cascade Trail is to the left. Take the left fork and approach Cascade Creek where the water roars and crashes over the boulders. Ascend through several switchbacks and cross Hell Canyon Creek over a sturdy bridge. Continue to climb through the montane forest. Pass large boulders, which are on the left and parallel Cascade Creek, which is on the right. At a fork and trail marker (3) the Buchanan Pass Trail is on the left and the Cascade Creek Trail is straight. Turn left on the Buchanan Pass Trail.

The trail is covered in loose rock and footing can be unstable. Follow this trail up the steep grade and climb toward Buchanan Creek. Meet the creek and parallel it through the valley. The creek is filled with large boulders and immense amounts of water flows causing a tremendous roar. Cross a small foot bridge and continue to parallel the creek through the woods to the fork and trail marker (4). The Buchanan Pass Trail continues straight and Gourd Lake is to the left. Turn left, ascend through several switchbacks, and traverse the hillside. There is a clearing with a view to the south of Thunderbolt Peak and to the southeast of Pawnee Peak and Paiute Peak. Head into the woods and no longer traverse the hillside, but take a more direct approach up the mountain to a small tarn (5). Continue to what appears to be another tarn, but is actually an arm (6) of Gourd Lake. A short distance further around the bend is Gourd Lake (7). This is a large deep lake with boulders surrounding the water's edge. Trees dot the rock hillside around the lake. There is a saddle above that leads to Marten Peak on the left and Cooper Peak on the right. Neither peak is visible from the lake.

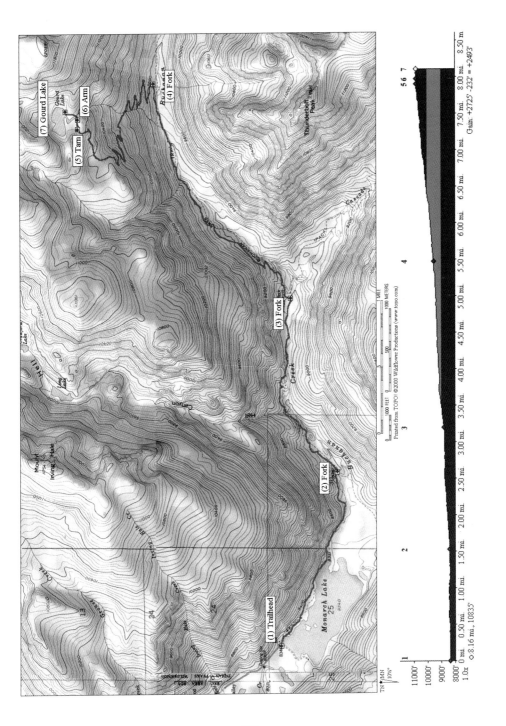

163

49. GOURD LAKE, FOX PARK, BUCHANAN PASS, AND SAWTOOTH MOUNTAIN LOOP

Level of Difficulty – More Difficult (Fox Park), Most Difficult (Buchanan Pass and Sawtooth Mountain)
Round-trip Mileage – 22.41 miles
Round-trip Hiking Time - 2-3 days
Altitude, GPS Reading at Trailhead – 8343', 40°06'39"N, 105°44'48"W
Altitude, GPS Reading at Gourd Lake – 10,839', 40°08'07"N, 105°40'14"W
Altitude, GPS Reading at Fox Park – 10,437', 40°07'57"N, 105°38'30"W
Altitude, GPS Reading at Buchanan Pass – 11,832', 40°07'51"N, 105°37'48"W
Altitude, GPS Reading at Sawtooth Mountain – 12,242', 40°07'35"N, 105°37'29"W
Trail Fee Required – Yes

🐾 Leash, ➤ Yes, ▲ Permit, **WD IP**

Trailhead Location – See Monarch Lake Loop Trailhead (1), Hike #43, page 142.

Trail Description – Follow the Gourd Lake Hike #48, page 162 description to (7). From Gourd Lake, either return to (4) and turn left toward Fox Park or take a short cut on a non-maintained well worn trail. The route described here is for the short cut, which is a cross-country traverse with a minimum drop in elevation.

Return to the arm (6) and head directly south. A worn trail is quickly found, but splits several directions. Head left (east) over a small knoll to a drop off. From this drop off Fox Park is visible in the distance below. Turn left at the drop off where the trail is easy to follow. Traverse the hillside and remain at a fairly constant elevation with only a few short climbs and drops. Follow the trail through the woods to a meadow with views of Buchanan Pass due east, Sawtooth Mountain to its right, and then Paiute Peak, Mt. Toll, Pawnee Peak and finally Thunderbolt Peak to the south. The trail fades in the grass, but continue east through the meadow down to the Buchanan Pass Trail (8). Follow the Buchanan Pass Trail left (north) through the trees and parallel Buchanan Creek. Leave the woods and cross the creek where there is a large meadow surrounded by trees. This is Fox Park (9). The meadow is filled with wildflowers. Looking up the drainage to the left is an unusual unnamed pinnacle and to the right are a number of building block shaped rocks perched on top of the Continental Divide.

Leave Fox Park and climb steadily through the spruce forest. Switchback several times up to timberline to a large meadow filled with creeks and tarns. The flowers are abundant in this wetland. At timberline there is a view of the top of Cooper Peak to the northwest and Mount Irving Hale to the west. Continue up the steep switchbacks across the tundra to Buchanan Pass (10). The views to the east are of the Front Range Mountains and are not as impressive as the views to the west. Looking north and counter-clockwise are Cooper and Marten Peaks, Mount Irving Hale, the Buchanan

Valley, Thunderbolt Peak, Mount Achonee, Mt. George, Fair Glacier, Apache Peak, Paiute Peak and Sawtooth Mountain.

Continue southeast along the ridgeline toward the summit of Sawtooth Mountain. The trail is well defined at the beginning, but disappears in the flat lichen covered boulders. Scramble over tons of boulders and pass several false pinnacles to the top of Sawtooth Mountain (11). The peak itself is flat with sharp drop-offs on three sides. The views to the east are much better from the top of Sawtooth Mountain than from Buchanan Pass. Looking south and counter-clockwise are Paiute Peak, Mount Audubon, and Coney Lake below. To the east are Beaver Reservoir, the Stapp Lakes, and several tarns.

Return to Fox Park (9), follow the trail into the spruce-fir forest and parallel Buchanan Creek. The creek drops rapidly and gains momentum through the valley. Descend through several switchbacks in an attempt to keep pace with the roaring creek. There are several cascading waterfalls through the narrow canyon (12). The forest quickly changes from subalpine to montane with lodgepole pine and aspen forests. In the next meadow there is a good view of Thunderbolt Peak on the left. At the Gourd Lake Trail fork (4), continue straight and follow the inbound trail back to the Monarch Lake Trailhead (1).

Gourd Lake

165

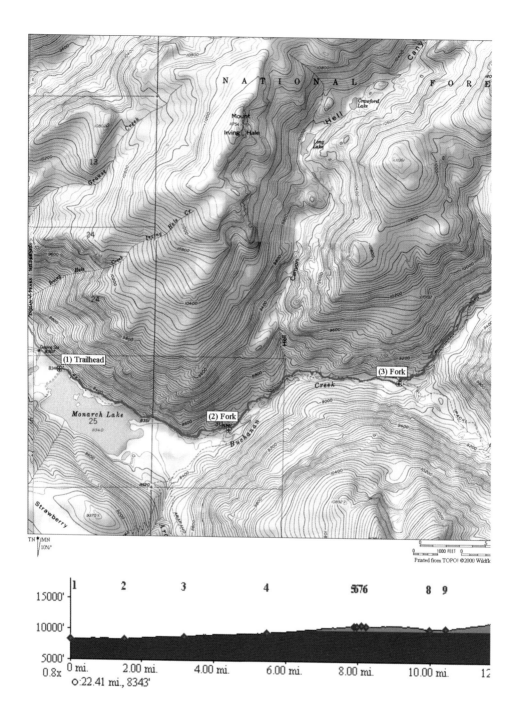

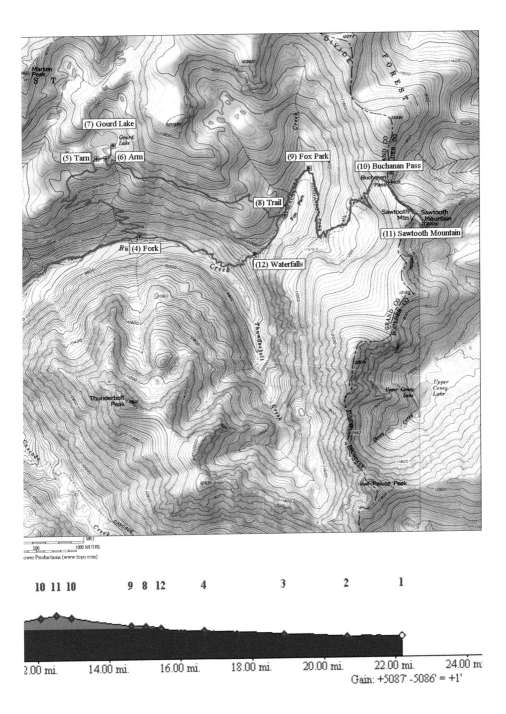

50. WATANGA LAKE

Level of Difficulty - Difficult
One-way Mileage – 4.12 miles
One-way Hiking Time – 3 hours
Altitude, GPS Reading at Trailhead - 8255', 40°07'46"N, 105°45'50"W
Altitude, GPS Reading at Destination – 10,790', 40°09'56"N, 105°44'05"W
Trail Fee Required – Yes

🐾 Leash, 🐟 Yes, ▲ Permit, **WD** IP

Trailhead Location – On US Hwy 34, between Granby and Grand Lake, between mile markers 5 and 6, turn east on CR 6 (FSR 125). Cross the Granby Dam and follow this road to mile marker 9. Turn left at the Roaring Fork Trailhead sign (CR 637). Continue for .9 miles to the Roaring Fork Trailhead parking area (1) on the right. These are all good dirt roads.

Trail Description – Hike through the montane forest of lodgepole pine and aspen trees. A fork and trail marker (2) identify the Knight Ridge Trail to the left and the Roaring Fork Trail to the right. Take the right fork. Sign in at the register box and cross into the Indian Peak Wilderness. Climb the very steep trail through the boulders. There are three switchbacks and then a long climb to the cascading waterfalls of the Roaring Fork Creek. Ripe thimbleberries line this section of the trail in August. The creek is appropriately named Roaring Fork because even in late summer this water still rumbles down the mountain with great force. From the falls, the grade is slightly easier. The montane forest begins with spruce and fir trees only near the water's edge, but eventually transforms into a spruce and fir forest leaving the lodgepole pine trees behind. Several cascading waterfalls are visible on the Roaring Fork Creek, including the occasional 15' fall. Cross the foot bridge and continue to climb parallel to the creek. At a clearing of willows, cross the Roaring Fork Creek again on a foot bridge. At a fork and trail marker (3), Watanga Lake is to the left and the Roaring Fork Trail continues on the right. Take the left fork. The trail levels off slightly in the dense spruce-fir forest. A view of Watanga Mountain is visible in the clearing. Cross Watanga Creek twice and climb steadily uphill. In the next clearing is a view of Mount Irving Hale to the southeast. Climb up several switchbacks and enjoy the views of the valley below and Twin Peaks to the west. Continue up the steep hillside through several more switchbacks. Follow the trail into the woods to Watanga Lake (4). The lake sits in a bowl with Watanga Mountain on the right (east). This is a beautiful lake that is surrounded by trees and is abundant with fish.

Historical Note – Watanga Lake was named after a famous Arapaho Indian.

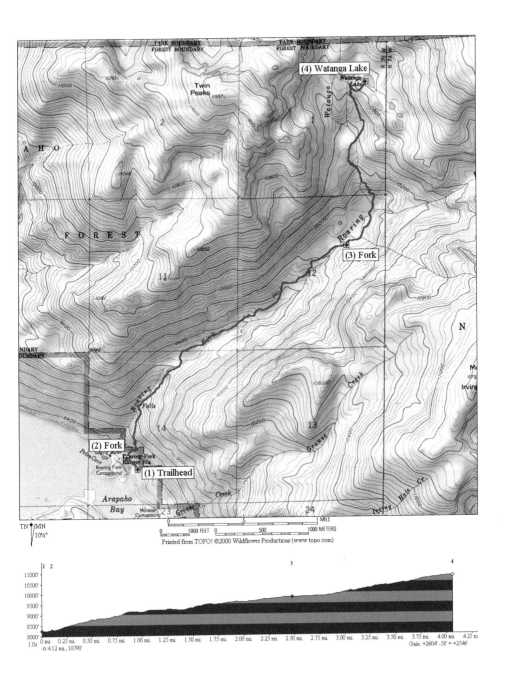

(4) Watanga Lake

(3) Fork

(2) Fork

(1) Trailhead

Arapaho Bay

51. MOUNT IRVING HALE

Level of Difficulty – More Difficult
One-way Mileage – 4.81 miles
One-way Hiking Time - 3 hours
Altitude, GPS Reading at Trailhead - 8255', 40°07'46"N, 105°45'50"W
Altitude, GPS Reading at Destination – 11,515', 40°08'16"N, 105°43'13"W
Trail Fee Required – Yes

🐈 Leash, 🎣 Yes, ▲ Permit, **WD** IP

Trailhead Location – See Watanga Lake Trailhead (1), Hike #50, page 168.

Trail Description – Hike through the montane forest of lodgepole pine and aspen trees. A fork and trail marker (2) identify the Knight Ridge Trail to the left and the Roaring Fork Trail to the right. Take the right fork. Sign in at the register box and cross into the Indian Peak Wilderness. Climb the very steep trail through the boulders. There are three switchbacks and then a long climb to the cascading waterfalls of the Roaring Fork Creek. Ripe thimbleberries line this section of the trail in August. The creek is appropriately named Roaring Fork because even in late summer this creek still rumbles down the mountain with great force. From the falls, the grade is slightly easier. The montane forest begins with spruce and fir trees only near the water's edge, but eventually transforms into a spruce and fir forest leaving the lodgepole pine trees behind. Several cascading waterfalls are visible on the Roaring Fork Creek, including the occasional 15' fall. Cross the foot bridge and continue to climb parallel to the creek. At a clearing of willows, cross the Roaring Fork Creek again on a foot bridge. At a fork and trail marker (3), Watanga Lake is to the left and the Roaring Fork Trail continues on the right. Take the right fork away from the creek and up the hill. There is a view of Twin Peaks on the left and Watanga Mountain ahead on the left. Zigzag and climb steeply through the woods. This is a long steady climb. The forest gives way to the meadows, leading to a saddle (4). Hell Canyon is ahead and Marten Peak is left of center with numerous pinnacles jutting on top. In the background are Paiute Peak, Mt. Toll, Pawnee Peak and Pass, Shoshoni Peak, Apache Peak, Fair Glacier, Mount George, and Mt. Achonee. From the saddle, Mt. Irving Hale is on the right (south) up the hill. The top of the mountain is barely visible from the saddle.

Head south and ascend the hillside along the ridgeline. Pass through the trees into the meadows and boulder fields. The boulders are abundant and no grasses remain. The boulders are huge and hiking over them is increasingly difficult. Beyond the false pinnacle is the top of Mount Irving Hale (5). The top is not wide, but the views are fantastic. Looking north and clockwise are the mountains in Rocky Mountain National Park, Watanga Mountain, Hiamovi Mountain, Upper and Stone Lakes nestled in the trees in Hell Canyon, Cooper Peak and Marten Peak, and Crawford and Long Lakes in Hell Canyon. Along the Indian Peaks Range are Paiute Peak, Mt. Toll, Pawnee Peak and Pass, Shoshoni Peak, Apache Peak, Fair Glacier, Mount George, and Mt. Achonee.

Looking south are Winter Park Ski Resort, the Vasquez Mountains, the Williams Fork Mountains and the Gore Range. Next are Strawberry Lake and Strawberry Bench below, the town of Granby, Lake Granby, the Never Summer Range, the Troublesome Valley, and Twin Peaks.

Historical Note – Irving Hale spent his summers as a youth between Grand Lake and Central City driving supplies over the Berthoud Pass wagon road. He later went on to become a General in the military and a hero.

Mt. Irving Hale

Views of the Indian Peaks Range from Mount Irving Hale

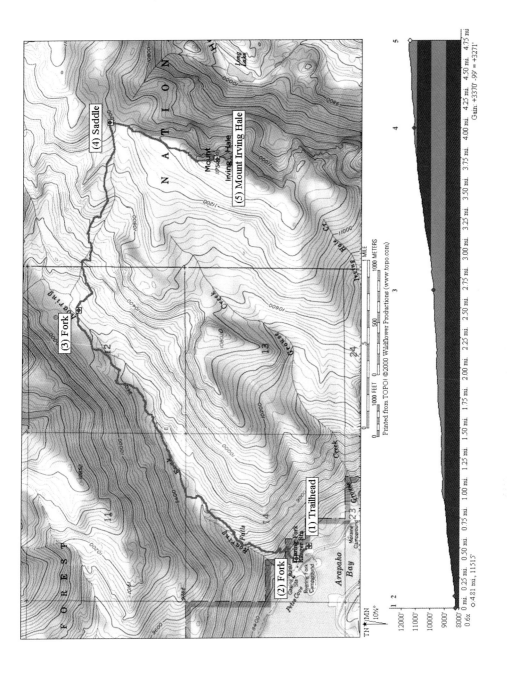

(4) Saddle

(5) Mount Irving Hale

(3) Fork

(2) Fork

(1) Trailhead

Printed from TOPO! ©2000 Wildflower Productions (www.topo.com)

173

52. ROARING FORK TO STONE AND UPPER LAKES

Level of Difficulty – More Difficult
One-way Mileage – 6.51 miles
One-way Hiking Time – 4 hours
Altitude, GPS Reading at Trailhead – 8255', 40°07'46"N, 105°45'50"W
Altitude, GPS Reading at Saddle – 11194', 40°08'51"N, 105°42'58"W
Altitude, GPS Reading at Upper Lake – 10,737', 40°09'18"N, 105°40'53"W
Trail Fee Required – Yes

🐾 Leash, ➤ Yes, ⚠ Permit, **WD** IP

Trailhead Location – See Watanga Lake Trailhead (1), Hike #50, page 168.

Trail Description – Hike through the montane forest of lodgepole pine and aspen trees. A fork and trail marker (2) identify the Knight Ridge Trail to the left and the Roaring Fork Trail to the right. Take the right fork. Sign in at the register box and cross into the Indian Peak Wilderness. Climb the very steep trail through the boulders. There are three switchbacks and then a long climb to the cascading waterfalls of the Roaring Fork Creek. Ripe thimbleberries line this section of the trail in August. The creek is appropriately named Roaring Fork because even in late summer this creek still rumbles down the mountain with great force. From the falls, the grade is slightly easier. The montane forest begins with spruce and fir trees only near the water's edge, but eventually transforms into a spruce and fir forest leaving the lodgepole pine trees behind. Several cascading waterfalls are visible on the Roaring Fork Creek, including the occasional 15' fall. Cross the foot bridge and continue to climb parallel to the creek. At a clearing of willows, cross the Roaring Fork Creek again on a foot bridge. At a fork and trail marker (3), Watanga Lake is to the left and the Roaring Fork Trail continues on the right. Take the right fork away from the creek and up the hill. There is a view of Twin Peaks on the left and Watanga Mountain ahead on the left. Zigzag and climb steeply through the woods. This is a long steady climb. The forest gives way to the meadows, leading to a saddle (4). Hell Canyon is ahead and Marten Peak is left of center with numerous pinnacles jutting on top. In the background are Paiute Peak, Mt. Toll, Pawnee Peak and Pass, Shoshoni Peak, Apache Peak, Fair Glacier, Mount George, and Mt. Achonee. From the saddle, Mt. Irving Hale is on the right (south) up the hill. (To reach the top of Mt. Irving Hale, refer to Mount Irving Hale Hike #51, page 170.)

Leave the saddle and descend east across the hillside. The wildflowers are thick and numerous along the trail. There is a small tarn on the right overlooking Hell Canyon. Follow the trail to a cabin beside a meadow (5). The cabin is perched on a knoll with a great view of the valley below. Martin Peak is clearly visible ahead. Descend more rapidly and approach Hell Canyon. Giant boulders and rocks are abundant. Many ferns grow along the trail where the area is moist. Stone cliffs loom above with fallen rock below. The hillside is steep and Marten Peak is the focal point. Water trickles from the rock faces on the left of the trail. The amount and size of the rocks are impressive. The trail is a maze and wanders through the boulders. From the meadow, a cascading waterfall flows from Round Lake, which sits out of sight on the shelf high above on the left. Follow the creek away from the falls where it flows into a tarn (6). Several creeks flow into this tarn which is beautiful with Marten Peak as a backdrop.

Follow the trail upstream and parallel Hell Canyon Creek to Stone Lake (7). This is an impressive lake surrounded by trees and boulders. Above are Marten Peak to the south (right), Cooper Peak to the east (ahead), the Continental Divide to the northeast, and Hiamovi Mountain to the northwest (far left). Follow the lake to the left around to the creek. The trail disappears, but follow the creek upstream to Upper Lake (8). There are trees on the perimeter of Upper Lake, but the rocks overtake the trees on the surrounding mountains. Hiamovi Mountain is immediately on the left, with a low pass in the center and the Continental Divide and Cooper Peak on the right.

Historical Note – Hell Canyon was named by a group of surveyors after a harrowing journey through the canyon during a storm.

Tarn near Stone Lake

175

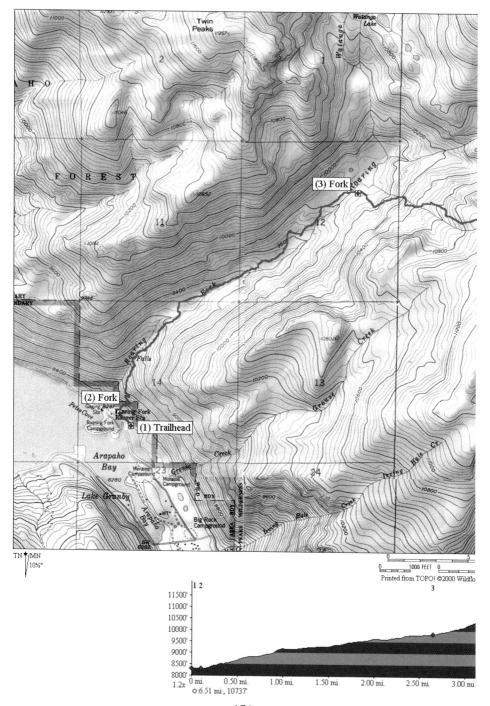

(3) Fork

(2) Fork

(1) Trailhead

TN ✶ /MN
10½°

0   5
0   1000 FEET   0
Printed from TOPO! ©2000 Wildflo

1 2
                                        3
11500'
11000'
10500'
10000'
9500'
9000'
8500'
8000'
1.2x   0 mi.   0.50 mi.   1.00 mi.   1.50 mi.   2.00 mi.   2.50 mi.   3.00 mi.
       O:6.51 mi., 10737'

176

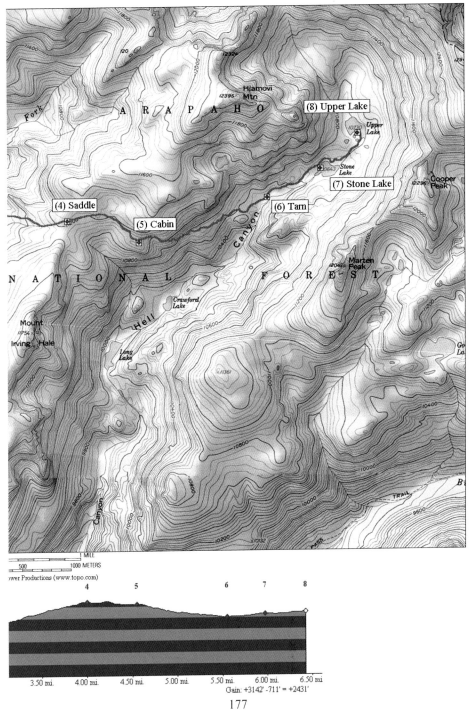

(8) Upper Lake

Upper Lake

(7) Stone Lake

Stone Lake

Cooper Peak

(4) Saddle

(5) Cabin

(6) Tarn

Marten Peak

Crawford Lake

Mount Irving Hale

Long Lake

Hell Canyon

Canyon

TRAIL

ARAPAHO

NATIONAL FOREST

Fork

MILE

500   1000 METERS

ower Productions (www.topo.com)

3.50 mi.   4.00 mi.   4.50 mi.   5.00 mi.   5.50 mi.   6.00 mi.   6.50 mi.

Gain: +3142' -711' = +2431'

53. KNIGHT RIDGE 🚐 🚐

Level of Difficulty - Difficult
One-way Mileage – 13.24 miles
One-way Hiking Time – 7 hours
Altitude, GPS Reading at Trailhead – 8273', 40°07'49"N, 105°46'00"W
Altitude, GPS Reading at Highest Point – 9029', 40°08'46"N, 105°48'01"W
Altitude, GPS Reading at Destination – 8391', 40°14'27"N, 105°49'31"W
Trail Fee Required - Yes

🐾 No, ➤ Yes, ▲ Permit, **WD** IP/RMNP

Trailhead Location – This hike is a one-way hike requiring two vehicles. It is described as a long *Two Lake Hike* and as a shorter *One Lake Hike*.

One Lake Hike 1ˢᵗ Car Parking - On US Hwy 34, between Granby and Grand Lake, between mile markers 11 and 12, head (southeast) toward the Green Ridge Complex, CR 66 and follow this road for 1.5 miles to the parking area at the end of the road (3A).
Two Lake Hike 1ˢᵗ Car Parking - On US Hwy 34 at the turnoff to Grand Lake, follow the signs to "Grand Lake and Village". Drive down the hill and turn right on Center Drive. At the stop sign, turn left on Marina and then turn right on Shadow Mountain Drive. Follow Shadow Mountain Drive to the lake and turn right on Jericho Road and cross the bridge. The East Shore Trail parking area is .4 miles past the bridge (4).
2ⁿᵈ Car Parking - From US Hwy 34, between mile markers 5 and 6 turn east on CR 6 (FSR 125). Cross the Granby Dam and follow this road to mile marker 9. Turn left at the Roaring Fork Trailhead sign (CR 637). Continue for .9 miles to the Roaring Fork Trailhead parking area on the right. These are all good dirt roads. DO NOT begin the hike at the Roaring Fork Trailhead. Continue on foot along the road toward the Roaring Fork Campground. Just beyond the camp host and small ranger station is a sign identifying the "Trail". Cross the bridge and follow the East Shore Trail (1) (Knight Ridge Trail).

Trail Description – This trail is also known as the East Shore Trail because it follows the east shore of Lake Granby and Shadow Mountain Lake. Cross the bridge and skirt the edge of Lake Granby through gently rolling hills of lodgepole pine and aspen forests. Move slowly away from the lake and climb in elevation. Cross over the top of Knight Ridge and descend into a fir forest with meadows and lily pad laden ponds. Cut across to Grand Bay where there is a defunct historic ranger station (2) at the water's edge with a picnic table conveniently located making this a great spot to rest. Leave the ranger station and follow the water's edge again. Across Grand Bay is a great view of the mountains in Rocky Mountain National Park. At the mouth of Columbine Bay, on the steep hillside across the water, an occasional Bald Eagle may be spotted flying above. Cross Columbine Creek and the spillway and continue along the Columbine Bay shore. This bay is appropriately named because of the hundreds of Colorado Columbines along this section of the trail in June and July. The bay leads to the Colorado River. Just after Pole Creek, there is a fork and trail marker (3). The sign identifies the East Shore Trail.

For the *One Lake Hike* take the left fork and follow this to the river. Follow the river upstream, cross over the river, and arrive at the Green Ridge Complex Parking area (3A).

For the *Two Lake Hike* take the right fork. Move away from the water and continue through more forests and meadows. Follow any signs referring to Grand Lake. Cross the large Ranger Meadow and then cross Ranger Creek. After Ranger Creek, there is a short section of marsh with very tall willows. Continue through more forests and meadows to Shadow Mountain Lake. Across the lake are great views of the harbors and the cottages dotting the shoreline. Hug the shoreline. Pass an Osprey nesting site high in the trees. Continue to the peninsula between Shadow Mountain Lake and Grand Lake to the East Shore parking area (4).

Note - The Bald Eagle is a federally protected species and the area between (3) and (3A) is closed from November 15 – March 1 each year to protect wintering bald eagles.

Historical Note – Harry Knight and his family visited this area for many years before he became a land owner. Knight was a friend of Charles A. Lindbergh and was also one of the financiers of the first crossing over the Atlantic by the Spirit of St. Louis.

Columbine flowers along Columbine Bay

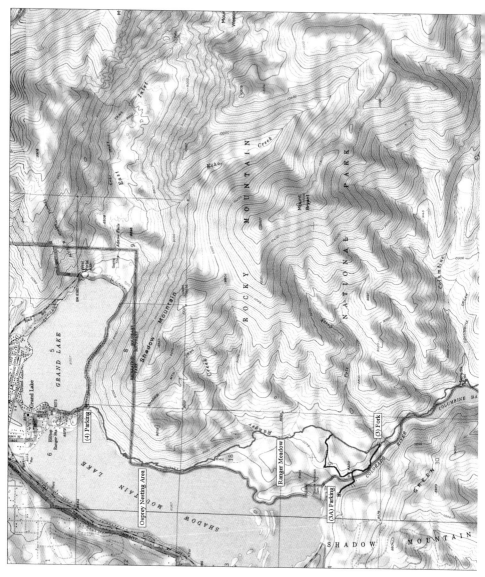

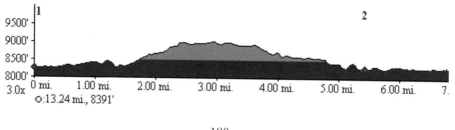

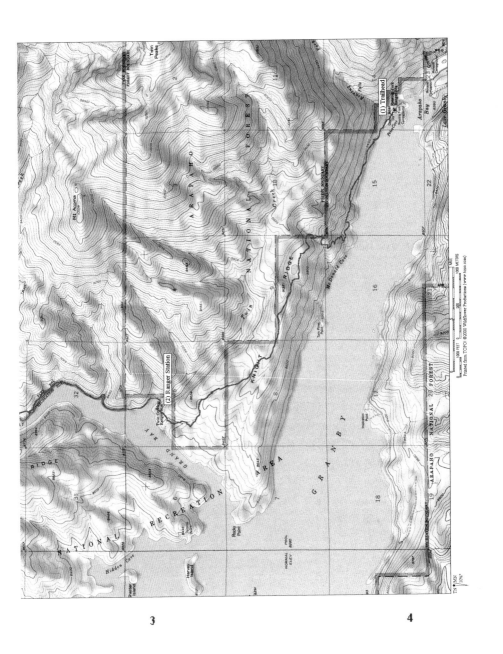

.00 mi.   8.00 mi.   9.00 mi.   10.00 mi.   11.00 mi.   12.00 mi.   13.00 mi.   14.00 m

Gain: +2924' -2809' = +115'

Barn near Bowen Gulch

NEVER SUMMER RANGE

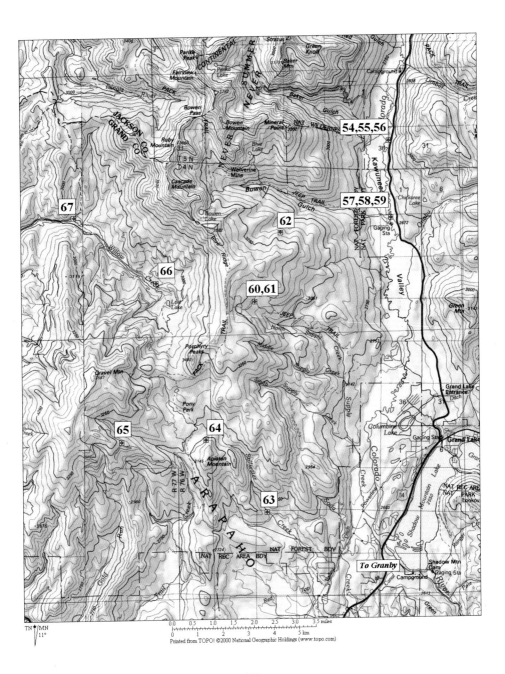

54. PARIKA LAKE AND PARIKA PEAK

Level of Difficulty – Difficult (Lake), More Difficult (Peak)
One-way Mileage – 5.61 miles (Lake), 6.67 miles (Peak)
One-way Hiking Time – 3 ½ hours (Lake), 4 ½ hours (Peak)
Altitude, GPS Reading at Trailhead – 8839', 40°21'17"N, 105°51'28"W
Altitude, GPS Reading at Lake – 11,444', 40°22'54"N, 105°56'12"W
Altitude, GPS Reading at Peak – 12,376', 40°23'07"N, 105°56'48"W
Trail Fee Required – Yes, included with RMNP entrance fee

🐕 No, 🐾 Yes, ▲ Yes, WD RMNP/NS

Trailhead Location – On US Hwy 34, north of Grand Lake, enter the west entrance of Rocky Mountain National Park, mile marker 15. Continue into the park about 1 mile further to the entrance fee station. From the Entrance Fee Station, it is 6.3 miles to the trailhead on the left (west) side of the road (1).

Trail Description – There is a marquee at the trailhead describing the trail. Cross over the Colorado River and pass around the "Road Closed" gate. Follow the road through a meadow. This meadow is part of the Kawuneeche Valley extending along the Colorado River from the headwaters to Grand Lake. After the meadow, pass two closed forks on the right. At the third fork and trail marker (2), Bowen Gulch Trail continues straight and Baker Gulch Trail is on the right. Turn right and follow the trail through the lodgepole pine forest. Leave Rocky Mountain National Park and enter the Never Summer Wilderness, where there is a register box (3). Register here and continue. Parallel the creek through the gulch, although the creek is not always audible. It is a moderate climb into the spruce-fir forest. At the top of the first switchback is a small pond (4). Beyond the pond is a clearing where Green Knoll is visible on the right. Look close to see the Grand Ditch. This aqueduct carries water from these mountains to the Long Draw Reservoir.

Meet the creek at the next set of switchbacks, where the creek bed drops dramatically from above creating a series of small waterfalls. At a clearing filled with boulders, Parika Peak is straight ahead with Baker Mountain on the right. In August, ripe raspberries line this boulder field. Climb out of the boulders and through several aspen stands where Bowen Mountain and Farview Mountain are visible. The spruce trees dominate the landscape. Climb up to the Grand Ditch (5). At the service road for the ditch, turn left and cross the foot bridge over the ditch. The meadows between the trees widen. Follow the trail across a swift creek to the next fork and trail marker (6). Baker Gulch Trail is on the right and Baker Pass Trail to Parika Lake is on the left. Continue left toward Parika Lake. The water in the creek cascades and the trail climbs. At the next fork and trail marker (7) the Baker Pass Trail is to the right and Parika Lake is to the left. Turn left where the trees are dramatically shorter and follow the trail to Parika Lake (8). This is a beautiful lake with Parika Peak behind it. The views looking back along Baker Gulch are spectacular with the mountains in Rocky Mountain National Park framing Longs Peak in the distance. To the left of Longs Peak in the foreground is Baker Mountain on the right and Farview Mountain on the left. The Englemann spruce trees are stunted around the lake at timberline and cling to the hillside in an effort to survive the cold and wind.

To reach Parika Peak, head left (south) of the lake where the trail is visible traversing the hillside between Farview Mountain and Parika Peak. The ground is covered in short grasses and flowers in this alpine zone with a few arctic willows near the trail. A beautiful creek above Parika Lake gathers water from the snow melt above. The marsh below provides a haven for flowers. Follow the trail across the hillside to the saddle (9). Both the saddle and Parika Peak are along the Continental Divide. To the left are Parkview Mountain and Radial Mountain. To the right is the valley known as North Park.

At the saddle, the well worn trail to the left leads to Bowen Pass, the CD Trail, and the Jack Park Trail. Turn right and follow the ridge. The alpine flowers disappear and are replaced with mosses and lichens. It is a steep climb and the summit seems to be at every next step.

From the top of Parika Peak (10) the views are unbelievable. Looking north and clockwise are Mount Cindy, the Never Summer Range, Mt. Cirrus, Howard Mountain, Mount Cumulus, Mount Nimbus, Mount Stratus, Baker Mountain, the Parika Lake Trailhead, Parika Lake, Longs Peak, Farview Mountain and Bowen Mountain. Continuing clockwise are the James Peak area, Winter Park Ski Resort, and the Vasquez Mountains. Looking south and continuing clockwise are Cascade Mountain, the Gore Range in the distance, the Troublesome Valley, Parkview Mountain, Radial Mountain, and North Park.

Historical Note – The Indian word Parika means "horn", describing the peak. Parika also describes the "horn" that the Indians would create by combing their hair straight up and applying paint and grease in an effort to intimidate their enemy.

Parika Peak

View of Farview and Bowen Mountain from Parika Peak

186

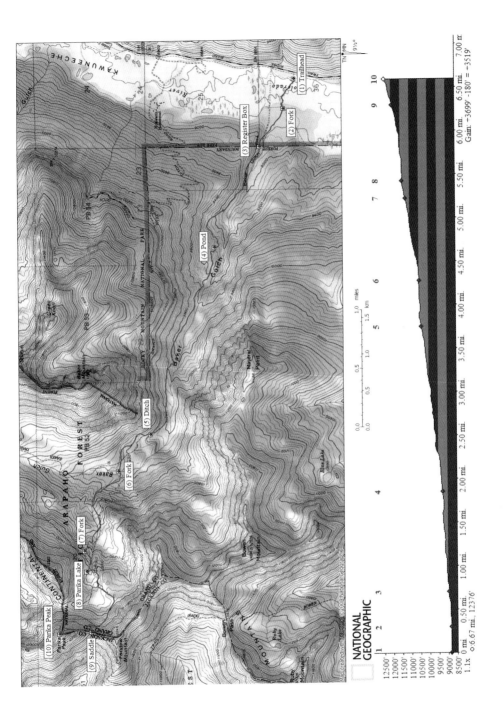

NATIONAL
GEOGRAPHIC

187

55. PARIKA LAKE AND BAKER PASS LOOP

Level of Difficulty – More Difficult
Round-trip Mileage – 14.18 miles
Round-trip Hiking Time – 7 hours
Altitude, GPS Reading at Trailhead – 8857', 40°21'17"N, 105°51'28"W
Altitude, GPS Reading at Baker Pass – 11,264', 40°24'07"N, 105°54'48"W
Trail Fee Required – Yes, included in RMNP entrance fee

🐾 No, 🐕 Yes, ▲ Yes, **WD** RMNP/NS

Trailhead Location – See Parika Lake and Parika Peak Trailhead (1), Hike #54, page 184.

Trail Description – Follow the Parika Lake and Parika Peak Hike #54, page 184, description to (8). From the lake, return to (7) and turn left (north) at the fork onto the Baker Pass Trail. Parallel the unnamed peaks along the Continental Divide at timberline. The left side of the trail is covered in scree and boulders. To the right are meadows covered with willows just above the trees. The trail is relatively level. The steep scree covered mountain ahead is Mount Cumulus. South of Mount Cumulus are Mount Nimbus, Mount Stratus, and Baker Mountain. At a small wet-land there is an old corral on the right. A short distance beyond the wet-land is a mine (9). This is the "Glow of the Rockies" lode also referred to as the "Mica Mine". Mica was excavated for use in stoves and windows and quartz was excavated for use in jewelry. Make a short descent to Baker Pass (10). The pass lies along the Continental Divide and from the pass looking left (north) is Mount Cindy. Continuing clockwise are the Michigan River Valley, the Never Summer Mountains, including Mount Cirrus, Howard Mountain, and Mount Cumulus. Next is a large saddle to the east and then are Mount Nimbus, Mount Stratus, and Baker Mountain. Continuing clockwise are Bowen Mountain, and Parika Peak.

From the pass, turn right (south) into Baker Gulch. This gulch is a beautiful valley with meadows and forest between two high mountain ranges. The trail is faint, but it is well marked with cairns. The gulch is abundant with alpine flowers. Hug the left (east) side of the gulch through the scree below Mount Nimbus, Mount Stratus and Baker Mountain. Move to the center of the valley and into an Englemann spruce forest along a ridge between more meadows. Approach a creek filled with flowers and willows. The valley narrows and the trail winds beside the creek through the woods and meadows. At the fork and trail marker (6), turn left and follow the inbound trail back to trailhead (1).

Parika Lake and Parika Peak

Baker Gulch

189

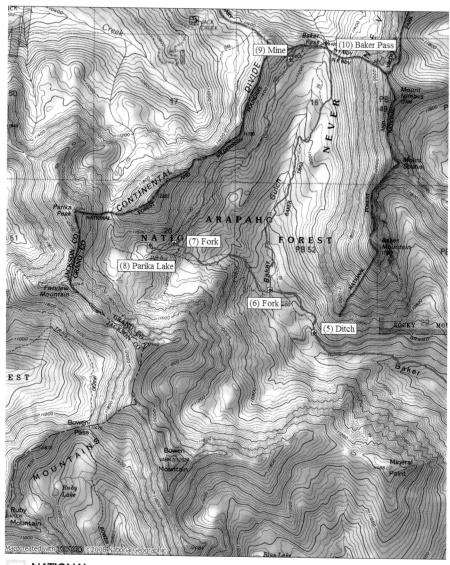

(9) Mine
(10) Baker Pass
(7) Fork
(8) Parika Lake
(6) Fork
(5) Ditch

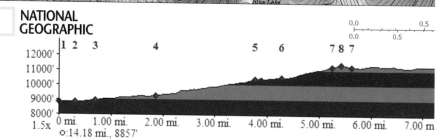

NATIONAL
GEOGRAPHIC

0.0   0.5
0.0   0.5

1 2   3   4   5   6   7 8 7

12000'
11000'
10000'
9000'
8000'

1.5x 0 mi.   1.00 mi.   2.00 mi.   3.00 mi.   4.00 mi.   5.00 mi.   6.00 mi.   7.00 m
○:14.18 mi., 8857'

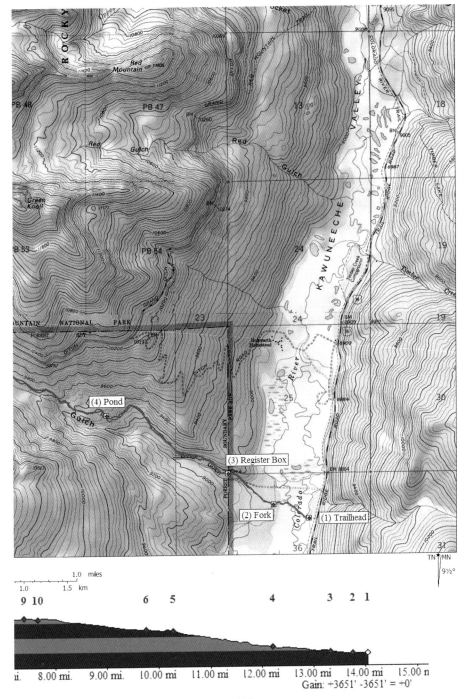

(4) Pond

(3) Register Box

(2) Fork

(1) Trailhead

1.0 miles
1.0
1.5 km

9 10   6   5   4   3   2 1

ii.   8.00 mi.   9.00 mi.   10.00 mi   11.00 mi   12.00 mi   13.00 mi   14.00 mi   15.00 n

Gain: +3651' -3651' = +0'

TN MN
9½°

56. BAKER MOUNTAIN

Level of Difficulty – More Difficult
One-way Mileage – 5.29 miles
One-way Hiking Time – 4 ½ hours
Altitude, GPS Reading at Trailhead - 8835', 40°21'17"N, 105°51'28"W
Altitude, GPS Reading at Destination – 12,222', 40°22'54"N, 105°54'22"W
Trail Fee Required – Yes, included in RMNP entrance fee

🐾 No, 🐾 Yes, ▲ Permit, **WD** RMNP/NS

Trailhead Location – See Parika Lake and Parika Peak Trailhead (1), Hike #54, page 184.

Trail Description – Follow the Parika Lake and Parika Peak Hike #54, page 184 description to (5). At the Grand Ditch service road, turn right and follow the water downstream. The views of Longs Peak and the mountains in Rocky Mountain National Park are beautiful along this service road. Where the water flows through a concrete pipe (6), look uphill (north) toward Baker Mountain to a pinnacle. Cross the ditch over the concrete pipe and hike to the left of the pinnacle above. The trail is faint and disappears on the steep terrain. Low growing shrubs are near the base of the mountain, but the ground cover quickly changes to stunted Englemann spruce trees. Follow the narrow strip of grass up through the spruce and boulders to the draw where the short subalpine grasses and flowers grow tight against the steep hillside. Boulders and trees line the narrow strip of grass on both sides restricting room for switchbacks. Above the stunted trees are an abundance of scattered boulders. This hike is very steep and there is no relief. At the ridge, there is a great view ahead (north) of Green Knoll and Mt. Stratus.

Head left up the ridgeline through the Englemann spruce trees, which look more like shrubs now. The ridgeline is increasingly more difficult to negotiate through the scree and boulders. The spruce trees and grasses completely disappear and the boulders dominate. There is an area of conglomerated mica and quartz between the granite boulders that appears to have been formed during the violent glacial carving of the mountain. Pass this mica/quartz formation and scramble over the large boulders to the top of Baker Mountain (7). This peak has fantastic 360° views. Looking north and clockwise are Mount Stratus, the mountains in Rocky Mountain National Park in the distance, Green Knoll, Longs Peak, the Kawuneeche Valley below, the Indian Peaks Range, Grand Lake, Shadow Mountain Lake, Winter Park Ski Resort, Lake Granby, the Vasquez Mountains, Williams Fork Mountains and the Gore Range, Porphyry Peaks, Elk Mountain, Cascade Mountain, Bowen Mountain, Farview Mountain, Parkview Mountain, Parika Lake and Mountain, North Park in the distance, Baker Gulch and Baker Pass below.

Historical Note - John Baker, a trapper and scout, was the first person to reach the top of Baker Mountain where he found a mine on the slope and filed claim to it.

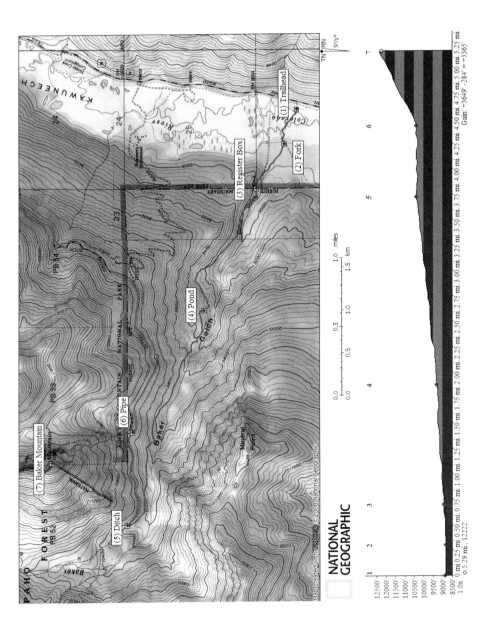

NATIONAL
GEOGRAPHIC

Map created with TOPO!® ©2008 National Geographic

193

57. BLUE LAKE AND MINERAL POINT

Level of Difficulty – Difficult (Lake), More Difficult (Mineral Point)
One-way Mileage – 5.59 miles (Lake), 7.66 (Mineral Point)
One-way Hiking Time - 3 hours (Lake), 4 hours (Mineral Point)
Altitude, GPS Reading at Trailhead – 8766', 40°19'42"N, 105°51'25"W
Altitude, GPS Reading at Lake – 10,711', 40°21'02"N, 105°55'16"W
Altitude, GPS Reading at Mineral Point – 11,485', 40°21'38"N, 105°54'16"W
Trail Fee Required – Yes, included in RMNP entrance fee

🐾 No, 🐟 Yes, ▲ Yes, **WD** RMNP/NS

Trailhead Location – On US Hwy 34, north of Grand Lake, enter the west entrance of Rocky Mountain National Park, mile marker 15. Continue into the park about 1 mile further to the entrance fee station. From the fee station drive 4.2 miles to a road on the left (west). Turn left and follow this road for .2 miles to a "T". The trailhead is at the gate on the right (1). Do not park in front of the gate.

Trail Description – Pass around the gate and follow the road over the Colorado River (Bowen Gulch Connector Trail). From the meadow are views of Cascade Mountain and Ruby Mountain on the left and an unnamed peak on the right. The road forks to the right, but remain straight (2). Pass the barn, which is on the left and continue through the Kawuneeche Valley. The willows grow thick in the marsh on the right. Near the far edge of the meadow stood the old town of Gaskill. Not much remains, however this was a bustling town that serviced the mining boom. Enter the woods and at the fork (3), bear right. This right fork is not well worn, but it is just prior to the creek. Climb up this old road that was built for the Wolverine Mine. It is wide in some places and single-track in others. Pass a second cabin, which is on the right nestled in the woods. Continue on this road through the woods and climb to the Bowen Gulch creek. Parallel this creek through the gulch, although it is not always audible. Leave Rocky Mountain National Park and enter the Never Summer Wilderness. At the next fork and trail marker (4), the trail to the right leads to the Bowen/Baker Gulch Trailhead, 1.3 miles away and straight is the Bowen Gulch Trail. Continue straight and follow Bowen Gulch through the woods with an occasional view of an unnamed peak and Bowen Mountain in the clearings. Cross Bowen Gulch creek (5) on a foot bridge, where the old wagon bridge lies in the creek. Cross the creek again further upstream on a foot bridge. Climb steadily beside the creek and then up a long switchback away from the creek. At the next fork (6) is another old road on the left. Bear right. After the trail switchbacks again, there is a fork and trail marker (7) on the right. The fork is a single-track trail that leads to Blue Lake. Straight continues up Bowen Gulch and to the Wolverine Mine (see below for the Wolverine Mine Side Trip). Turn right toward Blue Lake. The forest thins and the views open up. Climb higher through the meadows across the hillside. Head east and view the Bowen Gulch valley and Longs Peak. Continue across the steep hillside where the trees are thin as a result of the damage from fallen boulders. Approach the Blue Lake creek and when the trail is about 10 yards from the creek, a faint fork is visible on the right (8). This leads to Mineral Point and Bowen Mountain. Remain on the main trail for a short distance to Blue Lake (9). Blue Lake is surrounded by trees at the base with Bowen Mountain and an unnamed peak behind it. The fish are abundant here.

To reach Mineral Point, return to the faint fork next to the creek (8). Turn left and cross the creek. Follow the trail through the woods and at the next small clearing take the fork to the right (10). It is faint, but marked with small cairns. The trees thin where the trail leaves the subalpine and approaches timberline. Views of Blue Lake are visible below. Move away from the hillside and follow the trail to a meadow (11). Cross the creek and pass the small tarn. Bowen Mountain is straight ahead. Continue through the meadow, up the hill and follow the switchback that heads east toward Mineral Point. Climb higher in and out of the trees where the Englemann spruce trees significantly stunt in size. At a bend, the Blue Lake valley is left behind and the Mineral Point valley lies ahead. At this bend, a very distinct path crosses the trail (12). The left trail leads to the ridgeline of Bowen Mountain. (It is not the recommended route to Bowen Mountain because of an un-passable spire on the north end of this ridgeline. See the Bowen Mountain Hike #58, page 198 for peak access.) To reach Mineral Point, continue straight. Traverse the grassy hillside and descend into the meadow. The trail is faint in the meadow, but hug the left hillside to an old miner's cabin (13) where the old wood burning stove still remains. From the cabin, the trail to Mineral Point reappears. Follow the trail to the ridge. Baker Peak is straight ahead. Continue to the right (east) along the ridge through the dense spruce trees to the top of Mineral Point (14). The mineral "copper" was mined from this area. There is no marker identifying the top. For a good view, hike east below the trees. From the top of Mineral Point looking both north and east are the mountains in Rocky Mountain National Park. Continuing clockwise are Longs Peak and the Kawuneeche Valley below, the Indian Peaks Range, Grand Lake, Shadow Mountain Lake, Lake Granby and the James Peak area. Looking counter-clockwise from the north are Baker Mountain, Baker Gulch, Parika Peak, Farview Mountain, and Bowen Mountain.

Wolverine Mine Side Trip – At the fork (7), continue straight on the Bowen Gulch Trail. Travel a short distance to a clearing where an old road forks on the right (7A). Follow the old road where the trees have grown up through the gravel bed. This leads to the remains of the Wolverine Mine (7B). The mine has been filled in and lumber is strewn around the hillside where galena and sulfuret were once mined. Galena and sulfuret are used to make lead and silver. This side trip is about .37 miles each way.

Historical Note – Captain L.D.C. Gaskill was the superintendent of the Wolverine Mine. The town of Gaskill was named for him and was the headquarters for the mine.

Blue Lake and Bowen Mountain

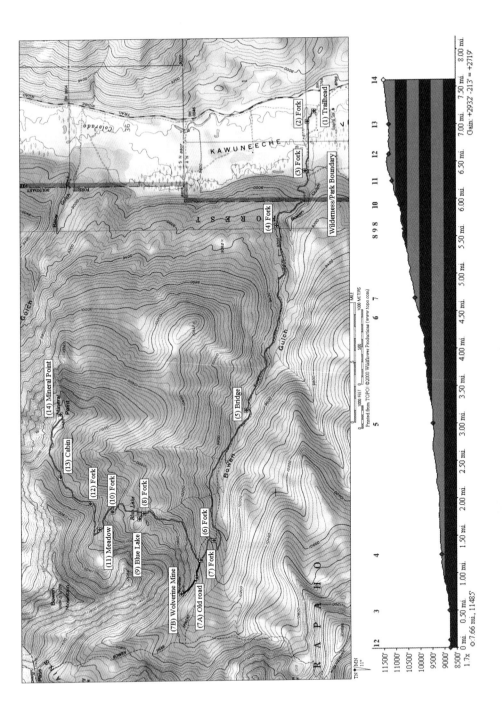

(1) Trailhead
(2) Fork
(3) Fork
(4) Fork
(5) Bridge
(6) Fork
(7) Fork
(7A) Old road
(7B) Wolverine Mine
(8) Fork
(9) Blue Lake
(10) Fork
(11) Meadow
(12) Fork
(13) Cabin
(14) Mineral Point

Wilderness/Park Boundary

KAWUNEECHE

ARAPAHO

FOREST

Printed from TOPO! ©2000 Wildflower Productions (www.topo.com)

Gain: +2932' -213' = +2719'

O: 7.66 mi, 11485'

197

58. BOWEN MOUNTAIN

Level of Difficulty – More Difficult
One-way Mileage – 7.25 miles
One-way Hiking Time – 5 hours
Altitude, GPS Reading at Trailhead – 8766', 40°19'42"N, 105°51'25"W
Altitude, GPS Reading at Destination – 12,391', 40°21'38"N, 105°56'00"W
Trail Fee Required – Yes, included in RMNP entrance fee

🐾 No, 🐟 Yes, ▲ Yes, **WD** RMNP/NS

Trailhead Location – See Blue Lake and Mineral Point Trailhead (1), Hike #57, page 194.

Trail Description – Follow the Blue Lake and Mineral Point Hike #57, page 194 description to (11). Cross the creek and pass the small tarn. Bowen Mountain is straight ahead. Do not continue on the worn trail up the switchback to reach the peak of Bowen Mountain. This route dead-ends at an un-passable spire just before the peak. Leave the worn trail, cross the meadow, and head west. Follow the grassy clearing on the left of the large white boulders. The rocks are numerous and the flowers are abundant. Hike to the top of this meadow where there are remains of an old prospect hole. Next, continue higher to a knoll surrounded by taller stunted Englemann spruce trees. In the middle of this knoll is another prospect hole (12) with the remains of an old stove, metal scraps, and scattered wood from a cabin. Continue west across the creeks and marshes. The subalpine zone is left behind and the alpine is approached. There is no trail here, but the easiest route is to hike up the grassy section between the rock faces. Once above the rock faces, the grassy hillside is scattered with boulders. The ascent is steep and the ground is covered in grasses and wildflowers. At a saddle (13) there are wonderful views ahead of Bowen Gulch below, Cascade Mountain on the left, Parkview Mountain in the distance, Ruby Mountain and Ruby Lake on the right, and North Park on the right in the distance. Turn right (north) and climb up the hillside. The terrain is very rocky and the small clumps of sod disappear. Although this section is not as steep, the boulders are difficult to negotiate to the top Bowen Mountain (14).

From the top looking north and clockwise are Baker Gulch, Howard Mountain, Mount Cumulus, Mount Nimbus, Mount Stratus, Baker Mountain, the Grand Ditch below Baker Mountain, and the mountains in Rocky Mountain National Park. Continuing east and clockwise are Mineral Point, Longs Peak, the Kawuneeche Valley, Blue Lake nestled in the trees, Grand Lake, Shadow Mountain Lake, Lake Granby and the unnamed peak. Next are the Fraser Valley and Winter Park area in the distance, along with the Vasquez Mountains, Porphyry Peaks, Blue Ridge, the Gore Range in the distance, and Gravel Mountain in the foreground. Cascade Mountain sits on the next ridge to the west with the Troublesome Valley behind. Ruby Mountain is directly ahead with Ruby Lake just below, then Parkview Mountain, Radial Mountain, North Park, Farview Mountain, and Parika Peak.

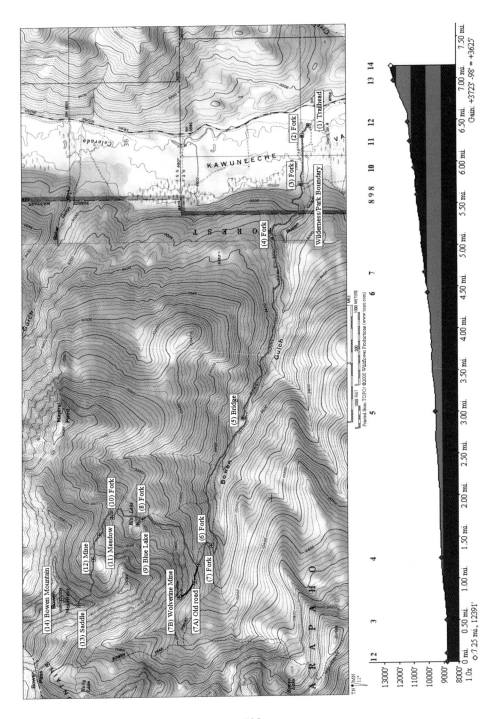

199

59. BOWEN GULCH TO BOWEN LAKE

Level of Difficulty - Difficult
One-way Mileage – 6.81 miles
One-way Hiking Time – 5 hours
Altitude, GPS Reading at Trailhead – 8766', 40°19'42"N, 105°51'25"W
Altitude, GPS Reading at Destination – 11,029', 40°19'51"N, 105°56'38"W
Trail Fee Required – Yes, included in RMNP entrance fee

🐾 No, ➤ Yes, ▲ Yes, WD RMNP/NS

Trailhead Location – See Blue Lake and Mineral Point Trailhead (1), Hike #57, page 194.

Trail Description – Follow the Blue Lake and Mineral Point Hike #57, page 194 description to (7). At this fork, continue straight along the Bowen Gulch Trail. After a short distance, there is a clearing and a fork (8) on the right leading to the remains of the Wolverine Mine (see below for Wolverine Mine Side Trip). Continue on the Bowen Gulch Trail and cross the foot bridge over the creek into the woods to the next fork (9). Bowen Pass is to the right and Bowen Lake is to the left. Turn left into the dense spruce-fir forest. Ascend out of the valley, gradually at first, but then steeply. Finally Bowen Lake is on the right (10). This is a wonderful lake with Cascade Mountain as its backdrop creating an amphitheater around the lake. Fishing is good and there are several great places to camp

Wolverine Mine Side Trip – At the fork (8), turn right and follow the old road where the trees have grown up through the gravel bed. This leads to the remains of the Wolverine Mine (8A). The mine has been filled in and lumber is strewn around the hillside where galena and sulfuret were once mined. Galena and sulfuret are used to make lead and silver. This side trip is about .2 miles each way.

Historical Note - Bowen Mountain was named after James Bourn, who along with Alexander Campbell, discovered the Wolverine Mine. Bourn's name was unfortunately mis-spelled by a clerk years ago and the mistake was never corrected.

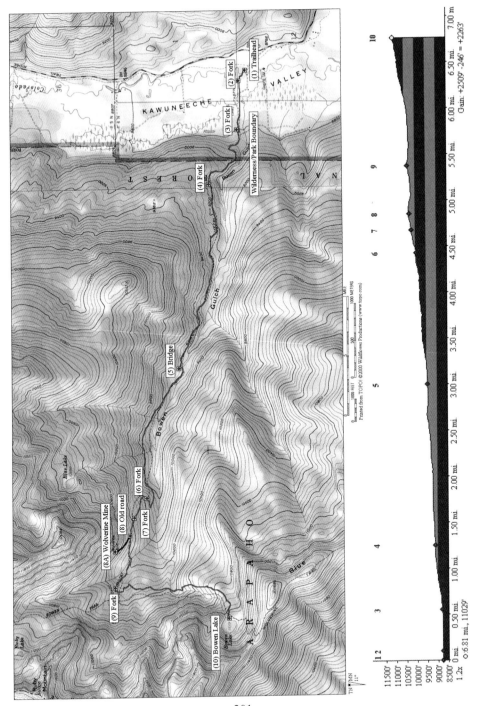

201

60. BLUE RIDGE TO BOWEN LAKE

Level of Difficulty – Difficult
One-way Mileage – 4.02 miles
One-way Hiking Time - 2 hours
Altitude, GPS Reading at Trailhead – 10,378', 40°18'00"N, 105°55'13"W
Altitude, GPS Reading at Highest Point – 11,579', 40°19'31"N, 105°56'07"W
Altitude, GPS Reading at Destination – 11,033', 40°19'51"N, 105°56'38"W
Trail Fee Required – No

🐾 Yes, 🐕 Yes, ▲ Yes, WD BG/NS

Trailhead Location – On US Hwy 34, southwest of Grand Lake, between mile markers 9 and 10, turn west onto CR 4. Follow CR 4 for 3.0 miles. Take the right fork (CR 455 also FSR 120 also Kawuneeche Road) toward the Never Summer Wilderness for 9.3 miles to the North Supply Trailhead (1). Both CR 4 and CR 455 are good dirt roads.

Trail Description - This trail begins as a common trailhead for motorized vehicles. Follow the trail to the fork and trail marker (2). The North Supply Loop Trail is on the left and the Blue Ridge Trail and Wolverine Trail are on the right. Take the right fork where motorized vehicles are not permitted. Immediately after this fork the trail enters the Bowen Gulch Protection Area. The sign identifies Blue Ridge Mountain Bike Trail on the right and the Blue Ridge Trail straight. Continue straight and at the next fork (3) turn right where the Blue Ridge Trail heads up the hill on the single-track trail. This part of the trail is steep and narrow. At the next fork (4), the Wolverine Trail is to the left and the Blue Ridge Trail is on the right. Turn right along the ridgeline. A short distance further is a fork (5) where the Wolverine By-Pass to Lost Lake is on the left. Continue straight and ascend the ridgeline. Next, pass the fork and trail marker for the Blue Ridge Mountain Bike Trail (6) on the right. Continue to ascend along Blue Ridge. Leave the woods and enter a clearing where Parkview Mountain, Radial Mountain, and Cascade Mountain are visible on the left. Bowen Mountain is straight ahead. To the right and clockwise are the mountains in Rocky Mountain National Park, Grand Lake and Shadow Mountain Lake, Indian Peaks, the James Peak area, and the Vasquez Mountains. Continue through a meadow where the trees thin near timberline. The next fork is at the Never Summer Wilderness boundary (7). Bikes are not permitted beyond this point. Cascade Mountain is on the left, with Farview Mountain ahead and Bowen Mountain on the right. The right fork leads to Bowen Lake and the left fork leads to Cascade Mountain. Take the right fork down the hillside through a couple of steep switchbacks into the forest to Bowen Lake (8). This is a wonderful lake with Cascade Mountain as its backdrop creating an amphitheater around the lake. Fishing is good and there are several great places to camp.

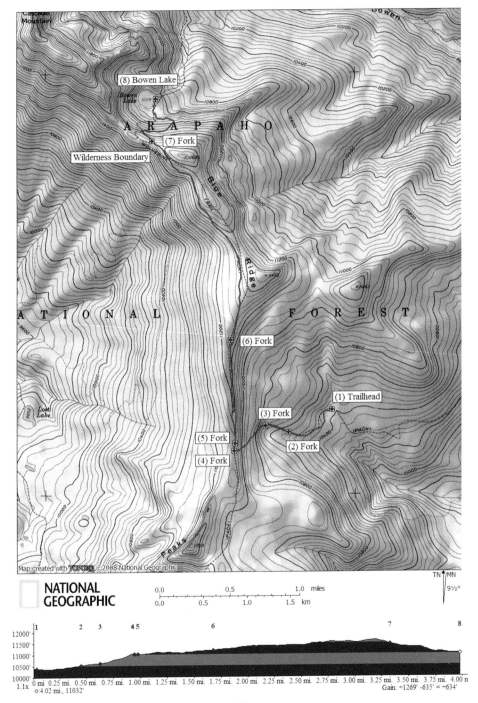

NATIONAL GEOGRAPHIC

61. CASCADE MOUNTAIN, BOWEN PASS, AND BOWEN LAKE LOOP

Level of Difficulty – Most Difficult
Round-trip Mileage – 13.94 miles
Round-trip Hiking Time – 9 hours
Altitude, GPS Reading at Trailhead – 10,387', 40°18'00"N, 105°55'13"W
Altitude, GPS Reading at Cascade Mt. – 12,251', 40°20'28"N, 105°57'34"W
Altitude, GPS Reading at Bowen Pass – 11,476', 40°21'50"N, 105°56'40"W
Altitude, GPS Reading at Bowen Lake – 11,027', 40°19'51"N, 105°56'38"W
Trail Fee Required – No

🐾 Yes, 🐟 Yes, ▲ Yes, WD BG/NS

Trailhead Location – See Blue Ridge to Bowen Lake Trailhead (1), Hike #60, page 202.

Trail Description – Follow the Bowen Lake Hike #60, page 202 description to (7). Continue left up the ridgeline to Cascade Mountain. The trail is faint and disappears in places. On the left are Porphyry Peaks, then Gravel Mountain, the Gore Range in the distance, and Parkview Mountain ahead. Climb through the alpine where the small flowers, mosses and lichens carpet the hillside. When the trail disappears, follow the cairns across the mountain side. Hike to the top of Cascade Mountain (8). From the top looking north and clockwise are Farview Mountain, Bowen Mountain, the mountains in Rocky Mountain National Park, Indian Peaks, Shadow Mountain Lake, the James Peak area, Porphyry Peaks, and Lost Lake below. Continuing from the south are the Vasquez Mountains, the Gore Range, Gravel Mountain, the Troublesome Valley, Parkview Mountain, Radial Mountain, the town of Rand, and North Park.

From the top of Cascade Mountain, head north down the ridgeline. Skirt the left side of the next unnamed peak and Ruby Mountain. Move closer to the ridgeline again where there is a small peak on the ridgeline (9) slightly off the trail with a wonderful view of Ruby Lake and the valley below. Continue down to Bowen Pass and the trail marker (10). Turn right (south) at Bowen Pass into Bowen Gulch through the arctic willows. Ruby Lake is on the right. The valley has an abundance of water from the snow melt creating a wonderland of flowers. Cross the creek flowing from Ruby Lake and remain high through the marsh and follow the cairns into the woods. Descend gently through the dense spruce-fir forest. The next fork and trail marker (11) identifies Bowen Lake straight ahead. The left fork leads to the remains of the Wolverine Mine (see below for Wolverine Mine Side Trip). Continue toward Bowen Lake through the dense spruce-fir forest. Ascend out of the valley, gradually at first, but then steeply. Bowen Lake is on the right (12). This is a wonderful lake with Cascade Mountain as its backdrop creating an amphitheater around the lake. Fishing is good and there are several great places to camp. Follow the trail south around the lake. The trail is a steep uphill climb with several switchbacks. At the ridge and fork (7), turn left and follow the inbound trail back to the trailhead (1).

Wolverine Mine Side Trip – At the fork (11), turn left and follow the trail over a creek to a clearing. At the clearing is an old road (11A) on the left. Turn left and follow this road where the trees have grown up through the gravel bed. This leads to the remains of the Wolverine Mine (11B). The mine has been filled in and lumber is strewn around the hillside where galena and sulfuret were once mined. Galena and sulfuret are used to make lead and silver. This is an additional 1.45 miles round-trip.

Creek along Bowen Gulch

205

Bowen Lake

Ruby Lake and Bowen Gulch

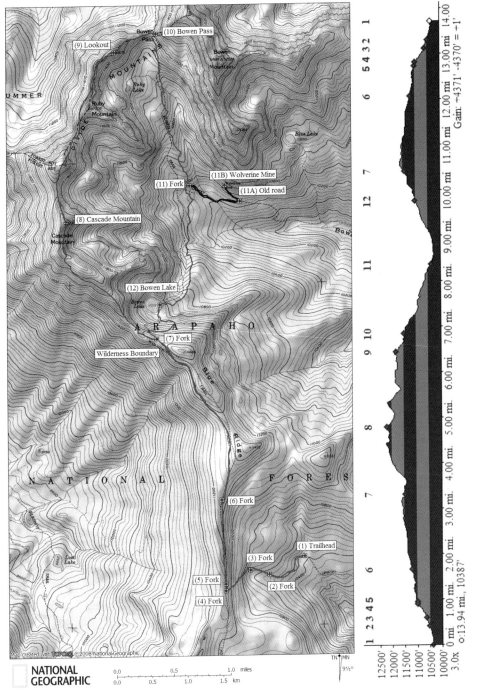

(9) Lookout

(10) Bowen Pass

Bowen
Pass

MOUNTAIN B

Bowen
Mountain

Ruby
Lake

UMMER

Ruby
Mountain

Blue Lake

DIVIDE

FOREST BDY
FOREST BDY

(11B) Wolverine Mine

(11) Fork

(11A) Old road

(8) Cascade Mountain

Cascade
Mountain

Bow

(12) Bowen Lake

Bowen
Lake

A R A P A H O

(7) Fork

Wilderness Boundary

Blue

N A T I O N A L

Blue
Ridge

F O R E S

(6) Fork

(1) Trailhead

(3) Fork

(5) Fork

(2) Fork

(4) Fork

Dodd
Lake

TRAIL

NATIONAL
GEOGRAPHIC

0.0   0.5   1.0   miles
0.0   0.5   1.0   1.5 km

TN MN

9½°

Gain: +4371', -4370' = -1'

0 mi   1.00 mi   2.00 mi   3.00 mi   4.00 mi   5.00 mi   6.00 mi   7.00 mi   8.00 mi   9.00 mi   10.00 mi   11.00 mi   12.00 mi   13.00 mi   14.00 mi

1 2 3 4 5   6   7   8   9 10   11   12   7   6   5 4 3 2 1

3.0x   o:13.94 mi., 10387'

12500'
12000'
11500'
11000'
10500'
10000'

62. BOWEN GULCH INTERPRETIVE TRAIL

Level of Difficulty - Easy
Round-trip Mileage – 1.22 miles
Round-trip Hiking Time – ½ hour
Altitude, GPS Reading at Trailhead – 10,467', 40°19'25"N, 105°54'30"W
Altitude, GPS Reading at Highest Point – 10,549', 40°19'11"N, 105°54'49"W
Trail Fee Required – No

🐾 Yes, 🐟 N/A, ▲ Yes, WD BG

Trailhead Location – On US Hwy 34, southwest of Grand Lake, between mile markers 9 and 10 turn west onto CR 4. Follow CR 4 for 3.0 miles. Take the right fork (CR 455 also FSR 120 also Kawuneeche Road) toward the Never Summer Wilderness for 7.9 miles to FSR 120.5. Follow this for 2.2 miles to the trailhead (1). CR 4 and CR 455 are good dirt roads. FSR 120.5 is rough for the first ¼ mile and a high clearance vehicle is recommended, but the remainder of the road is very good.

Trail Description – The Bowen Gulch Interpretive Trail is a great hike through an old growth spruce-fir forest that dates back as far as the 1500's. This is an easy hike with interpretive signs describing aspects of a mature spruce-forest. From the trailhead, walk down an old logging road to the first sign where there is a fork (2). The interpretive trail begins here. Take the left fork and follow the trail counter-clockwise.

The following information is copied from the "Bowen Gulch Interpretive Trail Guide" with permission of the USDA Forest Service, Sulphur Ranger District in Granby, Colorado. The pamphlet is available from the Granby office of the USDA Forest Service.

Trail Head – Sign 1
Bowen Gulch is a very special area in one of Colorado's largest spruce-fir old growth forests. From 1988-1990 there was a logging sale in this area. Public outcry stopped the sale. In August 1993, the Colorado Wilderness Act designated the "Bowen Gulch Protection Area" which protects Bowen Gulch from new road construction, logging, and mining.

Old Growth Forest Characteristics
Rocky Mountain Region – Sign 2
Old growth forests are unique ecosystems that are important for biological diversity. As you walk along the trail, look for these characteristics:
- Large, live trees
- Large standing dead trees which are home to insects and birds
- Large decaying trees lying on the ground
- A mix of young, medium-aged and old trees which form canopies at various heights

- Minimal evidence of disturbance from logging and fire
- Trees with broken tops or large cavities which provide nesting sites for birds and mammals

Tree Mortality – Sign 3
Tree death is an important part of the dynamics of an old growth forest. When a tree dies, it has served only one-third of its usefulness to the forest. Dead standing trees provide homes for a variety of insects, birds, and mammals. Fallen trees provide nutrients (decaying bark and wood) to the forest floor creating food and habitat for plants, insects and small mammals. When a tree falls, sunlight and space become available for existing trees and new growth.

Wildlife – Sign 4
The combination of wet (riparian) areas and old growth forests is very productive for wildlife. Many plants and animals, which depend on an old growth forest for part, or all, of their needs, are found in Bowen Gulch including pine-martens, boreal owls, goshawks, three-toed woodpeckers and red-backed voles.

Other wildlife found in this part of the Rocky Mountains include moose, elk, mule deer, coyote, red fox, red squirrel, osprey, mountain lion, black bear and mountain chickadee.

Rock Outcropping – Sign 5
Here is an old talus slope exposed at the bottom of a forested hill. Lichens and mosses grow on and between the rocks. Openings among the rocks provide cover for small mammals including mice, voles, and pikas.

Logging in Grand County – Sign 6
Hope of finding GOLD brought many people to Colorado. Most did not find gold, but some people found another resource – trees. As the railroad came through Grand County, logging camps flourished. Timber continues to be a valuable commodity in this area.

In 1891, the Forest Reserves, predecessor of the USDA Forest was created to manage federal lands and supply timber to the country. The Forest Service attempts to balance the need for timber with the health of forest ecosystems.

Timber Markings – Sign 7
You are in one of the cutting units of the former Bowen Gulch Timber Sale. The trees with the orange bands were scheduled to be cut. Trees with blue paint marked the boundaries of cutting units.

Riparian Zone – Sign 8
Water is a major ingredient in an old growth spruce-fir forest. Water from springs, snow melt, and rain seeps into the soils, into the dead and decaying material on the ground, and into dozens of small creeks. Creeks in old growth forests have low levels of

sedimentation (soil in the water) because the large mass of tree roots hold the soil in place. The wetness also protects the area from fires. Riparian areas provide very productive wildlife habitat because of the variety and number of plants, and the presence of water.

Meadow – Sign 9
A diversity of habitat within old growth forests is very valuable for wildlife. Meadows are wet, flat areas where the soil is too moist for tree growth. Notice the small trees at the edge of the meadow. If the meadow were slowly to dry out, trees would gradually replace the grasses.

Under Story Growth – Sign 10
Notice the trees of different ages, which form canopies of different heights. This characteristic of an old growth forest. The older trees form a high canopy, which protects and shades the younger trees and plants from the hot and drying effects of the sun.

Fire – Sign 11
In subalpine areas like Bowen Gulch, wildfire occurs every 500-1200 years. Because fire is infrequent, trees can grow to be very old. In this area the older spruce trees are more than 400 years old and the older fir trees are more than 300 years old.

The rare occurrence of fires along with the cool, north-facing slopes and wet soils are important factors in the development of an old growth forest.

Decomposition – Sign 12
Sometimes a fallen, decaying tree can become a nurse tree – a tree that provides nutrients so that a seedling is able to grow from it.

An important link between plants and animals is fungus. Many species of fungus thrive on fallen trees. Small mammals called Red-backed voles feed on fungus and distribute fungal spores in their droppings. These spores envelop roots and trees, share nutrients with the tree, and produce antibiotics, which protect the roots.

Re-Seeding Work – Sign 13
Before the logging sale was stopped, some roads were built into this area to bring logging equipment in and out. The road leading to this interpretive trail is an old logging road. Before leaving the areas, loggers built berms across the road to keep vehicles out. The logging company planted a special "Bowen Gulch" grass seed mix to help re-vegetate the area. As time passes, many new spruce and fir seedlings will grow.

Planning for the Future – Sign 14
Since old growth forests may be lost to fire, forest succession, wind and other natural factors, the Forest Service and other public agencies face a challenge to perpetuate old growth into the future.

Dateline – Sign 15

Many trees in the Bowen Gulch old growth area were alive during the following events:

- 1543 Copernicus publishes his work on the solar system.
- 1558 Elizabeth crowned Queen of England.
- 1588 Spanish Armada routed by the English Fleet.
- 1609 Galileo builds his telescope
- 1611 Shakespeare's "The Tempest" performed
- 1685 Birth of Johann S. Bach
- 1732 Birth of George Washington
- 1865 Civil War ends
- 1918 WW1 ends
- 1969 First humans land on the moon

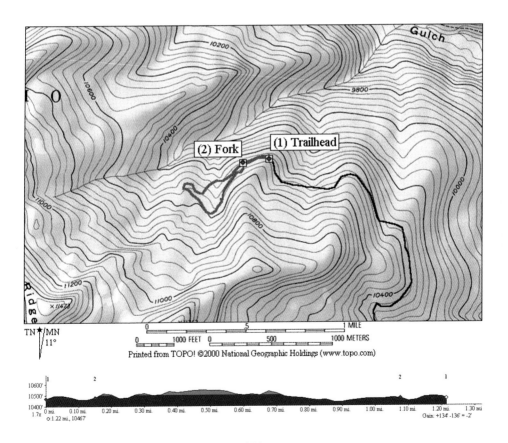

Printed from TOPO! ©2000 National Geographic Holdings (www.topo.com)

211

63. STILLWATER CREEK

Level of Difficulty - Moderate
One-way Mileage – 2.10 miles
One-way Hiking Time - 1 ½ hours
Altitude, GPS Reading at Trailhead – 8799', 40°13'40"N, 105°54'56"W
Altitude, GPS Reading at Destination – 9593', 40°15'06"N, 105°56'01"W
Trail Fee Required – No

🐾 Yes, 🐾 Yes, ▲ Yes, **WD** BG

Trailhead Location –
Access 1 – On US Hwy 34, southwest of Grand Lake, between mile markers 9 and 10, turn west onto CR 4 (FSR 123) for 4.5 miles. Turn right (north) onto an unmarked road for .2 miles. Park at the pullout near the end of the road (1). These are good dirt roads.
Access 2 – On CO 125, south of Willow Creek Pass, between mile markers 16 and 17, turn east onto CR 4 (FSR 123) for 18.1 miles. Turn left (north) onto an unmarked road for .2 miles. Park at the pullout near the end of the road (1). These are good dirt roads.

Trail Description – The trail along Stillwater Creek begins as a common trailhead for motorized vehicles. At the end of the road is a buck and rail fence. Pass around the fence and at the first fork, turn right. Follow this trail for a short distance up a steep hill to another fork and a buck and rail fence (2). Take the left fork around this fence where motorized vehicles are not permitted. This lodgepole pine forest quickly changes to a spruce-fir forest dotted with aspen trees. Approach Stillwater Creek, which is on the right and climb high above the creek. Climb through a few short steep sections. Cross Stillwater Creek and continue to parallel the creek. On a small knoll on the left is an old cabin overlooking the creek. This cabin is moderately preserved. Beyond the cabin is a shallow pond (3) surrounded by tall grass and trees with Apiatan Mountain behind it to the west. The larger pond beyond has dried up. The trail continues beside the creek, hugging the woods, but has no final destination.

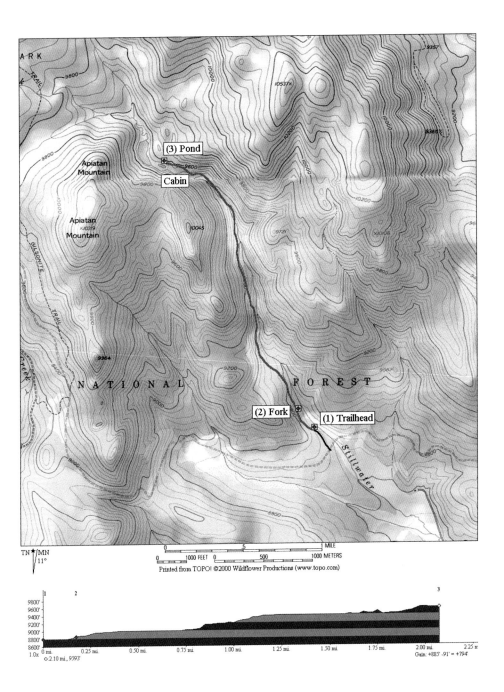

64. APIATAN MOUNTAIN

Level of Difficulty - Easy
One-way Mileage - .65 miles
One-way Hiking Time - ½ hour
Altitude, GPS Reading at Trailhead – 9948', 40°15'10"N, 105°56'37"W
Altitude, GPS Reading at Destination – 10,241', 40°14'46"N, 105°56'38"W
Trail Fee Required – No

🐾 Yes, 🛶 N/A, ▲ Yes, WD BG

Trailhead Location –
Access 1 – On US Hwy 34, southwest of Grand Lake, between mile markers 9 and 10, turn west onto CR 4 (FSR 123) for 8.9 miles. Turn right onto FSR 123-2B for .7 miles. Park at the end of the road at the pullout (1). The trailhead is unmarked. . CR 4 is a good dirt road, but FSR 123-2B is a rough road and a high clearance vehicle is recommended.
Access 2 – On CO 125, south of Willow Creek Pass, between mile markers 16 and 17, turn east onto CR 4 (FSR 123) for 13.7 miles. Turn left onto FSR 123-2B for .7 miles. Park at the end of the road at the pullout (1). The trailhead is unmarked. CR 4 is a good dirt road, but FSR 123-2B is a rough road and a high clearance vehicle is recommended.

Trail Description – Follow the road to the cliff (2) and turn right up the ridge. There is a faint trail through the woods to a steep rocky hillside. Hike up the hillside for a short distance where the trail is less steep and head back into the woods. Gradually ascend after this hill. Follow the ridgeline through the lodgepole pine forest where the trail is well worn in most places, but disappears in others. Follow the ridgeline to an open meadow, which is rocky and dotted with Englemann spruce trees. There is a large knoll ahead. Hike up to this false peak (3) where the views are limited and continue to the top of Apiatan Mountain. There are few trees on Apiatan Peak (4) and a short hike to the south provides a wonderful view. Looking north and clockwise are Porphyry Peaks, the mountains in Rocky Mountain National Park, Longs Peak, Mt. Craig, Shadow Mountain Lake, Lake Granby, the James Peak area, Winter Park Ski Resort, Sol Vista Ski Resort, the town of Granby, Byers Peak, the Gore Range, the Williams Fork Mountains, Elk Mountain and Corral Peaks in the Troublesome area, and Gravel Mountain.

Historical Note – Apiatan was the name of a Kiowa Indian chief who carried an apiatan (a ceremonial lance).

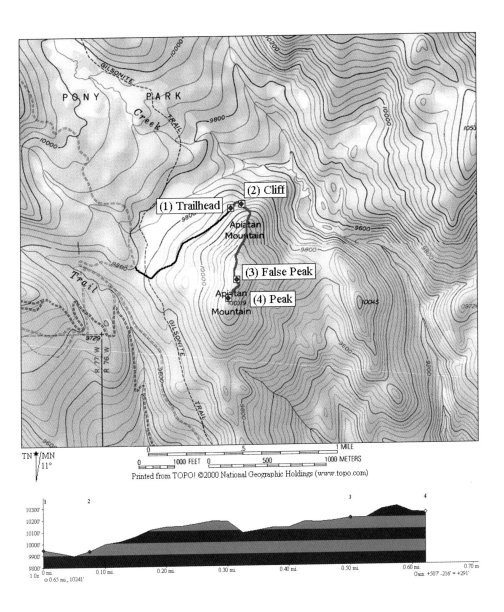

65. GRAVEL MOUNTAIN

Level of Difficulty - Difficult
One-way Mileage – 4.32 miles
One-way Hiking Time – 2 ½ hours
Altitude, GPS Reading at Trailhead – 10,502', 40°15'08"N, 105°58'59"W
Altitude, GPS Reading at Destination – 11,721', 40°16'32"N, 105°59'44"W
Trail Fee Required – No

🐕 Yes, ⋙ N/A, ▲ Yes, WD None

Trailhead Location –
Access 1 – On US Hwy 34, southwest of Grand Lake, between mile markers 9 and 10, turn west onto CR 4 (FSR 123) for 8.5 miles. Turn left onto FSR 190 toward Kauffman Creek for 2.2 miles and follow signs to Gravel Mountain. There is a trailhead on the left (1). CR 4 is a good dirt road, but FSR 190 is a very rough road recommended for high clearance vehicles only.
Access 2 – On CO 125, south of Willow Creek Pass, between mile markers 16 and 17, turn east onto CR 4 (FSR 123) for 14.1 miles. Turn right onto FSR 190 toward Kauffman Creek for 2.2 miles and follow signs to Gravel Mountain. There is a trailhead on the left (1). CR 4 is a good dirt road, but FSR 190 is a very rough road recommended for high clearance vehicles only.

Trail Description – Begin on an old logging road. Follow this main road to a secondary logging road, which forks to the right (2). This secondary road is distinct because not far from the fork is a very large tank trap. Pass around the tank trap and continue until the heavier grasses take over the road bed. Prior to the road disappearing in the tall grass, there is a faint jeep road, which forks to the right (3). Follow this faint jeep road, pass around a fallen tree blocking the road, and climb up the hill. Continue through the woods where the trees thin and the meadows widen. Englemann spruce trees line the edges of the meadow and the trail climbs steadily to timberline. The jeep road is filled with loose cobblestones, making footing unstable. The spruce trees stunt and the trail blends in with the grass fading near the ridgeline. When the trail fades completely, follow the ridgeline to the top of Little Gravel Mountain (4). The top is covered in large half buried boulders, short grasses, and lichen covered rocks. From the top of Little Gravel Mountain looking north and clockwise are Gravel Mountain, Blue Ridge, and Porphyry Peaks. To the east are Longs Peak, Shadow Mountain Lake, Lake Granby, the James Peak area, Sol Vista Ski Area, the town of Granby, the Vasquez Mountains, the Williams Fork Mountains, the Gore Range, Elk Mountain, Corral Peaks, the Troublesome Valley, Haystack Mountain, Parkview Mountain, North Park, and Radial Mountain.

From Little Gravel Mountain, continue north and follow the ridgeline down into a cluster of trees at the saddle between Little Gravel Mountain and Gravel Mountain. Pass through the forest, where small to medium boulders cover the ground, and of course gravel. Englemann spruce trees grow stunted on the ridgeline and on the slope to the left. The right slope is steep and rocky, but the taller spruce and fir trees grow further below. A shelf at the base of Gravel Mountain extending to Little Gravel Mountain is on the right, the result of glacial carving. Gravel Mountain is ahead, although there is no visible trail on the ridgeline. Continue up the hill where the grade increases, then levels off, and then ascends to the Gravel Mountain summit (5). From the top of Gravel Mountain, looking north and clockwise are North Park, Cascade Mountain and the Never Summer Range, the mountains in Rocky Mountain National Park, Porphyry Peaks, Longs Peak in the distance, Shadow Mountain Lake, Lake Granby, the James Peak area, the Winter Park Ski Resort, Sol Vista Ski Resort, the town of Granby, Willow Creek Reservoir, and the Vasquez Mountains. From the south and continuing clockwise are the Williams Fork Mountains with the Gore Range in the distance, Little Gravel Mountain, Elk Mountain, Corral Peaks, the Troublesome Valley, Haystack Mountain, Parkview Mountain, and Radial Mountain.

For an alternate return route, return to the saddle between Gravel Mountain and Little Gravel Mountain. Upon entering the woods there is a trail that runs to the left (6), traversing down the hillside. Take this trail through the woods to the base of the mountain. Continue to traverse the hillside just above the wetland along the shelf. The trail is faint, but remain between the wetland and the mountain base, back into the woods where the trail is well worn. In the woods the trail is faint, but hike downhill a short distance to the logging road. At the logging road, turn left and return to the trailhead (1).

Historical Note – Local residents gave Gravel Mountain its name for obvious reasons. The Colorado Geographic Board decided to rename the mountain Bennay after an Indian. The local residents objected strongly to this change and the name was returned to Gravel. Both names appear on many maps today.

Wild Mushrooms (not edible)

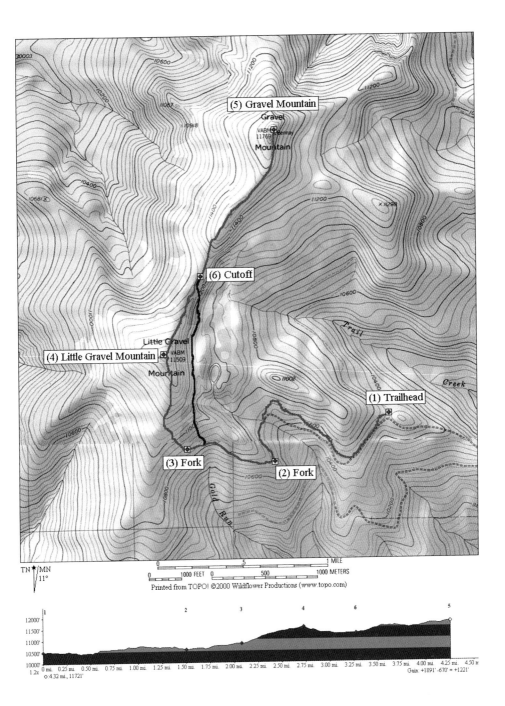

66. LOST LAKE

Level of Difficulty - Easy
One-way Mileage - .68 miles
One-way Hiking Time – ½ hour
Altitude, GPS Reading at Trailhead – 9454', 40°18'24"N, 105°57'59"W
Altitude, GPS Reading at Destination – 9658', 40°18'02"N, 105°57'38"W
Trail Fee Required – No

🐾 Yes, 🥾 Yes, ▲ Yes, WD BG

Trailhead Location –
Access 1 – On US Hwy 34, southwest of Grand Lake, between mile markers 9 and 10, turn west onto CR 4 (FSR 123) for 16.9 miles. Turn right onto FSR 123.3 for .7 miles. Follow signs for Lost Lake. The trailhead is at the end of the road (1). These are good dirt roads.
Access 2 – On CO 125, south of Willow Creek Pass, between mile markers 16 and 17, turn east onto CR 4 (FSR 123) for 5.7 miles. Turn left onto FSR 123.3 for .7 miles. Follow signs for Lost Lake. The trailhead is at the end of the road (1). These are good dirt roads.

Trail Description – Both the Gilsonite (Bike) Trail and the Wolverine Bypass (Bike) Trail use this same trailhead. Begin in a somewhat open montane forest. A short distance from the trailhead, cross into the Bowen Gulch Protection Area. At the first fork and trail marker (2), the left fork heads toward the Wolverine Bypass Trail and the right fork continues toward Lost Lake. Take the right fork to the top of the hill. Hike down the hill and view Porphyry Peaks across the meadow. Pass two small meadows to the next fork and trail marker (3). The right fork leads to the Gilsonite Trail. Continue straight and gently ascend through the woods to the next fork and trail marker (4). The Wolverine Trail continues left at the fork. Turn right and cross the creek. Hike uphill through the dense spruce-fir forest, where a high canopy provides shade. It is rocky through this section to the top where Lost Lake (5) lies surrounded by trees and boulders. Across the lake (southwest), Gravel Mountain stands in the distance. There is an unmaintained trail around the lake that is an additional .45 miles. It is easy to follow, but the trail crosses over many boulders. Across the lake to the east are Porphyry Peaks and to the north is Cascade Mountain.

Historical Note – Lost Lake was originally called Lake Solitaire

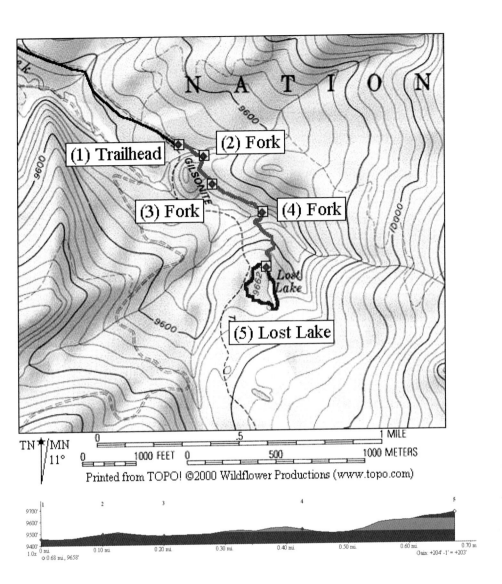

67. BILL CREEK

Level of Difficulty - Moderate
One-way Mileage – 3.48 miles
One-way Hiking Time – 2 hours
Altitude, GPS Reading at Trailhead – 9114', 40°19'46"N, 106°00'17"W
Altitude, GPS Reading at Destination – 9994', 40°22'11"N, 106°00'43"W
Trail Fee Required – No

🐾 Yes, 🐟 N/A, ▲ Yes, WD None

Trailhead Location –
Access 1 – On US Hwy 34, southwest of Grand Lake, between mile markers 9 and 10, turn west onto CR 4 (FSR 123) for 19.2 miles. Make a sharp right at the fork and continue for .4 miles. There is a trailhead marker on the left side of the road (1). Park at the wide spot in the road. There are private property signs, but the trailhead is prior to the private property. These are good dirt roads.
Access 2 – On CO 125, south of Willow Creek Pass, between mile markers 16 and 17, turn east onto CR 4 (FSR 123) for 3.5 miles. The road forks. Take the left fork and continue for .4 miles. There is a trailhead marker on the left side of the road (1). Park at the wide spot in the road. There are private property signs, but the trailhead is prior to the private property. These are good dirt roads.

Trail Description – This is a beautiful hike through the woods, but the view from the pass is obstructed due to the large size and number of trees. Hike up the short steep incline to the top of a knoll and back down to the barbed wire fence (2). This fence denotes the private property of Vagabond Guest Ranch. Please do not trespass inside the fence. At the fence, turn left and at the corner fence post, turn right. Follow the fence and pass the Vagabond Guest Ranch with its many solar panels and satellite dishes. Continue through the sage and lodgepole pine forested hillside until a small pond and cabin are visible on the right in the valley (3). At this point, leave the fence and make a sharp left up the hill. The trail previously crossed onto the Vagabond property at this point. Hike uphill a little left of north on the faint trail where it joins up with a well worn trail in the woods. The trail levels off slightly in the woods. Parallel the creek for a short distance and climb steadily through the montane forest. Cross the foot bridge, which is in poor condition. Continue to ascend higher and higher. Finally descend and cross over two more foot bridges, which are also both quite deteriorated. At a grassy clearing, the trail intersects the CD Trail and Ruby Mountain Trail (4). Turn left and follow the ridgeline north to Illinois Pass and the Illinois Pass Trail (5), (also accessible from FSR 123). This pass was used as a stock trail over the Continental Divide.

The Vagabond Ranch (also called the Cascade Ranch due to of its proximity to Cascade Mountain) was a youth camp in the 1950's and 1960's.

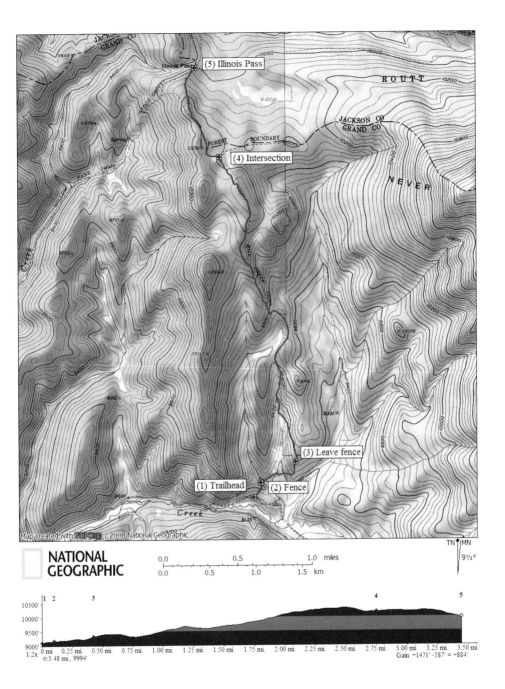

223

Parkview Mountain

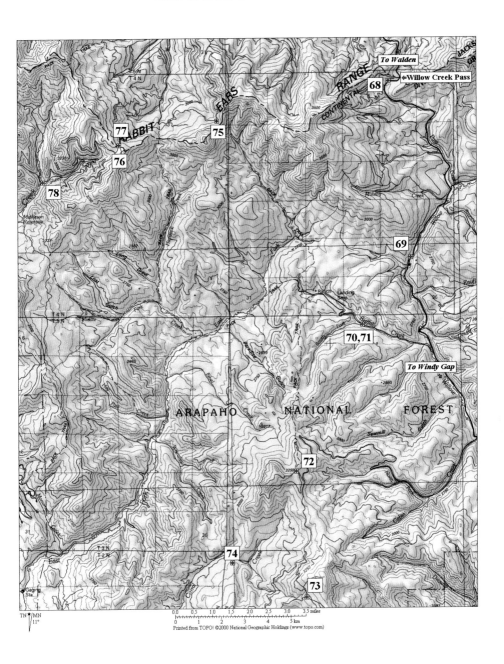

68. PARKVIEW MOUNTAIN AND LOOKOUT HOUSE 🚙 🚙

Level of Difficulty - Difficult
Round-trip Mileage – 10.07 miles
Round-trip Hiking Time – 6 hours
Altitude, GPS Reading at Trailhead – 9494', 40°20'56"N, 106°05'44"W
Altitude, GPS Reading at Destination – 12,265', 40°19'49"N, 106°08'10"W
Trail Fee Required – No

🐕 Yes, 🐟 N/A, ▲ Yes, WD None

Trailhead Location – This is a one-way hike requiring two vehicles.
1ˢᵗ Car Parking - On CO 125, south of Willow Creek Pass, between mile markers 16 and 17 on the west side of the highway is a jeep road, FSR 258-1. Park on the side of the highway at the Mulstay Jeep Road (10).
2ⁿᵈ Car Parking – On CO 125, south of Willow Creek Pass, between mile markers 21 and 22 on the west side of the highway is a jeep road, FSR 266-1H. Park at the pullout (1).

Both jeep roads FSR 258-1 and 266-1H are passable by jeep or high clearance vehicle. However, 266-1H is very steep and narrow and FSR 258-1 is very rough, not well marked, and has many high water bars. It is recommended to park beside the highway and continue on foot.

Trail Description – From the trailhead, follow the jeep road up the hill to the fork (2) and "Trail" sign on the right. This trail sign points to the southern route of the CD Trail. Turn left at the fork along the jeep road and follow the CD Trail to the north. Begin in a thick montane forest. It is a steady uphill climb. At the next fork (3), bear left. The road to the right leads to a camp. At a brief clearing in the trees is a view of the James Peak area. The trees change to Englemann spruce in this subalpine zone. This jeep road intersects another jeep road (4). At the "T", turn left and continue to the next fork (5). Remain right at this fork. Continue to climb in elevation and follow a long switchback. After the switchback, there is a great view of the Parkview Mountain bowl and the Lookout House on top. At the next fork (6), there is an old mine on the right, a road ahead, and a road on the left. Take the left road and cross the creek. The jeep road fades and the trail is passable only on foot. The trees thin quickly and the terrain changes to tundra grasses and scree, making footing unstable. Ascend through the center of the bowl and after the switchback, head south. The trail is difficult to find, but cairns lead the way. At the ridgeline of the bowl, pass through the stunted Englemann spruce trees and view the next valley below. This valley is encountered on the return route. Climb steeply up the ridgeline. The alpine flowers are abundant above timberline and are enjoyable to look at on this difficult ascent. The trail is not worn, but several cairns are visible above. Avoid walking single file through this area to reduce the impact on the fragile soil. Follow the ridgeline to the crest, where it intersects another ridgeline (7).

The Troublesome Valley is ahead and the Lookout House is on the right. Turn right toward the Lookout House to the top of Parkview Mountain (8). From the summit looking north and clockwise are North Park, Ruby Lake, the Never Summer Range, Radial Mountain, Parika Peak, Farview Mountain, Bowen Mountain, and Ruby Mountain. To the east are Cascade Mountain and Longs Peak. Continuing clockwise are the Indian Peaks Range, the James Peak area, Byers Peak, and Ute Peak. From the south and clockwise are Elk Mountain, Searight Mountain, and Corral Peaks, the Gore Range, the Troublesome Valley below, Grimes Peak, Sheep Mountain, Haystack Mountain, the Rabbit Ears Range, and the town of Rand.

The return route is not as steep and more leisurely. Follow the wooden tripod shaped winter trail markers southeast and descend across the tundra. The winter trail markers lead to the forest. At the edge of the forest, on the right is the Parkview Mountain Trailhead (9). Pass through the gate and into the forest to a jeep road. Follow this jeep road through a beautiful spruce forest. There are several side roads, but remain on the main road and continue to descend. The spruce forest gives way to the lodgepole pine trees. The forest floor is carpeted with lush undergrowth. Continue through the woods to a clearing of willows and cinquefoil. Behind the willows is Mulstay Creek on the right. Finally, the remains of an old cabin are on the right prior to reaching CO 125 (10).

Historical Note – The Lookout House was built as a watchtower for forest fires and was accessed from the Gilsonite Ranger Station, originally located just off CO 125 south of the Mulstay Jeep Road.

Note - The area between (9) and (10) is being logged. Please consult USDA Forest Service (970) 887-4100 for details.

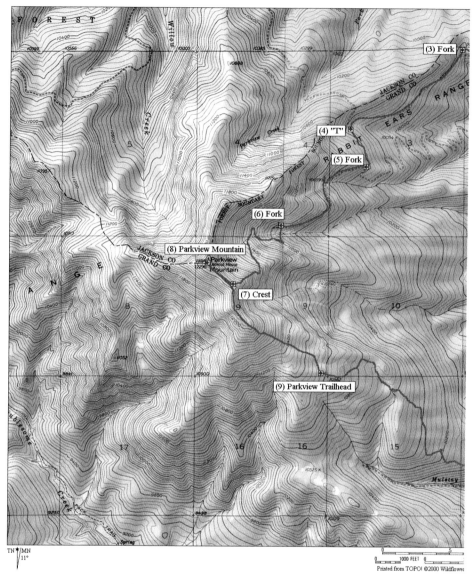

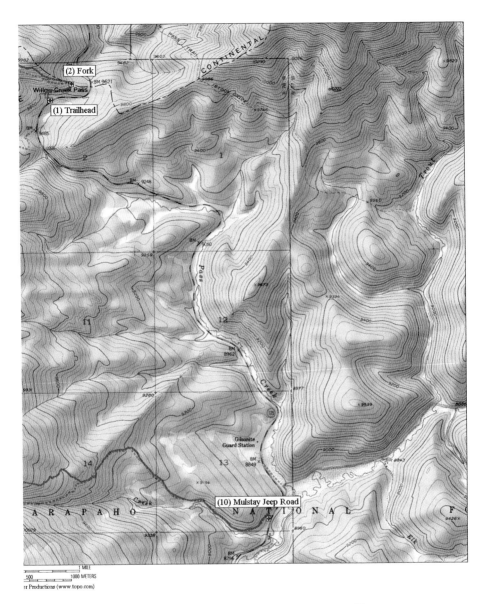

(2) Fork
Willow Creek Pass
BM 9621
(1) Trailhead
Gilsonite
Guard Station
(10) Mulstay Jeep Road
A R A P A H O   N A T I O N A L   F O

1 MILE
500   1000 METERS
er Productions (www.topo.com)

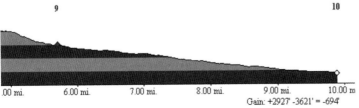

9   10

.00 mi.   6.00 mi.   7.00 mi.   8.00 mi.   9.00 mi.   10.00 m

Gain: +2927' -3621' = -694'

69. TRAIL CREEK, EAST FORK TROUBLESOME CREEK, HAYSTACK CREEK, AND MIDDLE FORK CREEK LOOP ☽

Level of Difficulty - Difficult
Round-trip Mileage – 23.67 miles
Round-trip Hiking Time – 3 days
Altitude, GPS Reading at Trailhead – 8661', 40°16'57"N, 106°05'04"W
Altitude, GPS Reading at Highest Point – 9926', 40°18'45"N, 106°11'12"W
Trail Fee Required – No

🐾 Yes, 🐟 Yes, ▲ Yes, **WD** None

Trailhead Location – On CO 125, south of Willow Creek Pass, between mile markers 14 and 15 is a parking area on the east side of the highway across Willow Creek. Directly west of the parking area is the trailhead (1).

Trail Description – Climb steeply through the sagebrush hillside into the lodgepole pine forest. The trail levels off after a short distance and follows the edge of a sagebrush meadow. There is a series of beaver ponds (2) and at the end of the last pond, before the small creek is a faint fork (3) on the right. Turn right and follow the creek upstream. This is the North Trail Creek Trail. The creek is lined with willows. Keep the creek on the left side of the trail. At the outfitter's camp (4) in the woods, the trail fades, but head north away from the creek where it will reappear. Continue through a stand of trees surrounded by two meadows to a sage meadow. Skirt the woods through the meadow and head west. Follow the trail into the woods to another camp (5). To the west is a very large sage and cinquefoil meadow. From the camp, head south through the sage to the edge of the woods to a trail (6). Left leads to the South Trail Creek Trail (21). Turn right and skirt the left edge of the large meadow. A great view of Parkview Mountain is visible across the meadow. Follow the trail through the woods into a meadow with cinquefoil and grass. Across the valley is a view of Haystack Mountain. Follow a fence uphill to a gate (7). Pass through the gate into the valley that was viewed from above. Follow the willow lined creek through the narrowing valley. There is a sage and aspen covered hillside on the right and a dense forest on the left. At the fork (8), the North Trail Creek Trail ends and intersects the Elk Mountain Trail. The left fork leads to the South Trail Creek Trail, (20). Continue straight to the next fork and trail marker (9). The Elk Mountain Trail ends and intersects the Troublesome Creek Trail. The left fork follows the East Fork Troublesome Creek downstream to (18). Take the right fork and follow the East Fork Troublesome Creek upstream. Around the bend is another fork. Both forks join 50' ahead, but the left fork is easier.

Parallel the creek and gently ascend through forests and meadows. There are a couple of small ponds near the creek and a couple of springs on the side of the trail. At the next fork (10) turn left, cross the East Fork Troublesome Creek, and head into the woods. This is a predominantly mature spruce and fir forest, but it changes back to a lodgepole pine forest again along the trail. At the next clearing is another good view of Haystack

Mountain. At the post in the meadow (11), make a sharp left. Head toward the second post. At the fork just past the second post, turn right and head into the woods. Wind through the woods and meadows and climb above the creek. There is another meadow with another post (12). Continue straight through this meadow to the post. From the post, count 35 paces up the hill. Make a sharp left turn and the trail will reappear in the woods. Continue through the woods where there are a few peek-a-boo views of the valley below and of Sheep Mountain. Descend and move away from Haystack Mountain. At the next fork and trail marker (13), Haystack Creek Trail is on the left and Troublesome Pass is straight ahead. Turn left and gently descend.

Across a very large meadow is a view of Corral Peaks in the distance. Pass through several aspen stands and lodgepole pine forests. Parallel Haystack Creek, which is on the left. The meadow is long and wide, but narrows when the trail nears Haystack Creek. At the creek, the willows and River Birch grow profusely in the moist terrain. When the valley widens, cross Haystack Creek. Further down the trail is a large pile of rocks on the right and a short distance further is a fork and trail marker (14). The Middle Fork Troublesome Creek Trail is on the right, but continue straight. Haystack Creek flows into the Middle Fork Creek here. Follow the trail into the large sage meadow where the willows line the creek on the right. Searight Mountain and Corral Peaks are visible ahead. The next fork does not have a trail marker (15), but the right fork crosses Middle Fork Creek and continues into the woods. This is a short cut leading downstream to the East Fork Troublesome Creek. Remain straight on the trail between the sage hillside and the willows along the creek. Middle Fork Creek flows into the East Fork Troublesome Creek. At the next fork (16), the Troublesome Creek Trail is on the right coming up the East Fork Troublesome Creek and merges with this trail. Continue straight and cross the East Fork Troublesome Creek. Cattle graze freely in this area and many cattle trails have been worn, but follow the main trail into the woods. At a sage meadow, there is a fork and trail marker (17) identifying the Paradise Creek Trail on the right. Continue straight through the sage meadow into the woods and parallel the East Fork Troublesome Creek where there is a great view of Parkview Mountain and the Lookout House on the top. The next fork and trail marker (18) identifies the Troublesome Creek Trail straight and the Troublesome Cutoff on the right. Take the right fork up the long steep hill into the woods. After a short descent, the cutoff ends at a "T" (19) and intersects the Elk Mountain Trail. Turn left and head uphill through a large stand of mature aspens. There is an unmarked fork on the left with a Forest Service sign in the distance. Bear right. The next fork (20) identifies the Elk Mountain Trail on the left and (South) Trail Creek Trail on the right. Take the right fork, where there is a great view of Parkview Mountain. Pass through the woods into a great meadow with tall grasses and cinquefoil bushes. Hug the edge of the meadow where the tall grass is replaced with sage. At the unmarked fork on the left (21), remain straight and continue to hug the edge of the meadow. When the trail approaches Trail Creek, the valley narrows. The willows are abundant along the creek. At the next fork (22), the right trail crosses the creek, but remain left and keep the creek on the right. Cross over a hill to another drainage, cross the creek (3), and follow the inbound trail back to the trailhead (1).

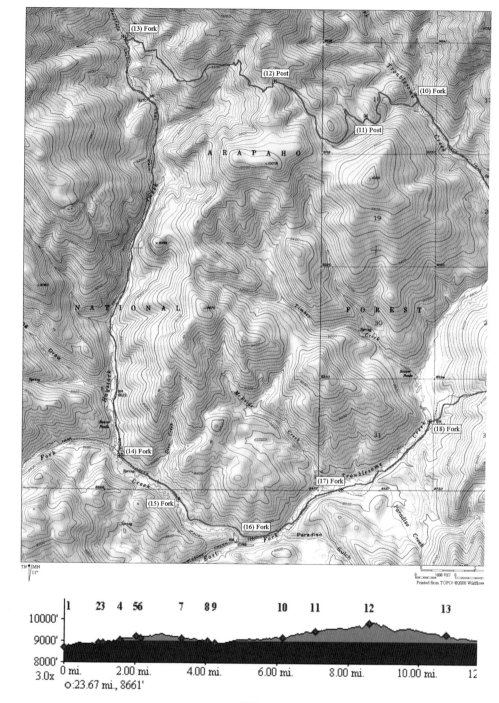

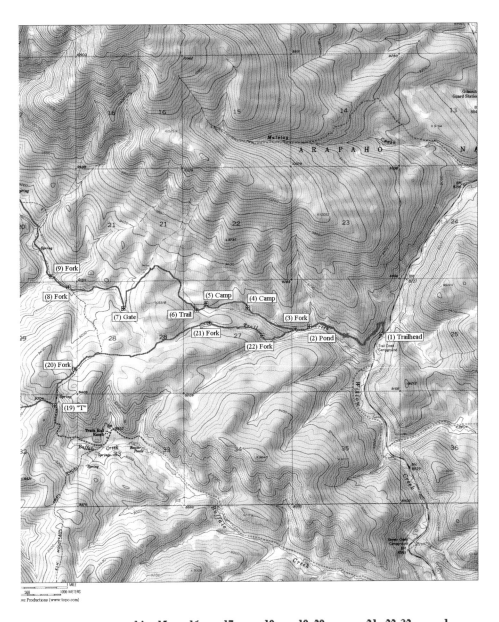

(9) Fork

(8) Fork

(5) Camp
(4) Camp

(7) Gate
(6) Trail
(3) Fork

(21) Fork
(2) Pond
(1) Trailhead

(20) Fork
(22) Fork

(19) "T"

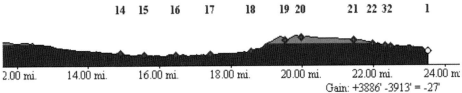

14   15   16   17   18   19 20   21 22 32   1

2.00 mi.   14.00 mi.   16.00 mi.   18.00 mi.   20.00 mi.   22.00 mi.   24.00 m:

Gain: +3886' -3913' = -27'

233

70. LOOKOUT POINT AND BUFFALO PARK LOOP

Level of Difficulty – Moderate
Round-trip Mileage – 7.98 miles
Round-trip Hiking Time – 5 ½ hours
Altitude, GPS Reading at Trailhead – 8776', 40°15'26"N, 106°06'33"W
Altitude, GPS Reading at Lookout Point – 9821', 40°14'09"N, 106°08'44"W
Trail Fee Required – No

🐾 Yes, 🐎 N/A, ▲ Yes, **WD** None

Trailhead Location – On CO 125, south of Willow Creek Pass, between mile markers 11 and 12 there is a road on the west side of the highway signed for King Mountain Ranch (FSR 108). Follow this road for 2.1 miles to the parking area on the right. Begin at the Bill Miller Trailhead (1) on the left side of the road. FSR 108 is a good dirt road.

Trail Description – Begin with a steady climb, traversing a sage hillside into a lodgepole pine forest. Descend and cross a creek (2). There are several side trails, but remain on the main trail and head uphill into the forest. At the first main fork and trail marker (3) the Paradise Creek Trail is on the left and the Bill Miller Trail is on the right. Follow the Paradise Creek Trail through the forest and climb steadily to the next fork and trail marker (4). Elk Mountain Trail is on the left and Paradise Creek Trail is on the right. Turn left and follow the Elk Mountain Trail through the woods. Climb to the next fork and trail marker (5). This sign identifies Lookout Point to the right and Elk Mountain Trail on the left. Take the right fork toward Lookout Point. Climb up to a ridge where there are many stunted aspen trees and pass an old camp to Lookout Point (6). Corral Peaks is straight ahead (south), Searight Mountain, the Continental Divide, Longs Peak, and Elk Mountain are on the left, Grimes Peak, Sheep Mountain, and Haystack Mountain are on the right, and Paradise Gulch is below.

Return to the fork (5) and turn right onto the Elk Mountain Trail. At the end of the aspen stand is a clearing. This clearing is the upper end of Buffalo Park. Cross the clearing to the trail marker at the base of the hill (7) identifying the Buffalo Park (Creek) Trail to the right and left and the Elk Mountain Trail up the hill. Turn left into the park and parallel the South Fork Buffalo Creek. Keep the creek on the right. Pass between the sage and cinquefoil meadow and the willows along the creek. Cross the creek and head into the woods. Hug the forest for the remainder of the trail to the Buffalo Park (Creek) Trailhead (8) near the Bill Miller Trailhead (1).

Historical Note – Bill Miller was a local rancher in the area.

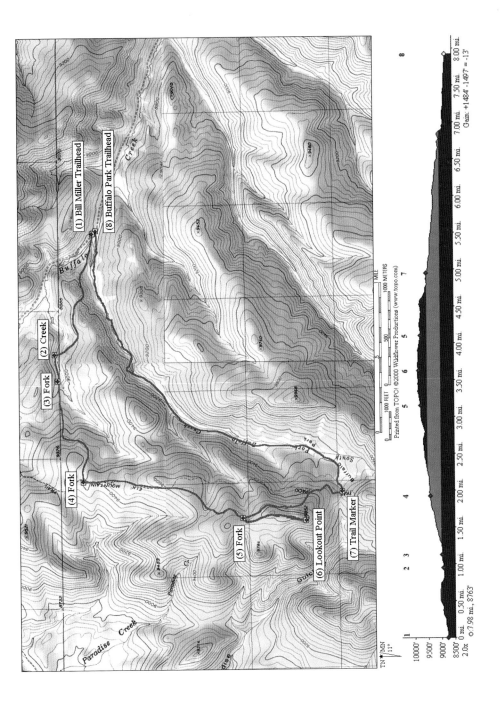

(1) Bill Miller Trailhead
(8) Buffalo Park Trailhead
(2) Creek
(3) Fork
(4) Fork
(5) Fork
(6) Lookout Point
(7) Trail Marker

Buffalo Creek
Buffalo Creek
South Fork Buffalo Park
ELK MOUNTAIN
Paradise Creek
Pinnacle Cr
Gulch

Printed from TOPO! @2000 Wildflower Productions (www.topo.com)

1000 FEET
1000 METERS
MILE

TN MN
11°

10000'
9500'
9000'
8500'

0 mi.   0.50 mi.   1.00 mi.   1.50 mi.   2.00 mi.   2.50 mi.   3.00 mi.   3.50 mi.   4.00 mi.   4.50 mi.   5.00 mi.   5.50 mi.   6.00 mi.   6.50 mi.   7.00 mi.   7.50 mi.   8.00 mi.
2.0x   ⋄ 7.98 mi, 8763'   Gain: +1484' -1497' = -13'

235

71. SEARIGHT MOUNTAIN LOOP

Level of Difficulty - Difficult
Round-trip Mileage – 11.44 miles
Round-trip Hiking Time – 6 ½ hours
Altitude, GPS Reading at Trailhead – 8776', 40°15'26"N, 106°06'33"W
Altitude, GPS Reading at Destination – 10,704', 40°12'28"N, 106°08'34"W
Trail Fee Required – No

🐾 Yes, 🐟 N/A, ▲ Yes, WD None

Trailhead Location –See Lookout Point and Buffalo Park Loop Trailhead (1), Hike #70, page 234.

Trail Description – Follow the Lookout Point and Buffalo Park Loop Hike #70, page 234 description to (5). This sign identifies Lookout Point to the right and Elk Mountain Trail on the left. Follow the Elk Mountain Trail left. At the end of the aspen stand is a clearing. This clearing is the upper end of Buffalo Park. Cross the clearing to the trail marker at the base of the hill (6) identifying the Buffalo Park (Creek) Trail to the right and left and the Elk Mountain Trail up the hill. From the sign, hike straight up the hill on a faded trail, just a little left of south for 50 paces. At a small red marker on a tree the worn trail reappears. Follow this trail through the woods and continue to ascend. The trail is quite steep for a short section with a few switchbacks. There is a clearing with a great view of Parkview Mountain to the far right, then Haystack Mountain, Sheep Mountain, Grimes Peak, and the Troublesome Valley below. After a short distance, Corral Peaks is visible ahead. Head into the wood, where the trail levels off slightly and then gradually descend. When the main trail bends left, a faint trail continues straight (7). The main trail leads to FSR 112. Follow the straight (south) trail toward Searight Mountain. Ascend steeply up several switchbacks. The Englemann spruce trees are stunted due to the harsh winds and high altitude. The hillside is bare and provides a great view to the west. Continue across the hillside to the top of Searight Mountain (8) with a view straight ahead of the north peak of Corral Peaks. Looking clockwise from Corral Peaks are the Wolford Reservoir, Slide Mountain, Grimes Peak, the East Fork Cow Camp in the East Fork Troublesome Creek Drainage, Rabbit Ear Range, Sheep Mountain, Haystack Mountain, and Parkview Mountain. There are peek-a-boo view to the east of Radial Mountain, the Never Summer Range, and the Continental Divide extending to Berthoud Pass.

Return to the Buffalo Park Trail marker (6). Turn right into the park and parallel the South Fork Buffalo Creek. Keep the creek on the right. Pass between the sage and cinquefoil meadow and the willows along the creek. Cross the creek and head into the woods. Hug the forest for the remainder of the trail to the Buffalo Park (Creek) Trailhead (9) near the Bill Miller Trailhead (1).

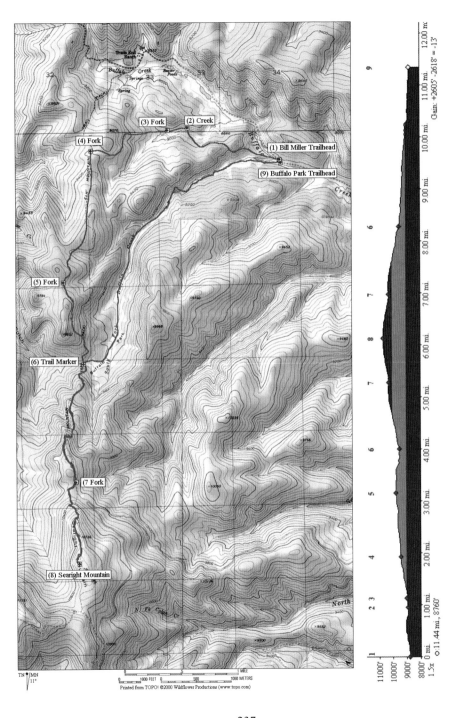

(3) Fork
(2) Creek
(4) Fork
(1) Bill Miller Trailhead
(9) Buffalo Park Trailhead
(5) Fork
(6) Trail Marker
(7 Fork
(8) Searight Mountain

Gain: +2605'-2618' = -13'
o 11.44 mi, 8760'
1.5x
1000 FEET
500
1000 METERS
MILE
Printed from TOPO! ©2000 Wildflower Productions (www.topo.com)

TN / MN
11°

72. CORRAL PEAKS LOOP

Level of Difficulty - Moderate
Round-trip Mileage – 3.04 miles
Round-trip Hiking Time – 2 ½ hours
Altitude, GPS Reading at Trailhead – 10,666', 40°12'07"N, 106°08'35"W
Altitude, GPS Reading at 1st Peak – 11,206', 40°11'46"N, 106°09'30"W
Altitude, GPS Reading at 2nd Peak – 11,164, 40°12'12"N, 106°09'13"W
Trail Fee Required – No

🐾 Yes, 🐟 N/A, ▲ Yes, WD None

Trailhead Location

Access 1 – On CO 125, north of the Windy Gap Wildlife Viewing Area, between mile markers 9 and 10 is Cabin Creek Divide (FSR 112) to the west. Follow FSR 112 for 10 miles. FSR 112 is a good dirt road. FSR 112-1A is on the right. The trailhead is .3 miles up this very rough jeep road. Either park on the side of the road and walk to the trailhead or drive up the jeep road and park at the right fork. The trailhead is at the left fork (1). *Access 2* - On US Hwy 40, just west of Parshall between mile markers 194 and 195, head north on CR 21 (FSR 112). Follow FSR 112 for 15.5 miles. FSR 112 is a good dirt road. At one point, FSR 12 forks to the left with a sign pointing to Corral Peaks. This road rejoins FSR 112 ahead, but FSR 112 has a great overlook near a small cabin next to the road. After 15.5 miles, FSR 112-1A is on the left. The trailhead is .3 miles up this very rough jeep road. Either park on the side of the road and walk to the trailhead or drive up the jeep road and park at the right fork. The trailhead is at the left fork (1).

Trail Description – Immediately after the trailhead, the trail forks. Take the left fork and follow the old jeep road up through the woods. At an opening in the trees along the hillside, there is a great view of Elk Mountain, Lake Granby, and the Continental Divide. Continue through the woods to a large meadow (2). Follow the jeep road to the left into the woods. At the base of the peak, the jeep road disappears and a single-track trail is on the right. Traverse the hillside, climb up a couple of short switchbacks, and follow the ridgeline to the top of the 1st Corral Peak (3). From the summit is a 360° view including the entire Troublesome Valley. Looking south and clockwise are the Williams Fork Mountains with the Gore Range behind them, Williams Fork Reservoir, and Grouse Mountain in the foreground. Next is the town of Kremmling and Gore Canyon. Continuing clockwise are Slide Mountain in the foreground, Wolford Reservoir, the East Fork Troublesome Valley, the East Fork Cow Camp below, Rabbit Ears Range, Sheep Mountain, Poison Ridge, Haystack Mountain, and Parkview Mountain. Next are Radial Mountain, the Never Summer Range, Porphyry Peaks, the Continental Divide, Shadow Mountain Lake, Longs Peak, Indian Peaks, the James Peak area, Elk Mountain in the foreground, Byers Peak, and Ute Peak.

To reach the 2nd Corral Peak return to the meadow (2) and instead of turning right, back into the woods, continue straight. The trail is faint, but head north through the meadows and trees. Cross over the boulders to the top of the 2nd Corral Peak (4). The ridge to the northeast is Searight Mountain.

Return to the meadow (2), turn left into the woods and follow the inbound trail back to the trailhead (1).

Historical Note – Corral Peaks was named after George Corral who was a homesteader in the area.

Note – Per the USDA Forest Service, access to this hike is scheduled to be decommissioned. Please consult USDA Forest Service (970) 887-4100 for details.

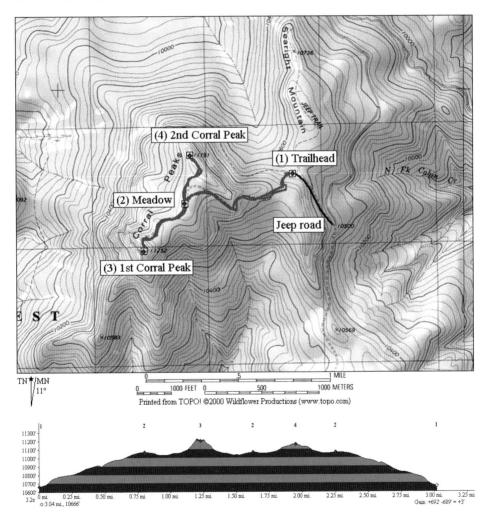

73. ELK MOUNTAIN LOOP

Level of Difficulty - Moderate
Round-trip Mileage – 2.68 miles
Round-trip Hiking Time – 2 hours
Altitude, GPS Reading at Trailhead – 10,577', 40º09'16"N, 106º08'17"W
Altitude, GPS Reading at Peak – 11,332', 40º09'43"N, 106º07'42"W
Trail Fee Required – No

🐕 Yes, 🐎 N/A, ▲ Yes, WD None

Trailhead Location –
Access 1 – On CO 125, north of the Windy Gap Wildlife Viewing Area, between mile markers 9 and 10 is Cabin Creek Divide (FSR 112) to the west. Follow FSR 112 for 14.7 miles to a logging road on the left. Follow this logging road for 1.4 miles (1). Park on the side of the road. These are good dirt roads.
Access 2 - On US Hwy 40, just west of Parshall, between mile markers 194 and 195, head north on CR 21 (FSR 112). Follow FSR 112 for 10.8 miles to the logging road on the right. Follow this logging road for 1.4 miles (1). Park on the side of the road. These are good dirt roads.

Trail Description – This is a short hike with spectacular views of the Continental Divide and Grand County. The trailhead is not identified, but begin on the old logging road on the left. Follow the logging road through the forest. It abruptly ends at a tank trap. Just prior to this tank trap is a small clearing (2) on the right. Turn into the clearing and hike uphill, where there is a large meadow on the right. The lodgepole pine forest quickly changes to a subalpine forest of spruce and fir trees. Ascend through the center of the meadow and follow a set of faint jeep tracks. The surrounding forest thins until there are no trees remaining through the barren meadow to the top of Elk Mountain (3). The best views of Grand County are from this summit. Looking north and clockwise are Parkview Mountain, Radial Mountain, the Never Summer Range, Longs Peak, Lake Granby, Indian Peaks, Sol Vista Ski Area, the Fraser Valley, the James Peak area, Sheep Mountain, Cottonwood Pass, Byers Peak, Ute Peak, Ute Pass, the Gore Range, and the Williams Fork Mountains. From the south and continuing clockwise are the Williams Fork Reservoir, Grouse Mountain below, Gore Canyon, Wolford Reservoir, the East Fork Troublesome Valley, Rabbit Ears Range, Corral Peaks, and Haystack Mountain.

Leave the summit and head south down the ridgeline into the woods (4). A faint trail appears and disappears, but continue to parallel the ridgeline. Directly on the ridgeline is a plaque (5) buried in the ground. It reads:

Hunting Grounds Of "Ute Bill"
March 26, 1849   March 19, 1926
In Memory By Henry Grafke-Otto Schott

William Jefferson Thompson "Ute Bill" was captured by the Ute Indians and was thought to have had his life spared because the Indians were amused by his long hair.

From the plaque, continue down the ridgeline through a meadow and then back into the trees. From the front edge of the second meadow (6), parallel the ridgeline for 50 paces and turn right (south west) down through this meadow. Bear right near the end of the meadow, where the trail reappears in the woods (7). Follow the trail to an old logging road (8). Turn right at the logging road and follow it to the trailhead (1).

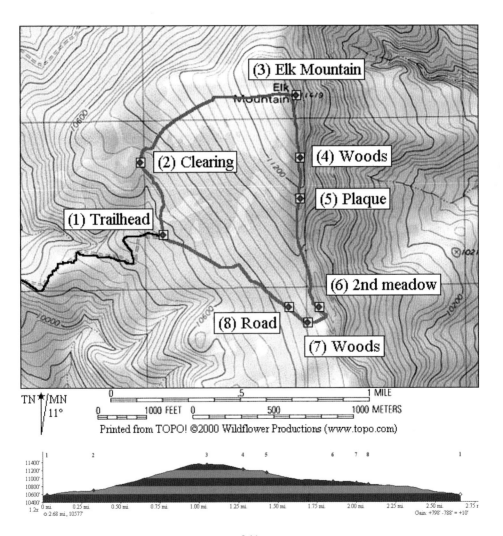

74. WHEATLEY HOMESTEAD AND COW CAMP LOOP

Level of Difficulty – Difficult
Round-trip Mileage – 16.25 miles
Round-trip Hiking Time – 2 days
Altitude, GPS Reading at Trailhead – 9234', 40°10'03"N, 106°10'33"W
Altitude, GPS Reading at Troublesome Creek
      at Road (11) – 8279',40°13'24"N, 106°12'35"W
Altitude, GPS Reading at Highest Point – 9984', 40°12'00"N, 106°10'11"W
Trail Fee Required – No

🐈 Yes, 🐟 Yes, ▲ Yes, **WD** None

Trailhead Location – On US Hwy 40, just west of Parshall between mile markers 194 and 195, head north on CR 21 (FSR 112). Follow FSR 112 for 6.9 miles and then turn left on FSR 12 toward Corral Peaks. Follow this road for 2.8 miles and then turn left on FSR 121 toward the Wheatley Creek Trail. Take FSR 121 for 2.5 miles to the end of the road (1). Do not park in front of the gate. These are all good dirt roads.

Trail Description – Pass around the gate and follow the fence, which is on the right. This fence runs a very short distance and then makes a sharp right turn at the corner post (2). Follow this fence down to Corral Creek. Just before the creek is a gate on the right. Pass through the gate and a post (3) and cross Corral Creek. Head north and gently climb through a meadow. Follow a small creek bed, which is on the left side of the trail. Continue through a mature aspen stand and pass a second post (4). The trail fades in places, but most of the trees are blazed with an "**i**" marking. Continue through the woods and cross several small creeks and meadows. At a marshy meadow with tall willows, the worn trail completely disappears. Hike north across the marsh and pass a third post (5), and another section of marsh. Clear this wet area and head northwest, where the trail reappears. Descend and pass two small frog ponds, which are on the right. At the "T" (6) the Wheatley Creek Trail continues on the left and the return trail from Ethel Creek is on the right. Head left and not far from this "T" is a trail marker identifying the Wheatley Creek Trail.

Descend into a great meadow and remain on the right side of the meadow. Pass an outfitter's camp, which is on the right and head down through the meadow. The meadow narrows and the trail moves to the left side into the woods (7). Pass through the woods onto a sage covered plateau. Turn around and view Corral Peaks. At the end of the plateau, make a sharp right turn (8) back into the woods and descend. A faint trail has been rerouted on the right, marked with white flags hanging from the trees (9). Turn right and follow this trail and flags through the aspen and lodgepole forests. Cross a creek bed (10) and immediately turn left out of the forest into the sage covered hillside with the forest and valley on the left. Follow the cairns across the hillside back into the forest. The trail makes a "U-turn" around a stone reinforcing wall. At the next sage meadow, turn around for another great view of Corral Peaks. Continue through several more areas of sage and woods and descend through several switchbacks. Follow the trail out of the woods along the sage covered ridge and head west toward the East Fork of the Troublesome Creek.

At the creek, head north (upstream) and find a shallow spot where it is safe to cross. Next, bear right (north) up the steep hillside and parallel the creek. After the gully, the trail ends at a road (11) where there is a view of Haystack Mountain ahead. Follow this road and parallel the creek until the road meets the creek at the Cow Camp property. The Cow Camp was used by cowboys during their stay while ranching cattle in the area. The Cow Camp is on "Private Property", but the trail skirts around it. Pass through the gate and cross the creek, where there is a path on the right of the road through the trees. Follow the path up the hill and away from the road to a second gate. Due north is Haystack Mountain. Pass through the gate (12) and follow the trail through the sage meadow. The mountain to the left is Sheep Mountain. The trail is lost among the cattle trails in the area, but cross the meadow and head east to the fence and the next gate (13). Pass through the gate and continue to head east. Follow the small creek bed and meadow up the valley. The meadow forks to the left and right. Follow the trail on the right side of the left fork back into the woods to Ethel Creek. Keep Ethel Creek on the left and continue along the edge of the woods. At the next clearing, Searight Mountain is visible straight ahead. Next is an area where a microburst has littered lodgepole pine trees on the forest floor like broken toothpicks. Hike around the debris and head toward the creek. Pass the aspen covered hillside, which is on the left and continue back through the woods to another outfitter's camp and another post (14). Cross the meadow and continue south into the woods. Ascend steadily to a small meadow on the right (15). This is the unidentified cutoff back to the "T" (6). At the front edge of the meadow, turn right and leave the worn trail. Skirt the edge of the woods where there is a tree blazed with a "J" marking. Follow the trail to the "T" (6). Turn left and follow the inbound trail back to the trailhead (1).

Historical Note - George and Forrest Wheatley explored Middle Park. George Wheatley built the Wheatley Homestead and Forrest built his homestead 1 ½ miles away beside the East Fork of the Troublesome Creek. Wheatley Creek is named after George.

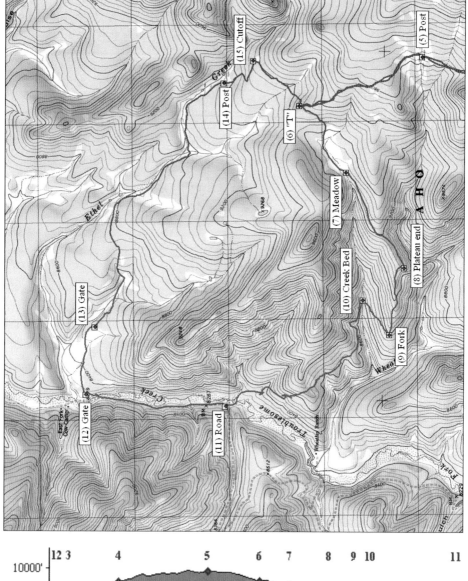

244

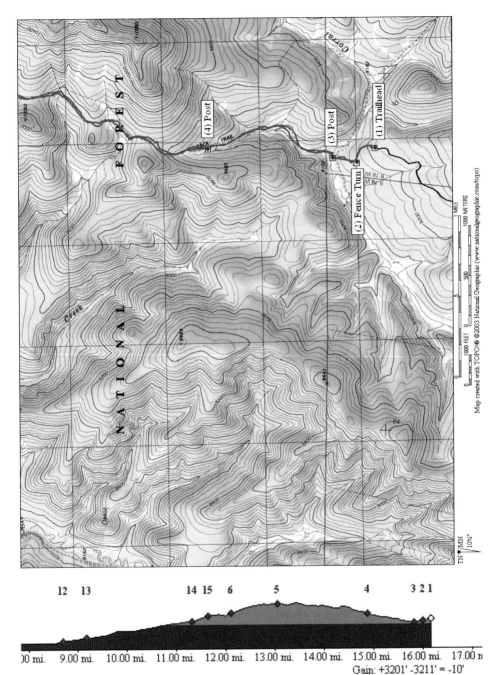

Map created with TOPO!® ©2003 National Geographic (www.nationalgeographic.com/topo)

Gain: +3201' -3211' = -10'

245

75. HAYSTACK MOUNTAIN

Level of Difficulty - Difficult
One-way Mileage - .71 miles
One-way Hiking Time – 1 hour
Altitude, GPS Reading at Trailhead – 10,278', 40°20'03"N, 106°10'59"W
Altitude, GPS Reading at Destination – 11,438', 40°19'38"N, 106°11'22"W
Trail Fee Required – No

🐾 Yes, 🐟 N/A, ▲ Yes, **WD** None

Trailhead Location - Access is from Jackson County. On CO 125, north of Willow Creek Pass, between mile markers 26 and 27, turn west on FSR 106 (also called Willow Creek Road). Follow FSR 106 for 9.9 miles. FSR 106 is a good dirt road. At the "T", turn left onto FSR 730. This is a rough road and is generally closed from September through November. Follow FSR 730 for 2.0 miles. There is no trailhead sign, but just above the culvert on the hill to the right is the trail (1). Park at the wide spot in the road.

Trail Description – Because of the rapid elevation gain in such a short distance, this hike is rated as difficult. This trail is extremely steep.

Not far from the trailhead, through the forest is a clearing on the right. This clearing is the side of Haystack Mountain (2). Turn right into the scree and hug the forest. Follow the ridgeline along the Continental Divide. The cairns that once marked the trail have fallen over and are difficult to distinguish from the rubble. Ascend slowly across the steep and unstable ground. Follow the ridgeline to a subalpine forest, where the ground is solid and easier to negotiate. Continue along the ridgeline and pass through the forest onto the tundra where the meadow is covered mostly with mosses and lichens. Follow the ridgeline to the top of Haystack Mountain (3). The views are spectacular. Looking north and clockwise are North Park and Ruby Lake, the mountains in Rocky Mountain National Park, Parkview Mountain, Porphyry Peaks, the Indian Peaks Range, East Fork Troublesome Creek below, the James Peak area, Vasquez Mountains, Elk Mountain, and Corral Peaks. Continuing from the south are the Williams Fork Mountains, the Gore Range, the East Fork Troublesome Valley below, Grimes Peak, Gore Canyon, Sheep Mountain, and Poison Ridge.

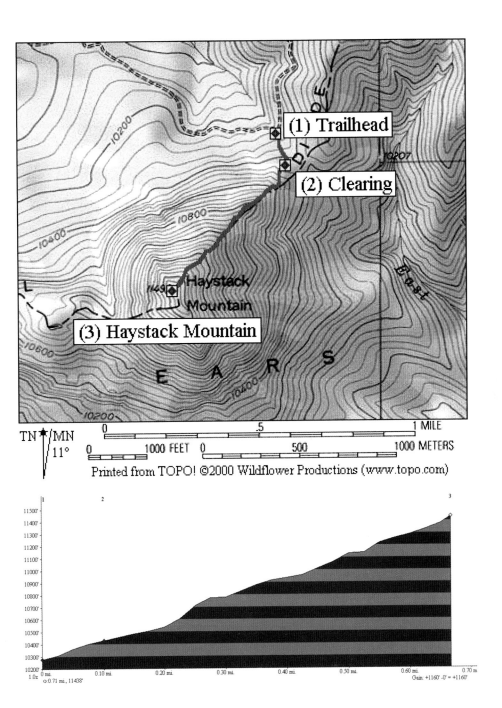

(1) Trailhead

(2) Clearing

Haystack
Mountain

(3) Haystack Mountain

Printed from TOPO! ©2000 Wildflower Productions (www.topo.com)

247

76. SHEEP MOUNTAIN

Level of Difficulty - Moderate
One-way Mileage – 1.43 miles
One-way Hiking Time - 1 ½ hours
Altitude, GPS Reading at Trailhead – 10, 590', 40°19'31"N, 106°14'00"W
Altitude, GPS Reading at Destination – 11,354', 40°18'32"N, 106°14'28"W
Trail Fee Required – No

🐾 Yes, ➤ N/A, ▲ Yes, WD None

Trailhead Location – Access is from Jackson County. On CO 125, north of Willow Creek Pass, between mile markers 26 and 27, turn west on FSR 106 (also called Willow Creek Road). Follow FSR 106 for 9.9 miles. FSR 106 is a good dirt road. At the "T", turn right onto FSR 730. This is a rough dirt road. Follow FSR 730 for 1.4 miles, where it forks. Take the left fork onto FSR 107 for another .7 miles to the saddle in a large meadow. Park on the side of the road. Begin on the left at the jeep road (1). There is no trailhead sign.

Trail Description – Follow the old jeep road. A few Englemann spruce trees survive, but the strong winds prevent much from growing in this sub-alpine zone. Not far up the hill from FSR 107, there is a tank trap (2). Pass around the tank trap and traverse up the side of the mountain through the trees. On the right is a view of Poison Ridge. After climbing up a switchback, approach the ridgeline where there is a great view to the east of Haystack Mountain and Parkview Mountain. Follow the trail near the ridgeline to the top of Sheep Mountain (3). Looking south and clockwise are the Gore Range, Grimes Peak, Wolford Reservoir, Hyannis Peak, and Poison Ridge. Continuing from the north are North Park, Haystack Mountain, Parkview Mountain, The Never Summer Range, Longs Peak, the Indian Peaks Range, the James Peak area, Searight Mountain, Corral Peaks, Elk Mountain, the East Fork Troublesome Valley, Vasquez Mountains, and the Williams Fork Mountains.

Note - There are three Sheep Mountains in Grand County. The second is just northwest of Poison Ridge on the Jackson County/Grand County boundary along the Continental Divide - see Poison Ridge Trail #77, page 250. The third is in the Vasquez Mountain Range – see Sheep (Snow) Mountain Trail #29, page 102.

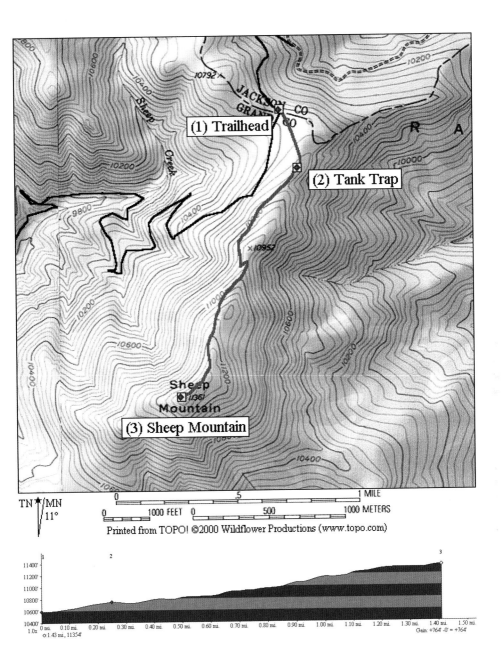

(1) Trailhead

(2) Tank Trap

(3) Sheep Mountain

JACKSON CO
GRAND CO

Sheep Creek

Sheep Mountain

x 10952

R   A

TN/MN
11°

0   .5   1 MILE

0   1000 FEET   0   500   1000 METERS

Printed from TOPO! ©2000 Wildflower Productions (www.topo.com)

1.0x
◇1.43 mi, 11354'
Gain: +764' -0' = +764'

77. POISON RIDGE

Level of Difficulty - Moderate
One-way Mileage – 1.56 miles
One-way Hiking Time – 1 hour
Altitude, GPS Reading at Trailhead – 10,599', 40°19'30"N, 106°14'02"W
Altitude, GPS Reading at Destination – 11,439', 40°20'21"N, 106°14'51"W
Trail Fee Required – No

🐾 Yes, 🐟 N/A, ▲ Yes, WD None

Trailhead Location - Access is from Jackson County. On Colorado 125, north of Willow Creek Pass, between mile markers 26 and 27, turn west on FSR 106 (also called Willow Creek Road). Follow FSR 106 for 9.9 miles. FSR 106 is a good dirt road. At the "T", turn right onto FSR 730. This is a rough dirt road. Follow FSR 730 for 1.4 miles, where it forks. Take the left fork onto FSR 107, for another .7 miles to the saddle in a large meadow. Park on the side of the road. Begin on the right side of the road at the CD marker (1).

Trail Description – This is a relatively short hike, but it is challenging and the views are rewarding. Begin through the meadow along the CD Trail. On the left is Sheep Mountain and ahead in the valley is Matheson Reservoir. Around the bend is a good view of Poison Ridge. Enter the forest of Englemann spruce and subalpine fir trees. Ascend slowly to the next meadow. Continue through the meadow to a rock outcropping on the right. This rock outcropping extends down to the trail (2). Pass the rock outcropping and a short distance further where the trail begins downhill, leave the worn trail and make a sharp right turn up the hillside. The hillside is carpeted with wildflowers and the ascent is challenging. Keep another large rock outcropping on the left and follow the ridgeline through the meadow to the top of Poison Ridge (3). The views are unmatched. Looking north and clockwise are North Park , the mountains in Rocky Mountain National Park, Parkview Mountain, Haystack Mountain, the Indian Peaks Range, the James Peak area, Elk Mountain, Corral Peaks, the Vasquez Mountains, and Sheep Mountain. Continuing from the south are the Williams Fork Mountains, the Gore Range, Wolford Reservoir, Matheson Reservoir in the foreground, Hyannis Peak, and Sheep Mountain.

Side Trip – From Poison Ridge, either continue northwest along the ridgeline or on the CD Trail to Sheep Mountain. The CD Trail continues into Jackson County beyond Sheep Mountain.

Historical Note – The exact origin of the name Poison Ridge is not known, but a lily called the Death Camas grows quite well in this area and is known to be poisonous to sheep and cattle. Also the delphiniums Monkshood and Larkspur grow well here and are known to be poisonous to cattle.

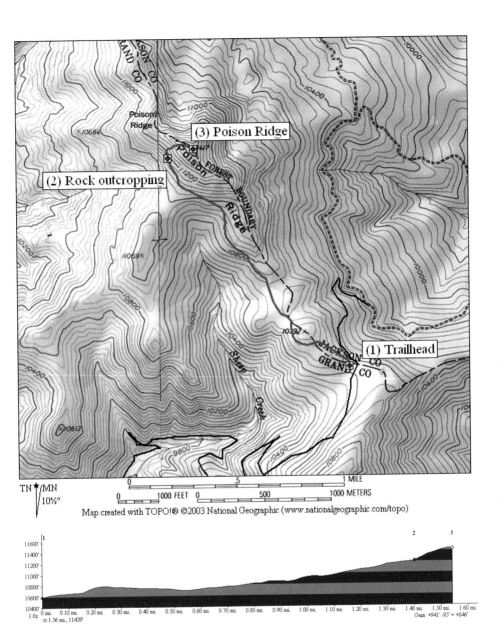

78. MATHESON RESERVOIR TO GRIMES PEAK

Level of Difficulty – More Difficult
One-way Mileage – 7.81 miles
One-way Hiking Time – 4 hours
Altitude, GPS Reading at Trailhead – 9174', 40°18'41"N, 106°16'20"W
Altitude, GPS Reading at Highest Point – 10,261', 40°14'15"N, 106°16'18"W
Altitude, GPS Reading at Destination – 10,009', 40°13'27"N, 106°15'45"W
Trail Fee Required – No

🐾 Yes, 🐟 N/A, 🔺 Yes, WD None

Trailhead Location - Access is from Jackson County. On CO 125, north of Willow Creek Pass, between mile markers 26 and 27, turn west on FSR 106 (also called Willow Creek Road). Follow FSR 106 for 9.9 miles. FSR 106 is a good road. At the "T", turn right onto FSR 730. This is a rough road. Follow FSR 730 for 1.4 miles, where it forks. Take the left fork onto FSR 107 for 5.1 miles. After the road crosses a saddle in a large meadow and begins downhill, it is very rough. A high clearance vehicle is necessary and 4-wheel drive is recommended. There are two very sharp turns at the beginning of the descent and one hairpin turn in the middle. The road forks at the end of the road. Park at the left fork. There is a tall white post in the small meadow. The trailhead is about 15 paces beyond the post at an opening in the willows at the creek on the left (1).

Trail Description – Cross the creek and follow the trail through the willows. Climb across a hillside and view the creek below. At the meadow is the Henricks Ranch on the right. This is private property, but the trail travels around the property. Turn left at the meadow toward the old road. The only view of the Matheson Reservoir is at the beginning of this road. Follow the old road into the woods. This road is closed to motor vehicles with the exception of the owners of the Henricks Ranch and maintenance of the Reservoir. There is very little water on this trail and many of the creeks dry up by July. Carry plenty of water on this hike. Climb rapidly through the woods. The first road on the right leads to the Matheson Reservoir (2). Remain straight and continue to climb steadily. There are several small meadows, but the best one is at the fork and trail marker (3) identifying the cutoff for the Middle Fork Troublesome Creek Trail on the left. (Some maps show this as the Siebert Creek Trail). From this meadow, there are great views of Searight Mountain, Corral Peaks, and Elk Mountain.

Remain straight and continue through the woods and small meadows along this roller coaster road. There are occasional peek-a-boo views of the mountains to the east. There is a fork to the left (east), but there is no trail marker (4). Continue straight and climb steadily again and remain on the old road. At the next fork and trail marker (5), the Siebert Creek Trail is on the left (east). (Some maps show this as the Hay Park Trail). Continue straight. The next landmark is difficult to find. A faint fork turns off the road to the left (east) (6). There are three posts in the ground not far from the fork, but they are not obvious. This is the turnoff to Grimes Peak. Leave the road and follow this trail up the steep hill to the top of an unnamed peak. This peak is higher than Grimes Peak, but doesn't have a view. Follow the trail down the other side of the peak. Climb uphill and pass two more unmarked forks (7 & 8). Near the top of Grimes Peak is an opening in the forest on the left where the entire East Fork Troublesome Valley is visible. Turn left off the trail, up to the ridgeline, and to the top of Grimes Peak (9). From the top of Grimes Peak looking north and clockwise are Poison Ridge, Sheep Mountain, Haystack Mountain, Parkview Mountain, the Never Summer Range, Searight Mountain, Corral Peaks, Wheatley Ranch below, Elk Mountain, the James Peak area, and the Vasquez Mountains.

Historical Note – George Henricks owned the ranch at Matheson Reservoir. He and his animals were killed in an avalanche while breaking trail through the snow in a canyon near his home. Freddy Grimes took over his ranch after the accident.

View from the top of Grimes Peak of Sheep, Haystack, and Parkview Mountains

254

(4) Fork
(5) Fork
(6) Fork
(7) Fork
(8) Fork
(9) Grimes Peak

Printed from TOPO! ©2000 Wildflower Productions (www.topo.com)

TN MN
11°

0 mi   0.50 mi   1.00 mi   1.50 mi   2.00 mi   2.50 mi   3.00 mi   3.50 mi   4.00 mi   4.50 mi   5.00 mi   5.50 mi   6.00 mi   6.50 mi   7.00 mi   7.50 mi   8.00 mi
2.4x   o:7.81 mi, 10000'   Gain: +1983' -1148' = +835'

255

Ute Peak Trail above Timberline

WILLIAMS FORK MOUNTAINS

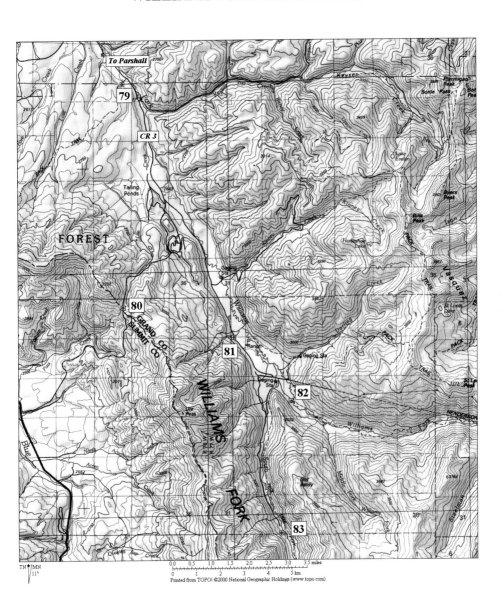

79. WILLIAMS PEAK

Level of Difficulty – More Difficult
One-way Mileage – approximately 7.11 miles
One-way Hiking Time – 4 ½ hours
Altitude, GPS Reading at Trailhead – 8421', 39°54'22"N, 106°06'19"W
Altitude, GPS Reading at Destination – 11,602', 39°51'19"N, 106°11'07"W
Trail Fee Required - No

🐾 Yes, 🛶 N/A, ▲ Yes, WD None

Note: Due to logging in late fall 2011, this trail has been rerouted (approximately points 2-3) and the description below does not accurately reflect the changes. Per the USDA Forest Service, follow the arrows on the brown vertical fiberglass post markers.

Trailhead Location – On US Hwy 40, just east of Parshall, between mile markers 197 and 198, turn south onto CR 3. Follow CR 3 for 14.5 miles to mile marker 15. Turn right (west) at the abandoned Horseshoe Guard Station. The trailhead is behind the building (1). CR 3 is a well-maintained dirt road.

Trail Description – This trail name is deceiving. There are two summits on the Williams Fork Mountain Range with the name of Williams. The first is "Williams" referring to the mountain and the second is "Williams Peak" located 2 ½ miles away. Some local residents refer to the south summit as the "Peak", but topographic maps refer to the south summit as the "Mountain". Both peaks are virtually the same elevation. Although the name of this trail is "Williams Peak", the destination according to the topographic maps is to "Williams" mountain. However, for the purpose of this trail description, the summit is referred to as Williams Peak.

Begin on a narrow single-track trail through a sagebrush covered hill to a gate. Pass through the gate. Cattle graze in this area, so leave the gate as it was found. The next five miles of the hike are on AMAX private property with trail right-of-way access. Hike though both fir and aspen forests. At the first clearing, Williams Peak is visible on the far right. It is the peak without trees on top. In this clearing is a fork (2). Take the right fork and follow this trail through both young and old forests of spruce and lodgepole pine trees.

(Please follow brown vertical fiberglass post markers through this logged section)

Follow the single-track trail (3). Approach Lost Creek, where the forest is lush. Follow the creek for a short distance and then cross over it (4). Turn left and follow the double track livestock trail. Move away from the creek. Distinguishing between the cattle trails and the hiking trail is difficult, but bear right and head uphill. There is a fork on the right (5), where a single-track trail is visible. Follow this single-track trail and ascend steadily. Continue on this trail through the lodgepole pine forest. Cross from AMAX property into National Forest land and climb through several switchbacks. At the Forest Service Road (FSR 200) (6), turn right and follow this road until the trail reappears on the left (7). Ascend through a meadow to a saddle. The Gore Range is on the left. Continue to the right to Williams Peak (8). Looking north and clockwise are the mountains in Rocky Mountain National Park and Longs Peak, the Indian Peaks Range, Ptarmigan Peak and Bottle Peak, the Henderson Mine Tailing Ponds, Byers and Bill's Peaks, the Vasquez Mountains, Ute Peak, Lake Dillon, the Gore Range, Green Mountain Reservoir, Williams Fork Mountains, and Williams Fork Reservoir.

Historical Note – Williams Peak and the Williams Fork area are named after Beverly D. Williams, who was the superintendent of the Russell, Majors, and Waddell's Leavenworth and Pike's Peak stage and express line. The Forest Service originally built the trail from the Horseshoe Guard Station to Williams Peak as an access route to the fire watch tower, which has long since been removed. Evidence remains of a phone line that ran from the Horseshoe Guard Station all the way to the watch tower.

Elk

(4) Creek Crossing

(5) Fork

(8) Williams (7) Trail

(6) FSR200

NATIONAL
GEOGRAPHIC

0.0		0.5		1
0.0	0.5	1.0	1.5	

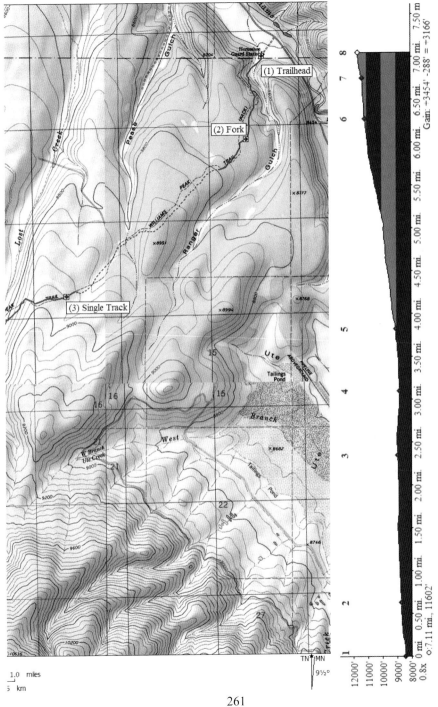

80. UTE PASS TO UTE PEAK

Level of Difficulty – Most Difficult
One-way Mileage – 5.79 miles
One-way Hiking Time – 5 hours
Altitude, GPS Reading at Trailhead – 9559', 39°49'25"N, 106°06'19"W
Altitude, GPS Reading at Destination - 12,307', 39°47'08"N, 106°04'37"W
Trail Fee Required – No

🐾 Yes, 🐟 N/A, ▲ Yes, **WD** None

Trailhead Location – On US Hwy 40, just east of Parshall, between mile markers 197 and 198, turn south onto CR 3. Follow CR 3 for 21.8 miles to the top of Ute. The trailhead is on the east (left) side of the road (1) in Summit County. CR 3 is a well-maintained dirt road.

Trail Description – Follow the trail into a predominantly fir and lodgepole pine forest. Pass through a gate and ascend steeply up several switchbacks. At a clearing is a fork (2). Turn left. From this sage clearing the view of the Gore Range and the valley below is spectacular. Pass through a second gate and climb steadily up more switchbacks. Continue through three small meadows, where the trail levels off slightly. After the meadows, the spruce trees appear and the trail descends slightly. At the next larger meadow is a great view of the side of Ute Peak. At the fork and trail marker (3), Williams Fork is on the left and Ute Peak is on the right. Turn right and continue to gain elevation. Pass two small ponds. Follow the ridgeline through the forest. The subalpine forest envelops the view, but the elevation gain is quite evident. The hike to timberline is difficult. Take time to rest and enjoy the solitude. At timberline (4), notice this location and any landmarks because the trail is not obvious when returning into the woods. Just above timberline look back at the view of the Williams Fork Reservoir on the right, and Williams Peak and Green Mountain Reservoir on the left. In the foreground are the Henderson Mill and its' settling pond. (The Henderson Mill processes molybdenum ore from a mine on the east side of the Continental Divide and conveys it through the mountains to the mill below.)

Above timberline, follow the cairns and switchbacks up and to the right across the tundra. The ground is covered in mosses and lichens with alpine flowers dotting the hillside. Cross the alpine meadow near the ridge, which is filled with daisies and buttercups in July. From the ridgeline, there are two peaks ahead. Ute Peak is the further peak on the left. Follow the trail just below the ridgeline to avoid the frequent stiff winds. Continue around to the right side of the first peak through the scree. Just beyond the scree, turn up the hill onto the ridgeline and follow the cairns to the base of Ute Peak. Finally, climb up the faint trail on the left through the loose rock to the Ute Peak summit (5). Looking to the west are the magnificent mountains of the Gore Range and the beautiful Blue River valley below. Continuing south and clockwise are Lake

Dillon, the Continental Divide, Jones Pass Road, St. Louis Divide and again the Continental Divide. This 360° view can't be beat anywhere in the county.

Historical Note – Ute Pass was one of the original Indian routes over the mountains.

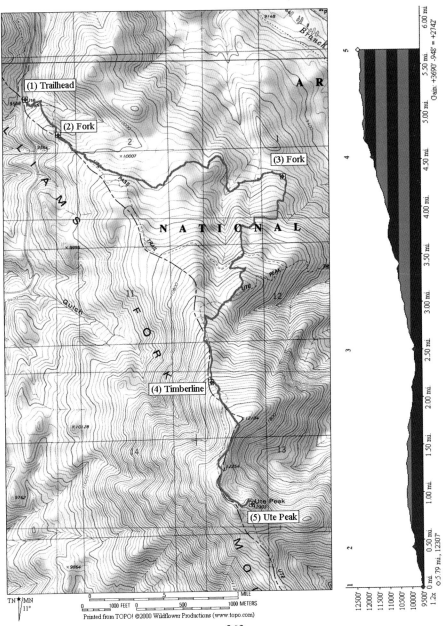

81. UTE PEAK

Level of Difficulty –Most Difficult
One-way Mileage – 4.72 miles
One-way Hiking Time – 3 ½ hours
Altitude, GPS Reading at Trailhead – 8871', 39°48'45"N, 106°03'02"W
Altitude, GPS Reading at Destination – 12,307', 39°47'08"N, 106°04'37"W
Trail Fee Required - No

🐗 Yes, 🥾 N/A, ▲ Yes, WD None

Trailhead Location – On US Hwy 40, just east of Parshall, between mile markers 197 and 198, turn south onto CR 3. Follow CR 3 for 17.9 miles, between mile markers 18 and 19 and head south onto CR 30 toward South Fork and Sugar Loaf Campgrounds. Follow CR 30 for 4.1 miles. Park at the pullout on the left. The trailhead is across the road from the parking area (1). Both CR 3 and CR 30 are well-maintained dirt roads.

Trail Description – Begin along a creek through a dense lush forest and quickly pass through a short tunnel under the Henderson Mill conveyor. This is one of the most diverse forests in the area with willows, lodgepole pine trees, fir trees, aspen trees, and spruce trees all intermingled creating a profuse montane life zone. The first mile of the trail is a moderate hike, but increases in difficulty with the gain in elevation. After the switchback, there is a fork and trail marker (2). The Ute Pass Trail is on the right and the Ute Peak Trail continues on the left. Bear left and pass two small ponds. Follow the ridgeline through the forest. The subalpine forest envelops the view, but the elevation gain is quite evident. The hike to timberline is difficult. Take time to rest and enjoy the solitude. At timberline (3), notice this location and any landmarks because the trail is not obvious when returning into the woods. Just above timberline look back at the view of the Williams Fork Reservoir on the right, and Williams Peak and Green Mountain Reservoir on the left. In the foreground are the Henderson Mill and its' settling pond. (The Henderson Mill processes molybdenum ore from a mine on the east side of the Continental Divide and conveys it through the mountains to the mill below.)

Above timberline, follow the cairns and switchbacks up and to the right across the tundra. The ground is covered in mosses and lichens with alpine flowers dotting the hillside. Cross the alpine meadow near the ridge, which is filled with daisies and buttercups in July. From the ridgeline, there are two peaks ahead. Ute Peak is the further peak on the left. Follow the trail just below the ridgeline to avoid the frequent stiff winds. Continue around to the right side of the first peak through the scree. Just beyond the scree, turn up the hill to the ridgeline and follow the cairns to the base of Ute Peak. Finally, climb up the faint trail on the left through the loose rock to the Ute Peak summit (4). Looking to the west are the magnificent mountains of the Gore Range and the beautiful Blue River valley below. Looking to the south and clockwise are Lake Dillon, the Continental Divide, Jones Pass Road, St. Louis Divide and again the Continental Divide. This 360° view can't be beat anywhere in the county.

Historical Note – The Ute Peak Trail was originally used as a stock drive trail over the Williams Fork Mountains. The name "Ute" is derived from the "Utah" Indians who lived in this valley before the white man arrived.

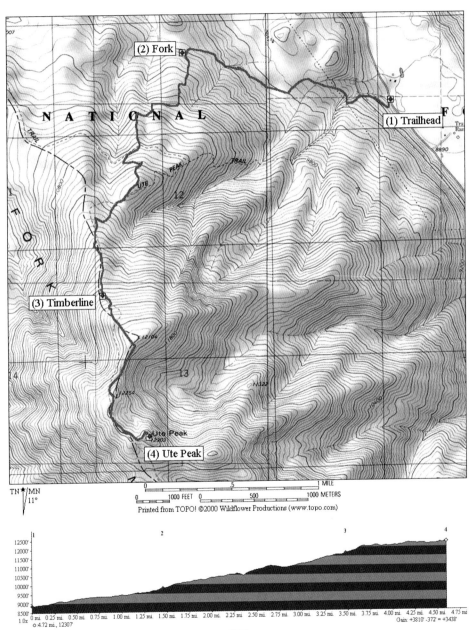

265

82. SOUTH FORK LOOP

Level of Difficulty -Difficult
Round-trip Mileage – 25.82 miles
Round-trip Hiking Time - 3 days
Altitude, GPS Reading at Trailhead – 8967', 39°47'48"N, 106°01'29"W
Altitude, GPS Reading at Pass – 12,267', 39°43'28"N, 105°55'52"W
Trail Fee Required – No

🐾 <u>Yes</u>, 🐾 <u>Yes</u>, ▲ <u>Yes</u>, WD <u>None</u>

Trailhead Location – On US Hwy 40, just east of Parshall, between mile markers 197 and 198, turn south onto CR 3. On CR 3, drive 17.9 miles, between mile markers 18 and 19 and head south onto CR 30 toward South Fork and Sugar Loaf Campgrounds. Follow CR 30 for 5.5 miles through the tunnel under the conveyor. Turn left to Darling Creek Road and parallel the conveyor for .4 miles to the trailhead (1). Both CR 3 and CR 30 are well-maintained dirt roads.

Trail Description – This hike is recommended as a 3-day backpacking trip, which does not include side-trips. However, both ends of the trail are beautiful day hikes. The nicest time of year for this hike is autumn because the temperatures are cooler and the weather is more dependable. It is not advisable to hike this area in the early spring since the snow melt can cause the creeks to flow dangerously high and fast. The trail description is divided into three sections (Days) because Day 2 is almost entirely above timberline and it is important to have the starting and ending points for that day clearly defined.

Day 1 - Begin near the entrance to the Henderson Tunnel. This tunnel transports molybdenum ore from the mine on the east side of the Continental Divide to the mill on the west side. From the chain link fence, head south, away from the tunnel around to the Williams Fork Creek. Follow the bank of the creek and pass several beaver ponds. A fork and trail marker (2) identifies the South Fork Trail on the right and Darling Creek Trail on the left. Take the right fork and follow the willows along the Williams Fork Creek. Meander through the woods and climb gently uphill. Cross the Williams Fork Creek twice and continue to a wonderful aspen stand. Ahead are peek-a-boo views of the Continental Divide and the road to Jones Pass. Cross a few meadows, which provide a clear view of the mountains to the right. A road is visible high up on the mountain to the right, which was used for access to a silver mine years ago. In the fall, the changing aspen leaves give contrast and great dimension to the mountains. Beyond the meadow on the left is a large exhaust vent (3) used by the Henderson Mine tunnel. Next is an old cabin on the left (4). Cross the next creek, where signs of an old road appear on the trail, probably used for installation and maintenance of the exhaust vent. Continue past several more old cabins (5 & 6) and creeks to a cairn. At the cairn, left leads to property of the Denver Water Board. Turn right at the cairn toward the Jones Pass Road. Pettingell Peak is visible along the Continental Divide. At the road and trail marker (7), the South Fork Trail continues to the right, Jones Pass Road (formerly the Jones Pass

Wagon Road) is straight, and McQueary Lake is to the left. McQueary Lake is a great side trip of about 5 ½ miles roundtrip (see McQueary Lake Hike #42, page 138). Turn right and follow the road for a short distance until the Bobtail Mine is visible. The land on both sides of the road and surrounding the mine are on private property. There is a camping area adjacent to the mine across Bobtail Creek; however, continuing further makes Day 2 easier. Look back at the St. Louis Divide, St. Louis Peak, and St. Louis Pass. Cross Bobtail Creek and follow it upstream. Pass the Bobtail Mine (8) and continue up the valley out of the trees and into the meadow toward Pettingell Peak. Cross Bobtail Creek again, where there is a good camp site on the left nestled at the edge of the trees (9).

Day 2 – It is necessary to get an early start for Day 2 because the hike is almost entirely above timberline. Hike through the large meadow. The meadow is swallowed up by the scree and boulders from Pettingell Peak on the left and the willows from the creek on the right. Hagar Mountain, also on the Continental Divide, is visible beyond Pettingell Peak. Cross the meadow, head west, and cross the creek. This is the last opportunity to gather water for the next 5 hours. Climb up the switchbacks through timberline. Several sets of switchbacks are cut along the hill. Head southwest if the switchback direction is unclear. This is a difficult grade, however the views are incomparable. At the pass is a fork and trail marker (10) identifying the northbound CD Trail to the left and the South Fork Trail straight ahead. Turn left up the hill for a better look at the mountains. From this pinnacle looking south are Coon Hill and the stark tundra valley below. To the left are Hager Mountain, Pettingell Peak, and Jones Pass. To the right of Coon Hill are the Williams Fork Mountains and the Gore Range in the background. Return to the pass (10) and follow the trail down the other side. It is quite steep and narrow. The trail levels off and the Steelman Creek Trail forks to the right (11). Bear left on the South Fork Trail and continue to traverse the hillside. When Coon Hill is in view again, turn right (west) and follow the cairns. There are several cairns in the distance where the worn trail disappears. Follow the cairns through the alpine meadow across the side of the mountains. The trail reappears along the ridgeline. Cross to the west side of the ridge. This is the high point of the trail. In the distance is a tall cairn sitting on top of a peak. Head toward this cairn. In the distance on the right (northwest) along a ridge, the Middle Fork Williams Fork (MFWF) Trail cuts off. Follow the South Fork Trail on the right of the peak with the tall cairn and descend. There is a large tarn on the right. Follow the trail to the saddle (12) and then turn left (south) down into a meadow. The trail is faint and the cairns are hard to follow. Remain on the right side of the creek where the trail reappears and head into the woods. It is a steep descent through many switchbacks to the South Fork Williams Fork Creek. Cross the creek, where there is a great place to camp (13).

Day 3 – This day is almost entirely downhill. Follow the trail west, downstream. Not far from camp is a fork and trail marker (14) identifying Ptarmigan Pass up the hill, and South Fork Campground ahead. Ptarmigan Pass is a great side trip of about 5.6 miles round-trip (see Ptarmigan Pass and Peak Hike #83, page 276 to (4) to (5)). Continue downstream on the South Fork Trail through the dense lush forest. The creek winds down the valley, never far from the trail. Pass several scree and boulder fields and low willows. There is a great view of Ute Peak in the distance and spectacular mountains on each side of the trail. At the next fork and trail marker (15), FSR 142 is to the left. (This Forest Road runs parallel to the trail and returns to the Henderson conveyor tunnel near the campground.) Continue straight. The South Fork Williams Fork Creek picks up speed and volume through the valley. Cross the creek on the log foot bridge and view Old Baldy on the right. Cross a second log foot bridge and a second boulder field. At the fork at the horse corral (16), continue straight and pass through the South Fork Campground. At the campground exit, turn left and follow the road. At Darling Creek Road, turn right and parallel the conveyor to the trailhead (1).

Historical Note – Bobtail Mine was in operation from 1882-1925 and produced gold ore, silver, and lead smelting ore.

Pettingell Peak was named after Jacob N. Pettingell who was a judge and prominent citizen of Grand County. Pettingell Peak is the highest peak in Grand County.

Hagar Mountain was named after George H. Hagar who was a mining promoter in the county.

Williams Fork River valley

Coon Hill

Tall Cairn on the Continental Divide

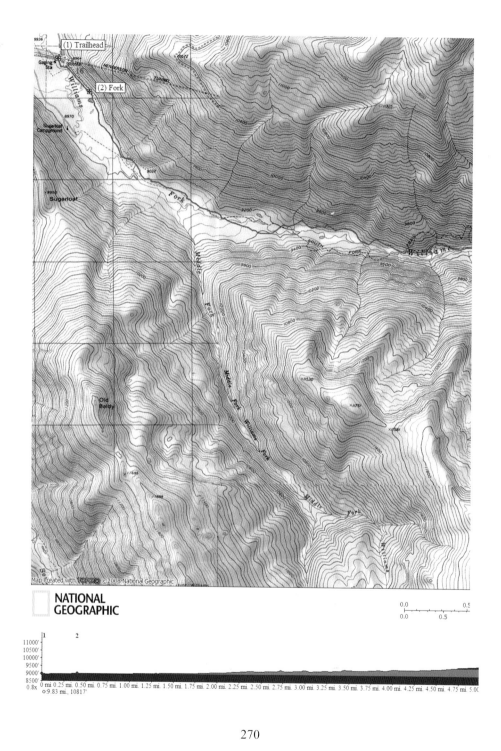

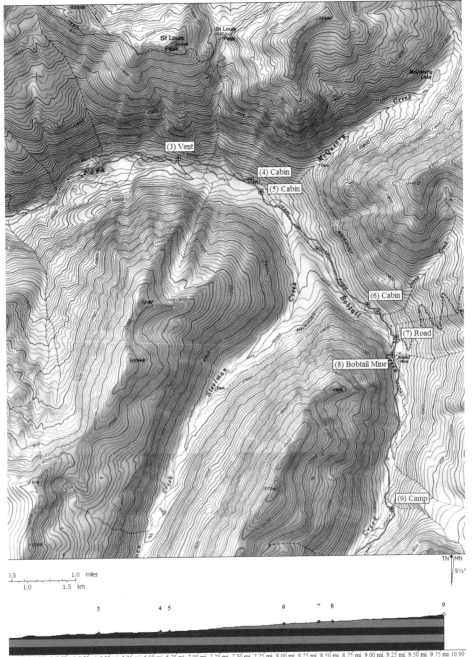

(3) Vent
(4) Cabin
(5) Cabin
(6) Cabin
(7) Road
(8) Bobtail Mine
(9) Camp

St Louis Peak
St Louis Pass
McQueary Lake

0.5   1.0   miles
1.0   1.5   km

TN   MN
9½°

3   4 5   6   7 8   9

5.00 mi. 5.25 mi. 5.50 mi. 5.75 mi. 6.00 mi. 6.25 mi. 6.50 mi. 6.75 mi. 7.00 mi. 7.25 mi. 7.50 mi. 7.75 mi. 8.00 mi. 8.25 mi. 8.50 mi. 8.75 mi. 9.00 mi. 9.25 mi. 9.50 mi. 9.75 mi. 10.00
Gain: +2228' -377' = +1851'

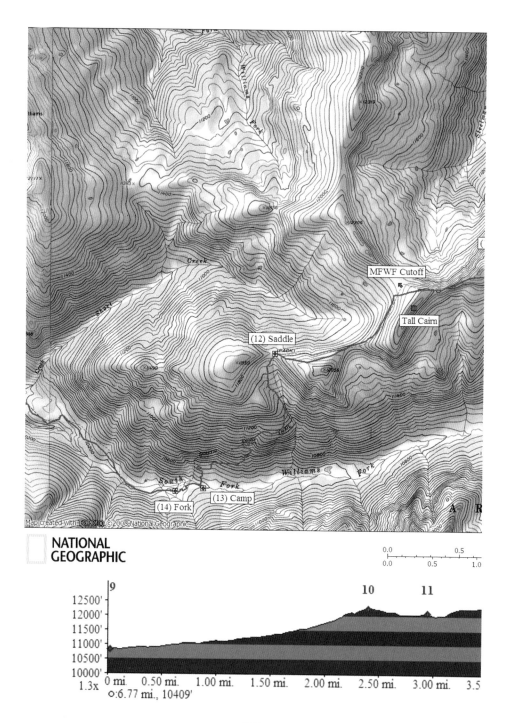

NATIONAL
GEOGRAPHIC

Map created with TOPO!® ©2008 National Geographic

MFWF Cutoff

Tall Cairn

(12) Saddle

(13) Camp

(14) Fork

272

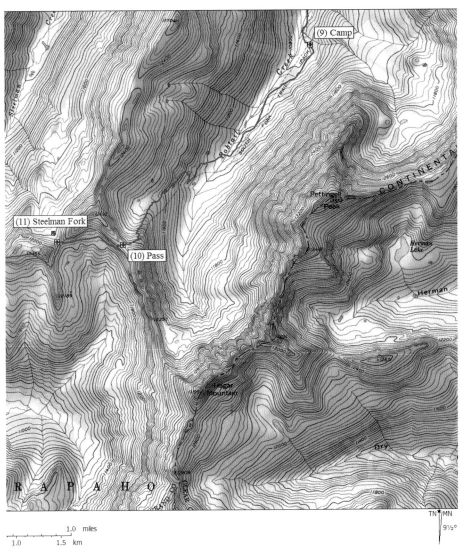

(9) Camp

(11) Steelman Fork

(10) Pass

Pettingell
Peak

CONTINENTAL

Herman
Lake

Herman

Hagar
Mountain

Dry

R   A   P   A   H   O

TN MN
9½°

1.0   miles
1.0   1.5   km

12   13

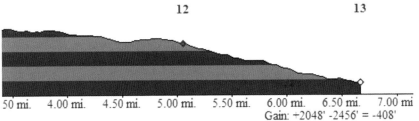

50 mi.   4.00 mi.   4.50 mi.   5.00 mi.   5.50 mi.   6.00 mi.   6.50 mi.   7.00 mi
Gain: +2048' -2456' = -408'

273

South Fork Williams Fork River

83. PTARMIGAN PASS AND PEAK

Level of Difficulty – More Difficult (Pass), Most Difficult (Peak)
One-way Mileage – 7.22 miles (Pass), 8.63 miles (Peak)
One-way Hiking Time - 4 hours (Pass), 5 hours (Peak)
Altitude, GPS Reading at Trailhead – 9512', 39°44'25"N, 106°01'39"W
Altitude, GPS Reading at Pass – 11,743', 39°41'11"N, 106°00'14"W
Altitude, GPS Reading at Peak – 12,503', 39°41'27"N, 106°01'35"W
Trail Fee Required – No

🐕 Leash, 🎣 Yes, ▲ Yes, **WD** PP

Trailhead Location – On US Hwy 40, just east of Parshall, between mile markers 197 and 198, turn south onto CR 3. Follow CR 3 for 17.9 miles, between mile markers 18 and 19 and head south onto CR 30 toward South Fork and Sugar Loaf Campgrounds. Follow CR 30 for 5.5 miles through the tunnel under the conveyor. Turn right, and follow the road for 4.8 miles along the South Fork Road to the trailhead (1). Both CR 3 and South Fork Road are well-maintained dirt roads.

Trail Description – This is a nice hike along a beautiful creek, up to a pass, and a peak with outstanding views. Begin in a montane forest and cross a foot bridge over the South Fork Williams Fork Creek. Just beyond the creek, the trail intersects the South Fork Trail at the fork and trail marker (2). South Fork Campground is to the left and Ptarmigan Pass is to the right. Turn right and begin a gentle ascent through the forest, parallel to the winding creek. Cross small creeks and small meadows filled with willows and tall grasses. Climb a few short steep sections and cross the South Fork Williams Fork Creek (3). Parallel the creek and gradually climb above it. In the clearing is a great view of Hagar Mountain and the creek valley with several beaver ponds and willows lining each side of the creek. Not far from the creek crossing is a fork and trail marker (4). The sign identifies Bobtail Mine straight ahead and Ptarmigan Pass to the right. Turn right and climb uphill. The ascent is steep with several sets of switchbacks. Pass back and forth through the woods and meadows and climb quickly. There are great views of the creek valley below and Hagar Mountain and Pettingell Peak to the northeast. At the boulder filled hillside, there is a clearing with Ute Peak in view to the northwest. Further up the trail, Ptarmigan Peak is visible. To the left of the ridgeline is a cirque with many trees downed, the result of winter avalanches. Continue to ascend steeply with a short descent through the woods to a large meadow. The trail is difficult to find in the meadow, but follow the cairns. Traverse the hillside through the tall grass to timberline and Ptarmigan Pass (5). From the pass is a spectacular view of Dillon Lake and the surrounding area. From the far left are Breckenridge Ski Area, the town of Dillon, Lake Dillon, the town of Frisco, and Hwy 70. The trail marker identifies Straight Creek down the hill on the right. This leads to Summit County and the town of Silverthorne. The trail from Ptarmigan Pass to Ptarmigan Peak follows the Ptarmigan Peak Wilderness boundary. Dogs must be leashed in this Wilderness Area. To reach Ptarmigan Peak, turn right and follow the ridgeline up the hill. The views to the left expand to include

Grays and Torreys Peaks and Keystone Ski Area. Above timberline, the ground is covered in tall grasses, small boulders, and short groundcovers. To the north is a good view of the St. Louis Divide with St. Louis Peak to the right and Byers Peak to the left.

The hike to Ptarmigan Peak is steep and slow. On the right side of the ridgeline is a great view of Ute Peak, the South Fork Valley, and Old Baldy. On the left of the ridgeline is Buffalo Mountain (a Summit County landmark). Also on the right are three tarns with one tucked into the trees. At the Ptarmigan Peak summit (6), the views are incredible. Looking south and clockwise are the towns of Breckenridge and Frisco, Hwy 70, the town of Silverthorne, Buffalo Mountain and the rest of the Gore Range. Next, are Ute Peak and the Troublesome Valley in the distance. To the north and clockwise are Byers Peak, the St. Louis Divide and Peak, Mt. Nystrom, Vasquez Peak, Jones Pass Road, Pettingell Peak, Hagar Mountain, the South Fork Williams Fork Valley looking upstream, Grays and Torreys Peaks, Keystone Ski Area, Mt. Gugot, and Bald Mountain.

Note - There are two Ptarmigan Peaks in Grand County. The other is in the Vasquez Mountains. Refer to the Bottle Peak, Bottle Pass, and Ptarmigan Peak Hike #24, page 90 or Bottle Pass, Bottle Peak, Ptarmigan Peak Hike #37, page 124.

Note – A Ptarmigan is an alpine grouse, which changes colors with the seasons to camouflage itself. The bird has feathered feet to adapt to walking on the deep snow. In the winter the bird's feathers are pure white to blend in with the snow. In the summer the feathers are speckled brown and white, blending in with the rocks and pebbles on the tundra.

Ptarmigan
277

Old Man of the Mountain found above timberline

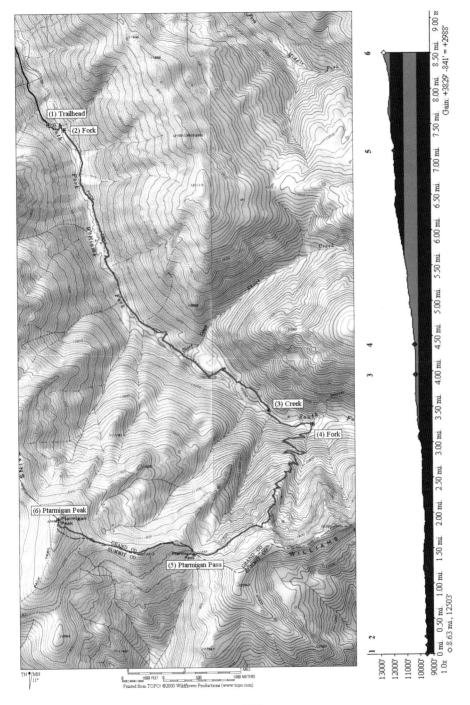

ADDITIONAL GRAND COUNTY HIKES

Additional Grand County hikes include the Routt Divide Trail and the
Gore Canyon Trail.

GORE CANYON AND ROUTT DIVIDE

Gore Canyon

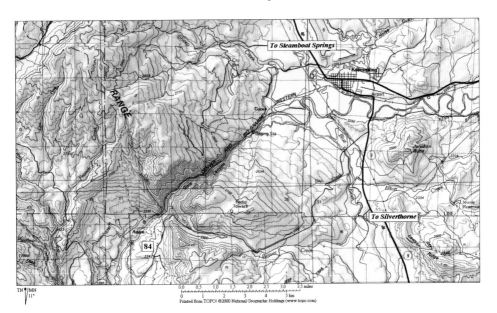

Routt Divide

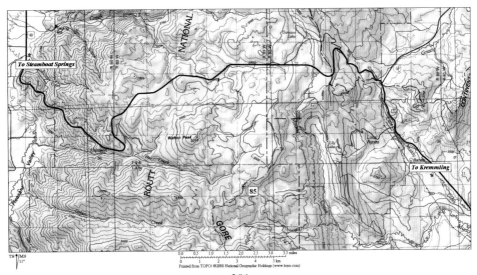

84. GORE CANYON

Level of Difficulty - Easy
One-way Mileage – 1.79 miles
One-way Hiking Time – 1 hour
Altitude, GPS Reading at Trailhead – 7002', 39°59'23"N, 106°30'29"W
Altitude, GPS Reading at Destination – 7032', 40°00'24"N, 106°29'16"W
Trail Fee Required – Yes

🐕 Leash, 🦴 Yes, ▲ Yes, **WD** None

Trailhead Location – From the town of Kremmling, head south on CO 9 for 2.1 miles. Turn west onto CR 1. Between mile markers 10 and 11 is the Pumphouse Recreation Area. Turn right and follow this road for 1.6 miles to the trailhead (1). These are good dirt roads.

Trail Description – Sign in at the register box and follow the trail upstream along the Colorado River. This trail is unique in that it is in the Foothill Life Zone. The plant life consists mostly of junipers, sage, cottonwoods, dogwoods, cedar, and pine. On the right side of the trail are high granite cliffs, which provide shade for the plant life to grow lush in this dry environment. There are several side trails leading to the river's edge for fishing access. Follow the main trail to a jeep road and follow it for a short distance parallel to the river. The jeep road turns to the right and heads uphill. Do not follow the jeep trail up the hill. Instead, continue to parallel the river to a trail marker (2) at the bottom of a hill, which points to the trail on the right. Climb to the top of the hill and continue to parallel the Colorado River about 50' above the water. This location provides a great view of the river and the rapids. Follow the cliff's edge. On the opposite side of the river is a railroad tunnel. Across the river from the tunnel, descend to the river's edge. The trail is steep and narrow. At the river, cross over many rocks and boulders. At the water's edge, below the tunnel is an old cabin. Continue upstream to a great grassy clearing (3). Beyond this point, the trail increases in difficulty and disappears through the narrow canyon.

Historical Note – Gore Canyon was named for Sir George Gore, an English Baronet, who came to Middle Park on a hunting expedition with scout Jim Bridger. He and his party killed thousands of animals for sport and were not looked upon fondly by locals by the time they left.

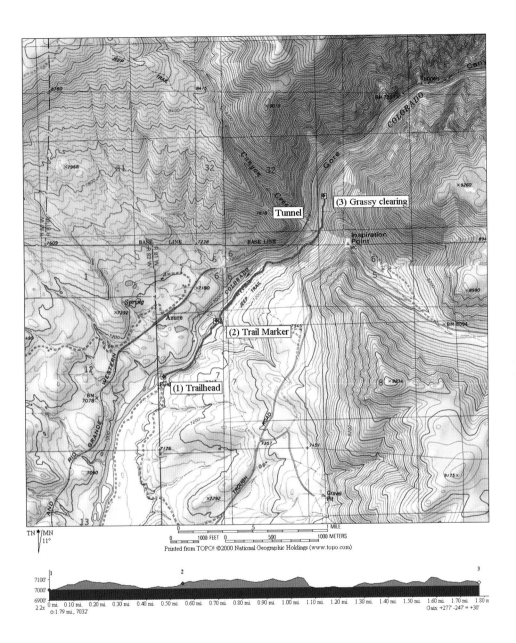

85. ROUTT DIVIDE 🚗 🚗

Level of Difficulty - Moderate
One-way Mileage – 8.68 miles
One-way Hiking Time – 3 ½ hours
Altitude, GPS Reading at Trailhead #1 – 9732', 40°19'51"N, 106°40'04"W
Altitude, GPS Reading at Highest Point – 10,056', 40°17'53"N, 106°40'05"W
Altitude, GPS Reading at Trailhead #2 – 9134', 40°16'21"N, 106°36'52"W
Trail Fee Required – No

🐕 Yes, 🐟 N/A, ▲ Yes, **WD** None

Trailhead Location – This is a one-way hike requiring two vehicles.
1st Car Parking – *Access 1* – On US Hwy 40, northwest of the town of Kremmling, between mile markers 178 and 179, head west on CO 134. Follow CO 134 to mile marker 23 and head north on CR 19 (FSR 100). Follow CR 19 to the Routt Divide Trailhead #2 (4) between mile markers 17 and 18. CR 19 is a good dirt road.
1st Car Parking – *Access 2* – On US Hwy 40, just west of Rabbit Ears Pass between mile markers 153 and 154, turn south onto CR 19 (FSR 100) to the Routt Divide Trailhead #2 (4) between mile markers 17 and 18. CR 19 is a good dirt road.
2nd Car Parking – On US Hwy 40, just west of Rabbit Ears Pass, between mile markers 152 and 153, turn south toward Harrison Creek (FSR 251). Follow FSR 251 for 2.1 miles to a fork. FSR 251 continues to the right and FSR 303 and FSR1108 are on the left. Take the left fork for 2.8 miles. There are two roads on the right and one on the left. Follow the left road with the "Trail" marker for .4 miles to the Routt Divide Trailhead #1 (1). FSR 251 is a rough dirt road and a high clearance vehicle is recommended.

Trail Description – The trail is a nice one-way hike with two cars since there is no lake or peak as a final destination. Immediately after the Trailhead #1 (1), there are a couple of tank traps to deter motor vehicles. Hike through this dense spruce-fir forest. Ascend slowly and follow a series of gently rolling hills. Make a short descent to a large meadow (2). From the meadow there are two hills ahead. Cross straight through the center of the meadow to the woods on the opposite side. Ascend steeply back and forth through the switchbacks and the boulder field. From the boulder field there is a clear view of Rabbit Ears and the valley below. Continue above the boulder field to the high point on the trail, which is on the back side of the second hill. Gradually descend through the continually changing spruce-fir and lodgepole pine forest. On a ridge, there is a large collection of huge boulders with views to the right and left (3). Continue to descend slowly through the woods. Follow the trail through the meadows and pass the aspen stands to the parking area and Trailhead #2 (4).

Historical Note – Routt was the governor of Colorado.

The Routt Divide Trail

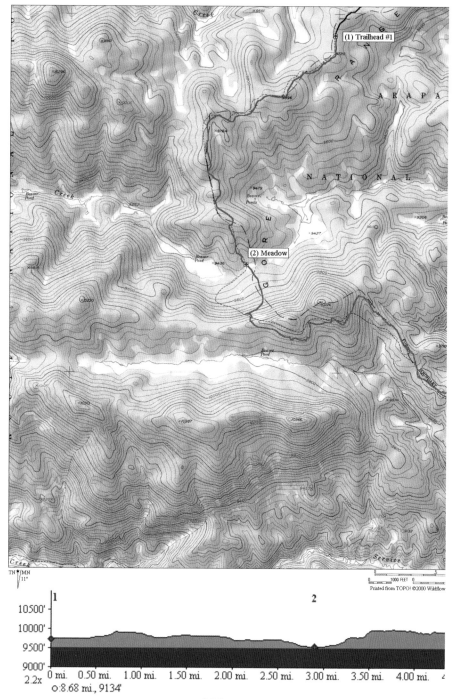

(1) Trailhead #1

(2) Meadow

TN / MN
/ 11°

1000 FEET
Printed from TOPO! ©2000 Wildflow

10500'
10000'
9500'
9000'
2.2x

0 mi.   0.50 mi.   1.00 mi.   1.50 mi.   2.00 mi.   2.50 mi.   3.00 mi.   3.50 mi.   4.00 mi.

○:8.68 mi., 9134'

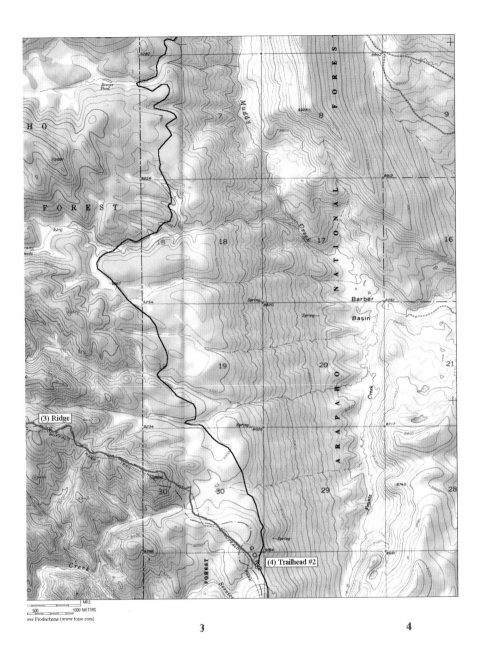

(3) Ridge

Barber

Basin

(4) Trailhead #2

1 MILE
500   1000 METERS
.ver Productions (www.topo.com)

3   4

4.50 mi.   5.00 mi.   5.50 mi.   6.00 mi.   6.50 mi.   7.00 mi.   7.50 mi.   8.00 mi.   8.50 mi.   9.00 m
                                                              Gain: +1087' -1685' = -598'

Lake Granby from Apiatan Mountain

Devil's Thumb Park

288

APPENDIX

Trail Name			Trails Illustrated Suggested Map	Level of Difficulty
Waypoint	Latitude (N) deg,min,sec	Longitude (W) deg,min,sec		

Winter Park

1. Berthoud Pass to Winter Park Ski Resort			103	Moderate
1	39,47,53	105,46,39		
2	39,48,11	105,47,17		
3	39,48, 6	105,47,37		
4	39,48,11	105,47,54		
5	39,48,40	105,48, 3		
6	39,51,27	105,46,33		
7	39,52,29	105,46,33		
8	39,53, 8	105,45,48		

2. Stanley Mountain, Vasquez Pass, and Vasquez Peak			103	Most Difficult
1	39,47,53	105,46,39		
2	39,48, 11	105,47,16		
3	39,47, 8	105,49,22		
4	39,47,16	105,49,45		
5	39,47,17	105,50,18		
6	39,47,22	105,50,31		
7	39,47,27	105,51, 7		
8	39,47,47	105,51,18		

3. Berthoud Pass Aqueduct to Second Creek			103	Moderate
1	39,48,8	105,46,38		
2	39,48,13	105,46,41		
3	39,48,23	105,46,42		
4	39,48,32	105,47,19		
5	39,48,33	105,47,24		
6	39,48,44	105,47,24		
7	39,48,50	105,47,17		
8	39,49,20	105,47,5		
9	39,49,32	105,47,6		
10	39,49,36	105,46,59		
11	39,49,22	105,46,11		

			103	Moderate
4. Seven Mile Ski Trail				
1	39,48, 9	105,46,26		
2	39,48,16	105,46,21		
3	39,48,38	105,46,26		
4	39,48,42	105,46,20		
5	39,49,19	105,45,44		
6	39,49,39	105,45,34		
5. Current Creek Loop			103	Moderate
1	39,48,35	105,46,47		
2	39,48,44	105,47,24		
3	39,48,52	105,47,28		
4	39,49, 0	105,47,24		
5	39,48,51	105,47,39		
6	39,48,43	105,47,43		
7	39,48,35	105,47,11		
6. Second Creek			103	Easy
1	39,49,22	105,46,11		
2	39,49,36	105,46,59		
7. Vasquez Creek to Vasquez Pass			103	Difficult
1	39,51,52	105,49,22		
2	39,49,28	105,49,39		
2A	39,49, 8	105,50, 7		
3	39,48,48	105,49,30		
4	39,47,15	105,49,44		

James Peak Area

			103	Most Difficult
8. Mt. Flora, Mt. Eva, Parry Peak, Mt. Bancroft, and James Peak				
1	39,47,52	105,46,36		
2	39,47,45	105,45,52		
2A	39,47,42	105,45,50		
3	39,47,51	105,45,36		
4	39,48,18	105,44, 7		
5	39,48,56	105,43,44		
6	39,49,38	105,43,11		
7	39,49,39	105,43, 6		
8	39,50,17	105,42,47		
9	39,50,15	105,42, 1		

10	39,51, 7	105,41,26		
11	39,51, 7	105,41,22		
12	39,51,22	105,41,22		
13	39,51,33	105,41,41		
14	39,52,14	105,41,51		
15	39,52,19	105,41,54		
15A	39,52,18	105,41,47		
16	39,52,22	105,41,57		
17	39,53,56	105,42,28		
9. Jim Creek			103	Moderate
1	39,52,55	105,45,17		
2	39,52,50	105,44,30		
3	39,51,38	105,42,24		
10. Rogers Pass and James Peak			103	Moderate/Difficult
1	39,53,56	105,42,28		
2	39,52,22	105,41,57		
3	39,52,19	105,41,54		
4	39,52,18	105,41,51		
5	39,52,18	105,41,47		
6	39,52,14	105,41,51		
7	39,51,28	105,41,28		
8	39,51,22	105,41,22		
9	39,51,07	105,41,22		
10	39,51,07	105,41,26		
11. Pumphouse, Deadman, and Corona Lakes			103	Easy
1	39,55,21	105,41,16		
2	39,55,32	105,41,22		
3	39,55,16	105,41,30		
4	39,56, 1	105,41,43		
12. Mt. Epworth			103	Moderate
1	39,55,21	105,41,16		
2	39,55,33	105,41,23		
3	39,55,21	105,41,45		
13. Rollins Pass Wagon Road			103	Moderate
1	39,55,21	105,41,16		
2	39,55,33	105,41,23		
3	39,55,48	105,41,36		
4	39,55,52	105,42,49		

14. Radio Beacon Site			103	Easy
1	39,55,36	105,41, 1		
2	39,55, 3	105,40,56		

15. King, Betty, and Bob Lakes			103	Moderate
1	39,56, 7	105,40,55		
2	39,56,16	105,41,14		
3	39,56,28	105,41, 8		
4	39,56,35	105,41, 7		
5	39,56,36	105,40,54		
6	39,56,55	105,40,47		
7	39,57, 6	105,41, 6		

16. Rollins Pass (Corona) to Devil's Thumb			103	Moderate
1	39,56, 5	105,40,58		
2	39,56,16	105,41,14		
3	39,58,29	105,41,22		
4	39,58,27	105,41,20		
5	39,58,44	105,41, 9		
6	39,58, 0	105,41,19		
7	39,56,25	105,41,37		

Fraser Valley

17. Devil's Thumb			103	Difficult
1	39,59,12	105,44,35		
2	39,59,11	105,43,52		
3	39,59, 1	105,43,10		
4	39,58,56	105,43, 2		
5	39,58,49	105,42,29		
6	39,58,27	105,41,20		
7	39,58,44	105,41, 9		
8	39,58,56	105,41, 6		

18. Columbine Lake			102	Moderate
1	40,2,40	105,43,55		
2	40,2,38	105,43,47		
3	40,2, 2	105,43,13		
4	40,1,46	105,42,36		
5	40,1, 2	105,41,56		

19. Mt Neva			102	More Difficult
1	40,2,40	105,43,55		
2	40,2,38	105,43,47		
3	40,2, 2	105,43,13		
4	40,1,46	105,42,36		
5	40,1, 2	105,41,56		
6	40,0,44	105,42, 3		
7	40,0,24	105,41,18		

20. Caribou Pass and Lake Dorothy			102	Moderate/Difficult
1	40,2,40	105,43,55		
2	40,2,38	105,43,47		
3	40,2, 2	105,43,13		
4	40,1,47	105,42,36		
5	40,1,10	105,41,27		
6	40,0,51	105,40,59		
7	40,0,47	105,41, 2		

Vasquez Mountains

21. Mt. Nystrom			103	Most Difficult
0	39,53,52	105,52,12		
1	39,51,49	105,51,51		
2	39,50,32	105,51,53		
3	39,50,16	105,52, 8		
4	39,49,50	105,52,21		
5	39,49,15	105,52,59		
5A	39,50,30	105,52,55		
6	39,48,44	105,53,30		
6A	39,48,19	105,53,15		
7	39,48,32	105,54, 7		

22. Byers Peak Loop			103	Difficult
0	39,53,19	105,55,31		
1	39,53, 1	105,56, 6		
2	39,52,36	105,56,22		
3	39,51,53	105,56,50		
4	39,53,26	105,56,28		
5	39,53,18	105,56, 6		

23. Byers Peak to Bill's Peak Loop			103	Most Difficult
0	39,53,19	105,55,31		

1	39,53, 1	105,56, 5
2	39,52,36	105,56,21
3	39,51,52	105,56,50
4	39,51,28	105,57,15
5	39,51,21	105,57,45
6	39,52,23	105,58, 3
7	39,52,29	105,57,57
8	39,52, 4	105,57,33
9	39,52,52	105,56,46
10	39,53,37	105,56,38
11	39,53,26	105,56,28
12	39,53,18	105,56, 6

24. Bottle Peak, Bottle Pass, and Ptarmigan Peak   103   Moderate

0	39,53,19	105,55,31
1	39,53,18	105,56, 6
MARKER	39,53,26	105,56,28
2	39,54, 8	105,56,11
3	39,54,11	105,56,31
4	39,54,22	105,56,53

25. St. Louis Lake   103   Difficult

0	39,51,6	105,54,37
1	39,48,53	105,55,51
2	39,48,28	105,57, 1
3	39,49,20	105,56,54

26. St. Louis Peak   103   Difficult

0	39,51,6	105,54,37
1	39,48,53	105,55,51
2	39,48,28	105,57, 1
3	39,48, 4	105,57,30
4	39,47,42	105,56,19

27. St. Louis Divide Loop   103   Difficult

0	39,51,6	105,54,37
1	39,48,53	105,55,51
2	39,48,28	105,57, 1
3	39,48, 4	105,57,30
4	39,48, 9	105,57,42
5	39,49,22	105,56,55

28. Mine Creek   103   Moderate

0	39,51,6	105,54,37		
1	39,49,25	105,55,43		
2	39,49,24	105,56,17		
3	39,49,29	105,56,25		
4	39,49,31	105,56,26		
29. Sheep (Snow) Mountain			103	Difficult
1	39,58,40	105,56,25		
2	39,58,22	105,56,19		
3	39,58,14	105,55,47		
4	39,57,40	105,55,31		
5	39,57,23	105,55,31		
6	39,57,12	105,55,18		
30. Nine Mile Mountain			103	Moderate
1	39,59,30	105,56,22		
2	39,59,25	105,56,53		
3	39,59,48	105,57, 3		
4	39,59,53	105,57,10		
31. Snow Mountain Ranch Waterfall			103	Easy
1	39,58,28	105,57,11		
2	39,58, 6	105,58, 4		
32. White Cliffs			106, 107, 103	Moderate
1	40, 1,53	106,2,13		
2	40, 1, 9	106,1,44		
3	40, 0,58	106,1, 6		
4	40, 0,23	106,1, 2		
5	39,59,51	106,0,37		
6	39,59,19	106,0,26		
7	39,58,49	106,0,15		
8	39,58,32	106,0, 1		
33. Bill's Peak to Byers Peak Loop			103	Most Difficult
1	39,53,37	105,57,23		
2	39,52,52	105,56,46		
3	39,52, 4	105,57,33		
4	39,52,29	105,57,57		
5	39,52,23	105,58, 3		
6	39,51,21	105,57,45		
7	39,51,28	105,57,15		
8	39,51,52	105,56,50		

9	39,52,36	105,56,21		
10	39,53,26	105,56,28		
11	39,53,37	105,56,38		
34. Lake Evelyn and Horseshoe Lake			103	Moderate/
1	39,53,37	105,57,23		Most Difficult
2	39,52,46	105,58,17		
3	39,52,24	105,58,17		
4	39,51,43	105,59, 6		
5	39,50,50	105,58,55		
35. Horseshoe Lake			107, 103	Moderate
1	39,51,14	106, 1, 0		
2	39,51,43	105,59, 6		
3	39,50,50	105,58,55		
36. Bill's Peak Loop			103	More Difficult
1	39,53,37	105,57,23		
2	39,52,46	105,58,17		
3	39,52,24	105,58,17		
4	39,52,23	105,58,10		
5	39,52,14	105,58, 2		
6	39,51,21	105,57,45		
7	39,52,23	105,58, 3		
8	39,52,29	105,57,57		
9	39,52, 4	105,57,33		
10	39,52,52	105,56,46		
37. Bottle Pass, Bottle Peak, and Ptarmigan Peak			103	Difficult
1	39,53,37	105,57,23		
2	39,53,32	105,56,58		
3	39,54,11	105,56,31		
4	39,54, 8	105,56,11		
5	39,54,22	105,56,53		
38. Keyser Ridge			107,103	Moderate
1	39,52,26	106, 1,15		
2	39,52,22	106, 1,8		
3	39,52,18	106, 0,15		
4	39,52,24	105,58,17		
5	39,52,22	105,58,3		
39. Darling Creek			107,103	More Difficult

1	39,47,48	106, 1,29		
2	39,47,35	106, 1,12		
3	39,48,18	106, 1,11		
4	39,48,53	105,59,46		
5	39,48,43	105,58,56		
6	39,48,34	105,57,58		
7	39,48,15	105,57,53		
8	39,48, 8	105,57,45		
9	39,48,10	105,57,41		
40. Jones Pass to Mt. Nystrom			103	Moderate
1	39,46,26	105,53,22		
2	39,47,50	105,53,13		
3	39,48,30	105,54, 0		
4	39,48,32	105,54, 7		
41. Jones Pass to Vasquez Peak			103	More Difficult
1	39,46,26	105,53,22		
2	39,47,50	105,53,13		
3	39,47,48	105,52, 1		
4	39,47,46	105,51,18		
42. McQueary Lake			103	Moderate
1	39,45,46	105,54,21		
2	39,46,54	105,55, 0		
3	39,46,56	105,54,58		
4	39,47,27	105,53,58		

Indian Peaks

43. Monarch Lake			102	Easy
1	40,6,39	105,44,48		
2	40,6,15	105,44,42		
3	40,5,59	105,43,52		
4	40,5,58	105,43,48		
5	40,6,16	105,43,19		
44. High Lonesome, Caribou, and Strawberry Creek Loop			102	Difficult
1	40,6,39	105,44,47		
2	40,6,15	105,44,42		
3	40,5,59	105,43,52		
4	40,5,33	105,44,13		

5	40,4,24	105,44,23
6	40,4,32	105,44,33
7	40,3,54	105,44,32
8	40,3,43	105,44,41
9	40,3,46	105,44,50
10	40,4,12	105,45,57
11	40,4,33	105,46,29
12	40,4,38	105,46,55
13	40,4,29	105,47,21
14	40,4,40	105,48,51
15	40,5,13	105,48,52
16	40,6,2	105,48,46
17	40,6,35	105,47,34
18	40,6,44	105,46,39
19	40,6,41	105,45,53

45. Arapaho, Caribou, and High Lonesome Loop			102	More Difficult
1	40,6,39	105,44,47		
2	40,6,15	105,44,42		
3	40,5,59	105,43,52		
4	40,5,58	105,43,48		
5	40,1,59	105,40,23		
6	40,1,18	105,40,53		
7	40,0,57	105,40,31		
8	40,0,52	105,40,41		
9	40,0,50	105,40,52		
10	40,0,51	105,40,59		
11	40,1,10	105,41,27		
11A	40,1,32	105,41,24		
12	40,1,47	105,42,35		
13	40,2, 2	105,43,13		
14	40,2,38	105,43,47		
15	40,2,41	105,43,55		
16	40,3,13	105,43,59		
17	40,3,15	105,43,55		
18	40,3,25	105,44, 1		
19	40,3,42	105,44,20		
20	40,3,54	105,44,32		
21	40,4,24	105,44,23		
21A	40,4,32	105,44,33		
22	40,4,38	105,44,10		
23	40,5,33	105,44,13		

46. Cascade Creek to Mirror Lake, Crater Lake, and   102   Difficult
    Lone Eagle Peak

1	40,6,39	105,44,48
2	40,6,16	105,43,19
3	40,6,35	105,41,50
4	40,6,32	105,41,42
5	40,6,10	105,41, 5
6	40,5,58	105,40,46
7	40,5,20	105,39,40
8	40,4,48	105,39,31
9	40,4,46	105,39,35
10	40,4,38	105,39,45
10A	40,4, 1	105,39,18
10B	40,4,13	105,39,13

47. Cascade Creek to Pawnee Lake and Pass   102   More Difficult/
    Most Difficult

1	40,6,39	105,44,48
2	40,6,16	105,43,19
3	40,6,35	105,41,50
4	40,6,32	105,41,42
5	40,6,10	105,41, 5
6	40,5,58	105,40,46
7	40,5,20	105,39,40
8	40,5,14	105,38,43
9	40,4,34	105,38, 7
10	40,4,31	105,37,59

48. Gourd Lake   102   More Difficult

1	40,6,39	105,44,48
2	40,6,16	105,43,19
3	40,6,35	105,41,50
4	40,7,31	105,40, 0
5	40,8, 2	105,40,23
6	40,8, 2	105,40,18
7	40,8, 7	105,40,14

49. Gourd Lake, Fox Park, Buchanan Pass, and   102   More Difficult/
    Sawtooth Mountain Loop   Most Difficult

1	40,6,39	105,44,48
2	40,6,16	105,43,19
3	40,6,35	105,41,50
4	40,7,31	105,40, 0
5	40,8, 2	105,40,23

6	40,8, 2	105,40,18		
7	40,8, 7	105,40,14		
8	40,7,39	105,38,43		
9	40,7,57	105,38,30		
10	40,7,51	105,37,48		
11	40,7,35	105,37,29		
12	40,7,24	105,38,59		
50. Watanga Lake			102	Difficult
1	40,7,46	105,45,50		
2	40,7,50	105,45,55		
3	40,9, 1	105,44,14		
4	40,9,56	105,44, 5		
51. Mount Irving Hale			102	More Difficult
1	40,7,46	105,45,50		
2	40,7,50	105,45,55		
3	40,9, 1	105,44,14		
4	40,8,51	105,42,58		
5	40,8,16	105,43,13		
52. Roaring Fork to Stone and Upper Lakes			102	More Difficult
1	40,7,46	105,45,50		
2	40,7,50	105,45,55		
3	40,9, 1	105,44,14		
4	40,8,51	105,42,58		
5	40,8,44	105,42,27		
6	40,8,58	105,41,32		
7	40,9, 7	105,41, 9		
8	40,9,18	105,40,53		
53. Knight Ridge			102, 200	Difficult
1	40, 7,49	105,46, 0		
2	40, 9,52	105,49, 8		
3	40,11,55	105,49,53		
3A	40,12,16	105,50,26		
4	40,14,27	105,49,31		

Never Summer Range

54. Parika Lake and Parika Peak			200, 115	Difficult/More
1	40,21,17	105,51,28		Difficult

2	40,21,22	105,51,45
3	40,21,33	105,52, 7
4	40,21,54	105,53, 5
5	40,22,24	105,54,53
6	40,22,39	105,55,14
7	40,22,55	105,56, 0
8	40,22,54	105,56,12
9	40,22,52	105,56,47
10	40,23, 7	105,56,48

55. Parika Lake and Baker Pass Loop 200,115 More Difficult

1	40,21,17	105,51,28
2	40,21,22	105,51,45
3	40,21,33	105,52, 7
4	40,21,54	105,53, 5
5	40,22,24	105,54,53
6	40,22,39	105,55,14
7	40,22,55	105,56, 0
8	40,22,54	105,56,12
9	40,24, 1	105,55, 5
10	40,24, 7	105,54,48

56. Baker Mountain 200, 115 More Difficult

1	40,21,17	105,51,28
2	40,21,22	105,51,45
3	40,21,33	105,52, 7
4	40,21,54	105,53, 5
5	40,22,24	105,54,53
6	40,22,22	105,54, 7
7	40,22,54	105,54,22

57. Blue Lake and Mineral Point 200, 115 Difficult/More Difficult

1	40,19,42	105,51,25
2	40,19,45	105,51,31
3	40,19,46	105,51,59
4	40,19,59	105,52,30
5	40,20,13	105,54,15
6	40,20,28	105,55,29
7	40,20,34	105,55,40
7A	40,20,36	105,55,50
7B	40,20,43	105,55,59
8	40,21, 0	105,55,13
9	40,21, 2	105,55,16

10	40,21,14	105,55,12		
11	40,21,20	105,55,22		
12	40,21,24	105,55, 7		
13	40,21,38	105,54,52		
14	40,21,38	105,54,16		

58. Bowen Mountain — 200, 115 — More Difficult

1	40,19,42	105,51,25
2	40,19,45	105,51,31
3	40,19,46	105,51,59
4	40,19,59	105,52,30
5	40,20,13	105,54,15
6	40,20,28	105,55,29
7	40,20,34	105,55,40
7A	40,20,36	105,55,50
7B	40,20,43	105,55,59
8	40,21, 0	105,55,13
9	40,21, 2	105,55,16
10	40,21,14	105,55,12
11	40,21,20	105,55,22
12	40,21,23	105,55,36
13	40,21,30	105,56, 3
14	40,21,38	105,56, 0

59. Bowen Gulch to Bowen Lake — 200, 115 — Difficult

1	40,19,42	105,51,25
2	40,19,45	105,51,31
3	40,19,46	105,51,59
4	40,19,59	105,52,30
5	40,20,13	105,54,15
6	40,20,28	105,55,29
7	40,20,34	105,55,40
8	40,20,36	105,55,50
8A	40,20,43	105,55,59
9	40,20,43	105,56,20
10	40,19,51	105,56,38

60. Blue Ridge to Bowen Lake — 200, 115 — Difficult

1	40,18, 0	105,55,13
2	40,17,52	105,55,34
3	40,17,54	105,55,45
4	40,17,48	105,55,59
5	40,17,48	105,56, 0

6	40,18,25	105,56, 2		
7	40,19,36	105,56,40		
8	40,19,51	105,56,38		

61. Cascade Mountain, Bowen Pass, and			200, 115	Most Difficult
Bowen Lake Loop				
1	40,18, 0	105,55,13		
2	40,17,52	105,55,34		
3	40,17,54	105,55,45		
4	40,17,48	105,55,59		
5	40,17,48	105,56, 0		
6	40,18,25	105,56, 2		
7	40,19,36	105,56,40		
8	40,20,28	105,57,34		
9	40,21,42	105,57, 5		
19	40,21,50	105,56,40		
11	40,20,43	105,56,20		
11A	40,20,36	105,55,50		
11B	40,20,43	105,55,59		
12	40,19,51	105,56,38		

62. Bowen Gulch Interpretive Trail			200	Easy
1	40,19,25	105,54,30		
2	40,19,24	105,54,39		

63. Stillwater Creek			106	Moderate
1	40,13,40	105,54,56		
2	40,13,46	105,55, 3		
3	40,15, 6	105,56, 1		

64. Apiatan Mountain			115, 106	Easy
1	40,15,10	105,56,37		
2	40,15,11	105,56,33		
3	40,14,51	105,56,35		
4	40,14,46	105,56,38		

65. Gravel Mountain			115	Difficult
1	40,15, 8	105,58,59		
2	40,14,54	105,59,45		
3	40,14,58	106, 0,20		
4	40,15,26	106, 0,29		
5	40,16,32	105,59,44		
6	40,15,49	106, 0,14		

66. Lost Lake			115	Easy
1	40,18,24	105,57,59		
2	40,18,22	105,57,53		
3	40,18,17	105,57,51		
4	40,18,12	105,57,39		
5	40,18, 2	105,57,38		

67. Bill Creek			115	Moderate
1	40,19,46	106, 0,17		
2	40,19,51	106, 0,14		
3	40,19,58	105,59,58		
4	40,21,41	106, 0,32		
5	40,22,11	106, 0,43		

Troublesome Valley

68. Parkview Mountain and Lookout House			115	Difficult
1	40,20,56	106,5,44		
2	40,21, 2	106,5,33		
3	40,21, 9	106,6, 2		
4	40,20,39	106,6,58		
5	40,20,25	106,6,50		
6	40,20, 3	106,7,33		
7	40,19,41	106,7,57		
8	40,19,49	106,8,10		
9	40,19, 8	106,7,12		
10	40,18,20	106,3,56		

69. Trail Creek, East Fork Troublesome Creek, Haystack Creek, and Middle Fork Creek Loop			115	Difficult
1	40,16,57	106, 5, 4		
2	40,17, 1	106, 5,49		
3	40,17, 0	106, 5,58		
4	40,17,10	106, 6,28		
5	40,17,12	106, 6,54		
6	40,17, 9	106, 7, 0		
7	40,17,10	106, 7,46		
8	40,17,20	106, 8,21		
9	40,17,25	106, 8,32		
10	40,18,42	106, 9,38		
11	40,18,32	106,10, 9		
12	40,18,48	106,11, 7		

13	40,19, 8	106,12,43		
14	40,15,53	106,12,43		
15	40,15,33	106,12, 5		
16	40,15,15	106,11,18		
17	40,15,38	106,10,22		
18	40,16,10	106, 9,26		
19	40,16,25	106, 8,30		
20	40,16,42	106, 8,17		
21	40,17, 3	106, 6,52		
22	40,16,57	106, 6,19		
70. Lookout Point and Buffalo Park Loop			115, 106	Moderate
1	40,15,26	106,6,33		
2	40,15,40	106,7,28		
3	40,15,39	106,7,40		
4	40,15,30	106,8,26		
5	40,14,32	106,8,43		
6	40,14, 9	106,8,44		
7	40,13,56	106,8,31		
8	40,15,25	106,6,32		
71. Searight Mountain Loop			116, 106	Difficult
1	40,15,26	106,6,33		
2	40,15,40	106,7,28		
3	40,15,39	106,7,40		
4	40,15,30	106,8,26		
5	40,14,32	106,8,43		
6	40,13,56	106,8,31		
7	40,13, 4	106,8,36		
8	40,12,28	106,8,34		
9	40,15,25	106,6,32		
72. Corral Peaks Loop			106	Moderate
1	40,12, 7	106,8,35		
2	40,11,59	106,9,15		
3	40,11,46	106,9,30		
4	40,12,12	106,9,13		
73. Elk Mountain Loop			106	Moderate
1	40,9,16	106,8,17		
2	40,9,30	106,8,23		
3	40,9,43	106,7,42		
4	40,9,31	106,7,41		

5	40,9,23	106,7,41		
6	40,9, 2	106,7,36		
7	40,8,59	106,7,39		
8	40,9, 2	106,7,44		

74. Wheatley Homestead and Cow Camp Loop			106	Difficult
1	40,10, 3	106,10,33		
2	40,10, 9	106,10,39		
3	40,10,17	106,10,37		
4	40,10,59	106,10,33		
5	40,12,17	106,10, 4		
6	40,12,59	106,10,25		
7	40,12,43	106,10,54		
8	40,12,23	106,11,35		
9	40,12,28	106,12,4		
10	40,12,37	106,11,49		
11	40,13,24	106,12,35		
12	40,14,12	106,12,30		
13	40,14, 9	106,12, 1		
14	40,13,25	106,10,16		
15	40,13,15	106,10, 6		

75. Haystack Mountain			115	Difficult
1	40,20, 3	106,10,59		
2	40,19,58	106,10,57		
3	40,19,38	106,11,22		

76. Sheep Mountain			115	Moderate
1	40,19,31	106,14, 0		
2	40,19,19	106,13,55		
3	40,18,32	106,14,28		

77. Poison Ridge			115	Moderate
1	40,19,30	106,14, 2		
2	40,20,19	106,14,59		
3	40,20,21	106,14,51		

78. Matheson Reservoir to Grimes Peak			115, 106	More Difficult
1	40,18,41	106,16,20		
2	40,17,35	106,16,54		
3	40,16,48	106,16, 7		
4	40,15,13	106,16,16		
5	40,15, 4	106,16,17		

6	40,14,36	106,16,17
7	40,13,47	106,15,50
8	40,13,41	106,15,51
9	40,13,27	106,15,45

Williams Fork Mountains

79. Williams Peak			107	More Difficult
1	39,54,22	106, 6,19		
2	39,53,54	106, 6,26		
3	39,53, 0	106, 7,50		
4	39,52,42	106, 8,26		
5	39,52,14	106, 8,57		
6	39,51,15	106,10,30		
7	39,51,20	106,10,57		
8	39,51,19	106,11, 7		

80. Ute Pass to Ute Peak			107	Most Difficult
1	39,49,25	106,6,19		
2	39,49,13	106,6, 4		
3	39,48,58	106,4,22		
4	39,47,49	106,4,55		
5	39,47, 8	106,4,37		

81. Ute Peak			107	Most Difficult
1	39,48,45	106,3, 2		
2	39,48,59	106,4,23		
3	39,47,49	106,4,55		
4	39,47, 8	106,4,37		

82. South Fork Loop			107, 103, 104, 108	Difficult
1	39,47,48	106, 1,29		
2	39,47,35	106, 1,12		
3	39,46,57	105,56,17		
4	39,46,48	105,55,38		
5	39,46,43	105,55,33		
6	39,45,58	105,54,37		
7	39,45,45	105,54,22		
8	39,45,38	105,54,24		
9	39,44,37	105,54,25		
10	39,43,28	105,55,52		
11	39,43,29	105,56,22		

12	39,42,57	105,58,17		
13	39,42,10	105,58,50		
14	39,42, 9	105,59, 3		
15	39,44,23	106, 1,29		
16	39,47,37	106,1,51		

83. Ptarmigan Pass and Peak			104, 108	More Difficult/
1	39,44,25	106, 1,39		Most Difficult
2	39,44,22	106, 1,30		
3	39,42,15	105,59,29		
4	39,42, 9	105,59, 3		
5	39,41,11	106, 0,14		
6	39,41,27	106, 1,35		

Additional Grand County Hikes

84. Gore Canyon			120, 106	Easy
1	39,59,23	106,30,29		
2	39,59,42	106,30, 5		
3	40, 0,24	106,29,16		

85. Routt Divide			118	Moderate
1	40,19,51	106,40, 4		
2	40,18,15	106,40,53		
3	40,17,19	106,38,48		
4	40,16,21	106,36,52		

WEB SITE

Please check http:// backcountrybound.home.mindspring.com for the following information.

1. Any permanent trail changes that are not reflected in the latest edition.

2. Any and all corrections of the book.

3. Ordering information for additional books.

4. Links to TOPO! mapping software, Trails Illustrated, and National Geographic web sites.

Columbine Lake

PAWNEE PASS – CONTINENTAL DIVIDE
ELEVATION 12,550 FEET
ARAPAHO NATIONAL   ROOSEVELT NATIONAL
← FOREST   FOREST →

← PAWNEE LAKE   2
← CRATER LAKE   5
← MONARCH LAKE   11

LAKE ISABELLE   2 →
LONG LAKE   3 →
BRAINARD LAKE   4 →

Pawnee Pass

HIKE LOG

Hike Name   **Date**   **Comments**

_____

_____

_____

_____

_____

_____

_____

_____

_____

_____

_____

_____

_____

_____

_____

_____

_____

_____

_____

_____

GRAND COUNTY

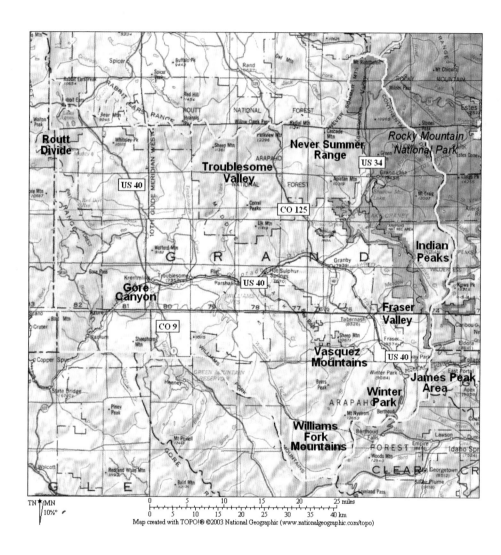

Map created with TOPO!® ©2003 National Geographic (www.nationalgeographic.com/topo)